———————————— SANTIAGO'S CHILDREN ————————————

SANTIAGO'S CHILDREN

What I Learned about Life at an Orphanage in Chile

by STEVE REIFENBERG

foreword by PAUL FARMER

UNIVERSITY OF TEXAS PRESS

AUSTIN

Requests for permission to reproduce material from this work should be sent to:
Permissions
University of Texas Press
P.O. Box 7819
Austin, TX 78713-7819
www.utexas.edu/utpress/about/bpermission.html

♾ The paper used in this book meets the minimum requirements of ANSI/NISO Z39.48–1992 (R1997) (Permanence of Paper).

Library of Congress Cataloging-in-Publication Data

Reifenberg, Steve, 1959–
   Santiago's children : what I learned about life at an orphanage in Chile / Steve Reifenberg ; foreword by Paul Farmer. — 1st ed.
      p.   cm.
   ISBN 978-0-292-71742-8

      1. Orphanages—Chile—Santiago.   2. Orphans—Chile—Santiago.   I. Title.
   HV1100.S26R44   2008
   362.73—dc22

                                                                    2007030042

This book is dedicated to two families: the children at the Hogar Domingo Savio, a family that Olga Díaz helped create in Santiago, Chile; and to my wife, Chris Cervenak, and children, Natasha, Alexandra, and Luke.

Hay un país extenso en el cielo
con las supersticiosas alfombras del arco-iris
y con vegetaciones vesperales:
hacia allí me dirijo, no sin cierta fatiga,
pisando una tierra removida de sepulcros un tanto frescos,
yo sueño entre esas plantas de legumbre confusa.

—PABLO NERUDA
RESIDENCIA EN LA TIERRA, I (1933)
CABALLOS DE LOS SUEÑOS

There is a country stretched across the sky
strewn with the rainbow's superstitious carpets
and evening's vegetation:
that way I go—not without some fatigue,
treading grave loam, fresh from the spade,
dreaming among these doubtful greens.

—PABLO NERUDA
RESIDENCE ON THE EARTH, I (1933)
DREAM HORSES

CONTENTS

CONTENTS

CONTENTS

FOREWORD
Paul Farmer

There are five reasons I jumped at the chance to write a foreword for Steve Reifenberg's memoir about living and working in the early 1980s in a home for Chilean children who would otherwise have ended up in a large institutional orphanage. Five reasons, five areas of curiosity, five questions.

First, anyone who works in countries or regions where there are many orphans—that is, in places where young parents are apt to die—needs to know more about how best to raise these children humanely. You don't have to read Dickens to doubt that large orphanages would be the best way to raise, for example, the millions of AIDS orphans now living in some of the places where I work as a physician.

A second reason I wanted to read *Santiago's Children* was that I knew its author had had an experience similar to mine: shortly after graduating from college, Reifenberg set off for a country far from home, a troubled but beautiful place in which he became engaged in a noble enough task. With only the vaguest of references and less than a hundred dollars in his pocket, he found himself helping run, under the guidance of a remarkable Chilean woman who said she was opposed to "the warehousing of children," a group home for a dozen poor children. I expected to read a lyrical account of two often frustrating and sometimes emotionally wrenching years, the story of a journey south to a place he didn't know, a journey with and among people, most of them children, who had known none of the security he'd enjoyed in a rock-solid, middle-class American family. Epiphany or, at the very least, illumination seemed sure to follow. I wanted to know more about Reifenberg's coming of age and to compare notes.

I knew that Steve—Tío Esteve to the Chilean children and to the tiny band of their fearless adult protectors—had arrived in Santiago, the tumultuous capital city of Chile, at a fairly harrowing time in the country's history. So, third: How would Chile's political crisis figure in so personal a memoir? Coming a decade after the coup of 1973 that put an end to Chile's experiment with socialism, Steve's tenure occurred at the time of a devastating economic downturn, a time of police interrogations, a time of curfews and harsh military repression of demonstrations, often involving deadly force. Would the book be solely about the joys of learning, however painfully, a new language? of making warm and enduring connections with children who'd seen the worst of a rapidly changing society? Or would Steve bring into relief, through his own experience and those of the children and their kin, the ways in which antidemocratic governance makes itself known in everyday life, sometimes through explosive violence and sometimes through less-than-subtle symbols of power, such as the tanks parked at the end of the road in full view of the orphanage? Would he somehow weave these strands together?

Fourth, would this be a good book to use in teaching? Scholarly treatises and historical accounts of difficult times rarely try to capture the everyday feel, the gritty anxiety of living on the edge, financially, with a dozen children to look out for; academic accounts are not good at rendering the texture of everyday life as violence and repression intrude. Teaching about the travails of democracy in Latin America is difficult to do when we are left to choose between shrill polemic, superficial journalism, and dry, experience-distant accounts. Certain novelists have managed to capture the texture of life under military rule, as has the occasional memoir. But Reifenberg was both an eyewitness and an externally placed observer, and he also learned a good deal about what was happening in Chile from materials gathered in his own country. On political issues, the often supine U.S. press was still better than the censored reporting that existed in the early 1980s in Chile, where newspapers, magazines, and human rights offices that called into question military rule or human rights abuses were shut down or worse.

Finally, I knew that the book had been conceived in journals written over twenty years ago. But Reifenberg had finished *Santiago's Children* much more recently, back in Santiago, where he once again lives. I was dead curious to see if he'd been able to follow the fates of all the children one would get to know in the telling. What were they all up to now? What relationship did this dark Chile of the early 1980s have with the impressive advances of Chile today?

Santiago's Children is immensely satisfying on all five scores: for young Americans—and for young people from many other places who find themselves able, through the luck of the draw and accident of birth, to travel to places like Chile or Haiti or Rwanda—this memoir will serve as a gentle and self-deprecating guidebook. What happened to its author, the ways he grew and learned more about his strengths and weaknesses, are all there. The book is pitch perfect, as far as humor and detail go.

First, there are the children. You get to know them and to see them grow. Reifenberg spent two years as a surrogate parent and teacher in the home inauspiciously baptized Domingo Savio. (The name took hold before its founder, a vividly depicted young Chilean woman named Olga Díaz, discovered that the new namesake was an Italian boy who didn't live to celebrate his fourteenth birthday and was the patron saint of choirboys.)

Some of the kids were right off the street; all of them were in what Chileans termed "irregular situations." Some had been abandoned by a parent not able to get by; others were orphaned by political violence or by the grinding violence of poverty and economic crisis. Reifenberg lets us know what it's like to get more than a dozen kids ready for school each morning, and what it feels like to try, twice, in a desperate bid to raise money, to launch a family farm only to see the water cut off or, worse, your newly acquired draft horse die before the field is fully plowed. We see how tempers sometimes flare in tight quarters, sense the anxiety that accompanies a trip to the beach with a dozen unruly kids. Please God, the reader thinks, let no one drown! (No one does.) And always, the narrator's frustration at not mastering Spanish quickly enough, often to the amusement of the kids and neighbors.

Of course, it's not all fun and games at the Domingo Savio house. Bedwetting and fights occur; there are kids who don't want to do their homework and don't get along. There are also Steve's and Olga's painful speculations about what past traumas might account for current problems at the home or in school. There are kids who miss their families but know them to be too poor and fractured to care for them. The reader wonders if the orphans aren't somehow better off. Indeed, most painful of all are the tenuous links many of the children have with their own families: siblings in precarious homes; a drunken father here, a beleaguered and beaten-down mother there; a revolutionary older brother caught up in the dangerous struggle against the regime of Augusto Pinochet.

Through these stories, we actually get to know a dozen children. The portraits are built piecemeal, but by the end of *Santiago's Children* we're left with memorable characters: the irrepressible Carlos and his brother Patricio, whose father is in jail and whose mother cannot take care of them; the studious and preternaturally mature Verónica; the naughty and spirited Marcelo; Andrés, a boy who can be relied on to carry out any threat and whose fear of horses is born when the doomed draft horse nips him prior to going to her great reward; Big Sonia, the amateur philosopher: "So, why do they always call God a he? It makes me furious!"; the quiet Karen, whose occasional utterances surprise Steve.

My favorite portrait is that of Sebastián, one of the older boys, whose down-on-her-luck mother and dissolute father are only a bus ride away. During Reifenberg's second year in Chile, Sebastián, by then fourteen, tries to be a parent to his younger cousin, whom he brings to the home on weekends. "Do you think it's possible," he asks Steve anxiously, "that maybe we could, maybe, let Daniel live here?" No, not everything goes well at the Domingo Savio house.

Despite the ordeals, it really is a loving home. Only the most stone-hearted will not be deeply moved by the account of Tío Esteve's departure, delayed for a year when he declines admission to a U.S. law school. The pain, his own and the kids', of his leaving Domingo Savio is lessened only when we learn in the epilogue at least something about each of the children he came to know and love.

Reifenberg is careful to focus on the children themselves in the first half of the book. But as the narrative moves forward easily and with a great deal of humor, political violence seeps into its pages. By that time the reader is a fierce partisan of these children and their neighbors, who live in a poor part of town. We start to ask harder questions. Wasn't it this repression that rendered some of these orphans parentless? What is the narrator to do when one of the mothers of the thousands of disappeared young activists entreats him, the American, to help her find her son? The wave of disappearances laps frighteningly close to the home. By the second half of the book the constant attack on civil and political liberties is as expertly blended into the text as the household struggles for access to the one bathroom and the arguments about who's going to do what chores.

Finishing the book, we discover we've learned a good deal about Chile. The country is in some ways emblematic of other troubled places in Latin America. The socialist government of Salvador Allende came to power in 1970 through democratic elections. In a pattern observed in many countries in Latin America, wealthy citizens joined forces with the military, which often benefited from generous overt and covert assistance from the U.S. government, to quash popular democracy. El Salvador, Guatemala, Honduras, Nicaragua, Haiti, even Argentina and Brazil—all traveled that *vía dolorosa*, with great loss of life and wounds that never fully heal.

Following the coup of September 11, 1973, General Pinochet ruled Chile with an iron fist for the next seventeen years. During the next decade, the period just prior to Reifenberg's arrival, the repression was so ruthless—many opponents (or presumed opponents) of the regime were disappeared—that public protest within Chile was muffled. Outside that terrified nation, however, Chile became the defining case in the international struggle for human rights. And if in fact the writer's goal was to understand the human rights situation in Chile, Reifenberg showed up at just the right time: by 1982, with the economy bottoming out as a result of ill-considered economic prescriptions from helpful American experts, he witnessed the first bubbling forth of public opposition.

On May 11, 1983, Reifenberg watches, both moved and perplexed, as the residents of his barrio, after nearly a decade of silence, begin banging together pots and pans, joining other neighborhoods to produce a din that roars through the poor parts of the city. These noisy protests sometimes attracted indiscriminate gunfire (generating, in a single instant, two more orphans to take into the crowded house). Tío Esteve's neighbors were not alone in their opposition to the military government; students and church groups, the mothers of the disappeared, and many union leaders also pressed for the restoration of democratic rule.

Reifenberg uses personal narrative to examine, through his own experience and that of the children and their surviving families, the seedy and violent side of military rule: disregard for civil and political rights; widespread practice of torture and assassinations; and exile. But we also see the resilience of both children and adults, and their willingness to make sacrifices at great personal cost. As the epilogue suggests, Chile has made great strides since the end of the dictatorship in 1990. In 2006 Chile elected Michelle Bachelet, not only its first woman president, but also a socialist doctor who lost her father to torture under Pinochet's auspices.

An American friend in Chile gives Steve Reifenberg a scrap of paper with a few lines from the German poet Rainer Maria Rilke copied on it. The poet's advice has served Steve well: "Ah! but verses amount to so little when one writes them young. One ought to wait and gather sense and sweetness a whole life long. . . . For verses are not, as people imagine, simply feelings (those one has early enough)—they are experiences." By waiting a couple of decades to write about his voyage south, Reifenberg is able to offer something much more than an affecting account of his experiences in the Domingo Savio home and personal glimpses of military rule in Chile.

As Reifenberg later discovered at Harvard, where he came to serve as executive director of the David Rockefeller Center for Latin American Studies, so many students are trying to figure out how to make a contribution in some meaningful way. We're all liable, especially when young, to undertake quests in search of a personal sense of self-efficacy—to feel that we've made a meaningful contribution. It's possible to focus excessively on the process—Reifenberg touches on this in a rueful but kindly consideration of another group of young Americans trying to "live in solidarity with the poor" by avoiding hot showers. His own rich experiences standing in line outside the Domingo Savio bathroom, waiting his turn behind a lot of squirming kids, led him to conclude that this was a conversation, no matter how earnest, that he'd just as soon be spared. Being desperately sick for a time taught him how little he could do to meet lofty goals when he was incapacitated and led him to the realization of how often the poor are sick. Through his book, we see him coming to understand just how huge the obstacles are. The book is also honest about the frustrations. Surrounded by lives trammeled by poverty and repression, he begins to see just how privileged and protected the lives of North Americans are. More honestly still, Reifenberg traces the links between such privilege and the privations of others. In the case of Chile, the connections are direct and damning.

Reifenberg's central message, though, is optimistic, encouraging. The effort doesn't have to be Herculean, he seems to be telling an audience contemplating great deeds in faraway places. A big step in the quest is taken, simply enough, by investing time and energy in something decent and then sticking with it. It's important to be willing to engage in things you care about, even if those efforts do not always lead to obvious victories, and to continue learning in the process.

For this reason, especially, the book will be a wonderful resource for students, young and old. I now teach mostly medical students and physicians, but in my experience their concerns are not very different from those Steve felt, as did I. It's hard to imagine someone who finds himself an outsider in one of the tougher neighborhoods of Latin America or Africa or other foreign parts of the world—or someone interested in learning about one of those places—who would not find this book immensely instructive and moving.

The world changes. For the past several decades, the United States has had unfettered influence in Latin America and in many other parts of the world. If an empire exists today, it has been built by the United States. All empires come to an end, it's said. Over the past decade, dramatic, violent events—war and terrorism and even genocide, as in Rwanda in 1994 and Darfur today—seem to have occurred whether the United States willed it or no, a never-ending cycle of disasters that turns ordinary citizens into helpless viewers. But it's not necessarily so.

It is a good sign that there seems to be growing interest among students and many others in understanding what the rest of the world is like and how it got to be that way, and thinking about ways to try to make it better.

Santiago's Children reminds us that even modest efforts like those of Steve Reifenberg might at least palliate the pain encountered in a place like Pinochet's Chile. Certainly efforts such as his, and the lessons drawn for this kind of international experience, would be preferable to the current ham-fisted approach to U.S. foreign policy and to the conventional development enterprise. Often these policies are steered, and none too gently, by economic ideologues who don't often apologize when they make yet another about-face whose costs are borne by others. I can't help but wonder what might have transpired if we'd approached these same problems and policies with the good will, humility, and willingness to learn that run through this book.

ACKNOWLEDGMENTS

I landed in Santiago, Chile, in November 1982, just before a critical turning point in that nation's history, although I didn't realize it at the time. I was twenty-three years old and very new to Latin America. The repression in Chile had been so severe in that first decade since the coup of September 11, 1973, that very few citizens living in Chile dared speak out against the military government. Six months after my arrival, in May 1983, I witnessed the first of a series of public protests across the nation that ultimately led to the peaceful return of democracy in 1990.

While it was a coincidence that I arrived at such an important historical moment (that I could understand only in hindsight), I knew almost immediately that I was experiencing something remarkable at the Hogar Domingo Savio. That I had the good fortune to land at the *hogar* and to get to work with Olga Díaz and the children who lived there, I am eternally grateful.

I am honored that my friend and colleague Paul Farmer wrote the foreword to this book, and I'm even more appreciative having learned that he stayed up all night while working in Rwanda to do so. A professor at the Harvard Medical School and a founding member of the international health and social justice organization Partners in Health, Paul has long inspired me and most everyone with whom he comes in contact. His remarkable story is told in Tracy Kidder's book *Mountains Beyond Mountains: The Quest of Dr. Paul Farmer, a Man Who Would Cure the World*.

The first article I ever published about these kids and the political conditions in Chile ran in the *Notre Dame Magazine* in 1983. I used a pseudonym, as I was afraid my descriptions of what was happening in

Chile might somehow harm the *hogar*. Kerry Temple, the *Notre Dame Magazine* editor who published that and subsequent articles, gave me encouragement and guidance, as he has ever since.

This book began as a series of vignettes that tried to capture something of the lives of these remarkable children at the *hogar*. My participation in the W. K. Kellogg Foundation National Fellowship Program, and wonderful colleagues from that program, helped carve out some space from my professional life to get the writing project going. The Kellogg Fellowship Program also introduced me to two talented writers, Martín Espada and William Zinnser, who led inspiring workshops with small groups of us Kellogg Fellows in the early 1990s. Both also helped me to turn these early musings into a book.

A wonderful group of family and friends read the manuscript as it developed and gave valuable feedback and encouragement along the way. Thanks go to Shawn Bohen, Gregor Brodsky, James Brodsky, Michaela Bruzzese, Donna Cervenak, Morrie Conway, Cristian Correa, Kathleen Cushman, Ophelia Dahl, Robin Dunnigan, Susan Eckstein, Paul Farmer, Debi Gero, Ronda Gomez, Merilee Grindle, Karla Hodge, Elizabeth Jensen, Peter Johnson, James and Jane Levitt, Abraham Lowenthal, Paulina Massa, Lora-Ellen McKinney, Pilo Mella, Brian Milder, Juan Esteban Montes, J. A. Murphy, Terry Phelps, Josh Pilz, Jane Pitz, Lisa Popik Coll, Cathy Raines, Phil Reifenberg, Rick and Sara Reifenberg, Jean and James Reifenberg, Catherine Reilly, Marcela Rentería, Sydney Rosen, Tom Sanders, David Seitel, Fraser Seitel, Neil Shister, Helen Claire Sievers, Sara Sievers, Susan Smith, Bob Stewart, Chris Sturgis, Alex Wilde, Carola Wilder, and Sophie Wollocombe.

Marjorie Agosín, a talented Chilean poet and Spanish professor at Wellesley College, read the stories and thought the University of Texas Press would be a good home for them. Theresa May, an editor at the University of Texas Press at the time and now editor in chief, first saw these initial stories a decade ago and encouraged me not only to turn them into a book, but also to broaden the story so that in addition to touching on the lives of the kids, it set their story in the wider social and political context. I believe that encouragement helped me tell a more significant story. Leslie Tingle and Larry Kenney were great to work with in the copyediting process.

These stories are true, but in a few cases I have changed the names of the children because some of the situations I describe are of an extremely personal nature.

I want to express enormous gratitude to my wife, Chris Cervenak, who encouraged me to have these stories see the light of day. Fortunately for me, among her many talents, she is an excellent editor.

A most special thanks goes to Olga Díaz, who continues to inspire many through her work with children from extremely difficult circumstances in the same neighborhood in La Granja where I lived more than twenty years ago and with whom I have had the pleasure and privilege to work all these years.

SANTIAGO'S CHILDREN

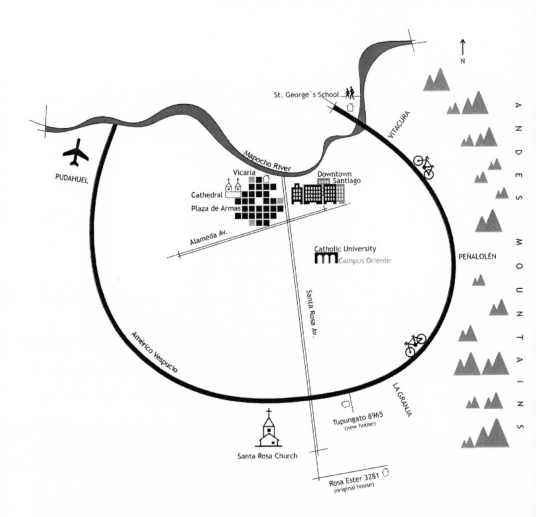

N

St. George's School

VITACURA

PUDAHUEL

Mapocho River

Vicaría

Cathedral

Plaza de Armas

Downtown Santiago

Alameda Av.

Catholic University
Campus Oriente

PEÑALOLÉN

Santa Rosa Av.

Américo Vespucio

LA GRANJA

Tupungato 8965
(new house)

Santa Rosa Church

Rosa Ester 3281
(original house)

A N D E S   M O U N T A I N S

〰

ONE

VISIONS OF A FAMILY FARM

〰

Geraldo is vomiting green paint," eight-year-old Carlos announced to everyone in the house. It was the first time I learned the goat had a name.

We found Geraldo panting on his side behind the orphanage's toolshed, his stomach bloated and his whole body shaking. A half dozen children stood around silently in a semicircle. His goat beard was covered with green bile.

Even before taken ill, this goat was no spectacular specimen. A mangy creature with big bald spots on his back, he'd regularly twist his head around in strange ways to chew. And he chewed most anything he could get his mouth around and gnawed off the green paint from one side of the toolshed. The goat regularly munched clothing hanging on the line to dry, having a particular affinity for mine. As I was down to just a few pairs of briefs, I had taken to hanging my underwear to dry on a tree branch, presumably out of reach of Geraldo's insatiable appetite.

"Somebody ate a pair of Tío Esteve's underwear," Carlos yelled across the dinner table one evening. Carlos's voice could always be heard above those of the other twelve children living at the orphanage. He was laughing so hard he could barely get the words out, his voice cracking, milk dribbling out of the side of his mouth: "Guess who ate it?"

The goat's body shook violently. Out came more green vomit, followed by tattered pieces of white cloth. Then the goat was still. From between his clenched teeth hung the shredded remains of my underwear, identifiable by its red elastic band. Carlos looked at me knowingly. Surprisingly, he remained silent.

Our next-door neighbor, Don Alvaro, a three-hundred-pound baker, was deemed the right person to consult on what to do. Wearing his flour-covered white apron, he leaned over and put his nose close to the goat's. Then, standing up, he gave a swift kick to the goat's belly. The goat didn't react. Don Alvaro bowed his head for a moment, confirming our worst fears, and went back to baking bread.

We dragged Geraldo to the farthest corner of the property, dug a deep hole, and rolled him into the grave. He hit the bottom with a thump, legs sticking up. Each of the six girls from the orphanage arrived with little bouquets of dandelions and wild daisies.

"Drop the flowers in the grave," one of the older girls instructed the mourners. The flowers fell on Geraldo's stomach, a few sticking to the green paste around his mouth.

"Now, throw a handful of dirt on top," she said.

Four-year-old Karen, who rarely uttered a word, threw her dirt and muttered, "Cabra estúpida" (Stupid goat) as she walked away.

The next morning the burial had to be repeated, this time without ceremony. During the night, Jackie, the German shepherd watchdog, left her litter of puppies and dug up Geraldo. She gnawed off a piece of calf and hoof that the next morning she carried proudly in her mouth. Twelve-year-old Sebastián chased Jackie around the field until he could grab her. Jackie's jaws were wrapped so tightly around the goat's leg that every time Sebastián pulled it, her milk-heavy tits would shake. A tug of war ensued. Finally, with a mighty pull that landed him on his back, Sebastián wrenched the goat leg free. We reburied the leg with the body and, with that, said our final goodbye to Geraldo.

I was full of ideas even before I met the thirteen children who lived at the orphanage Domingo Savio in Santiago, Chile, where I worked for more than two years in the early 1980s. I would teach the younger kids how to make potato prints and paint watercolors, the older ones calligraphy and woodworking (not that I knew anything about calligraphy or woodworking). There would be storybooks and history books and a copy of *The Little Prince* in Spanish. I would teach them how to play volleyball, and I would teach them English. If there was any land, even a small plot, we could have a garden.

And land there was. Behind the small three-bedroom adobe structure that housed the orphanage, there was an acre of rich Chilean soil in a plot long and narrow like a skinny football field. Beans and corn had once grown there, but weeds had now taken over.

I imagined bushy rows of peas and beans, ripe red tomatoes, yellow squash, striped cucumbers, and silky green stalks of corn climbing to the sky. This was coupled with my vision of the orphanage as a family farm where all the children, even the youngest, would work the land together, planting the seeds that would become the vegetables they harvested, learning how things grow and how to be self-reliant.

There was a single plum tree that produced only small, sour fruit. I debated planting more fruit trees, but that seemed, even to me, a little long-term given the orphanage's month-to-month lease. The goat's demise did not deter me from this vision of a family farm, nor did the fact that Chile was suffering one of its worst economic crises of the twentieth century.

The thirteen children living at Domingo Savio were all from *situaciones irregulares,* or "irregular situations." Most came from extremely unstable families, often related to parents who had problems with alcohol or drugs. A few of the children had been completely abandoned. Many had endured some type of abuse. All were poor. Without exception, this was the first time they had ever lived with a *gringo.*

I explained my ideas about the family farm to them in my broken Spanish.

"Everybody's going to help in the garden for half an hour a day," I instructed them one warm November afternoon a few weeks after I had arrived to work at the *hogar,* and only days after Geraldo's passing.

"It gets real hot here in the summer," Carlos said. "This is still spring, not even summer, and you've never been here in the summer. I don't know if this is such a good idea."

"We'll worry about that when it gets hot. Then you can work early in the morning or in the evening."

"Great, Tío, I can't wait," Carlos said. *Tío* literally means "uncle" but is an all-purpose Spanish word used to address adults.

I directed the troops, aged two to twelve, into the field and explained how to prepare the soil for planting. There were only two hoes. I gave one to Sebastián, who at twelve was the oldest, and I took the other.

"Where's my hoe?" Carlos asked.

"To start with, you'll just have to help by pulling up the weeds with your hands."

"Tío, these weeds have thorns," said Carlos about thirty seconds later, and then, "Sebastián is trying to chop off my hand with the hoe!" he cried.

3

"¡Mentiroso! Liar! I'm not trying to chop it off," Sebastián responded indignantly. "I'm just trying to see how close I can get without hitting it."

Carlos tugged at a big weed. It didn't come up. He stopped pulling.

"Is our time up?" he asked, after three minutes.

Sebastián and Patricio continued working, sharing one hoe. "Tío, they're just little kids," said Patricio, Carlos's ten-year-old brother. "You can't expect much out of them."

I'd often get up early, retrieve the hoe from the shed, and go out into the field alone while the ground was still damp, the morning cool. I liked the smell of freshly turned soil and the way the fog clung low to the ground as the sun climbed from behind the Andes mountains.

We bought one bag of white bean seeds, one bag of yellow corn seeds, and one bag of tiny white onion bulbs. Don Alvaro, the neighbor who spent his days baking little loaves of bread called *marraquetas* that pull apart into four fist-sized pieces, gave us thirty tiny tomato seedlings.

"Carlos, do you want to help me plant these tomatoes?" I asked.

"Do I have to?" he said. "I still have to do my homework."

Gradually I abandoned the idea of having all the kids become involved in the garden. With the help of the oldest two boys, Sebastián and Patricio, I planted five rows of onions, ten rows of beans, and twenty rows of corn. We planted the seedling tomatoes and a few squash and pumpkin seeds. Sebastián and Patricio became my faithful field hands in the late afternoon. They taught me Chilean songs, intentionally picking ones with lots of rolled "rrr's" so they could laugh at my pronunciation. But in other ways they emulated me. They would spit when I spat, knock the dirt off their shoes when I did, and wipe their brows when I wiped mine.

"You little kids just don't know how to work," Patricio told his younger brother Carlos.

Some of the little kids, though, liked to work in the fields. Two-year-old Andrés dug up and reburied half the tomato plants, leaves and all, under the plum tree.

"The tomatoes were getting hot in the sun," Andrés explained. When not burying tomatoes or digging holes and filling them with dog manure, Andrés stood in the field and asked questions.

"Tío, why do plants grow up and not down?" Without waiting for a response, he asked, "Where do seeds come from?"

"Is there a button we can push to turn that kid off?" Patricio asked.

"Tío, why did the goat eat your underwear?" Andrés was indefatigable.

"Andrés, we're going to irrigate the field right now, so you have to go back to the house," I told him.

"Will the goat get wet?" Andrés asked.

The back edge of our field, near Geraldo's final resting place, was bordered by an irrigation canal. Twice a week, Tuesday morning and Friday afternoon, we were allowed to open the canal gate to our field. The water gushed through the gullies between the rows of plants, making the soil dark and rich. The older boys and I stood in the canal and pushed the water with pieces of plywood down the rows. The sun, reflecting off the water, made the garden a lush green.

By mid-January that summer, we ate our first plate of green beans from the garden. They tasted wonderful. Then one Tuesday in late January, the hottest days of the summer, there was no water in the irrigation ditch. I talked with Don Alvaro, who had difficulty understanding my Spanish, and I his. But about the irrigation problems he was clear.

"No plata, no agua. No money, no water."

The farmers and families whose property backed up to the irrigation canal hadn't been paying their water bills to the local water authority. There was no water that Friday or the next Tuesday. The sun beat down, and there was no rain. The soil hardened and then cracked. We salvaged some tomatoes by carrying out buckets of water from the house. The corn stalks dried up. The beans shriveled.

"We worked really hard, didn't we," Patricio commented one afternoon in late summer as we stood looking at the dried remains of the garden. I wasn't sure if it was a question or a statement. By the end of the summer, the only things alive were the weeds and the plum tree with its sour fruit. The kids organized races down the empty irrigation ditch and played hide and seek among the dried corn stalks.

ᔕ

THE ARRIVAL

ᔕ

I had signed up to start law school in Indiana in the fall of 1982 but instead on a sunny November afternoon found myself newly arrived in Santiago walking down a dirt road toward an orphanage where I had agreed to work for the coming year.

It happened like this. A year after graduating with a philosophy degree from the University of Notre Dame, I was finishing my first year teaching at a Catholic boys' school in Canon City, Colorado. The veteran teachers at the school told me that the first year was the hardest, that as a more experienced second-year teacher my class management would improve, and that after a while you simply got used to the unkind things written about you and your family in indelible ink on the bathroom walls. Even with those assurances, I decided I wanted a break from teaching overstimulated teenage boys. Therefore, going to law school in the fall seemed a sensible, if not particularly exciting, option.

Those plans were dramatically altered when a college friend, Nathan Stone, visited me while traveling through Colorado in early May 1982. A few years ahead of me at Notre Dame, he had worked in Chile as part of the Holy Cross Associates, a volunteer program not unlike the Peace Corps that was run by the Holy Cross priests of Notre Dame.

When I was a senior at Notre Dame, I had applied to the same program that had taken Nathan to Chile. At the end of the interview process, the selection committee informed me that because I had never lived or studied overseas (the furthest south I had ever been was Florida), they were concerned about my ability to adjust to such a radically different culture. Instead, I was offered a position in one of the university's volunteer programs in the United States. Not wanting to take what I considered a second-best offer, I went on my own to teach in Colorado.

Nathan's visit reignited my interest in Chile, and we stayed up until 4:00 a.m. talking. He had spent two years teaching in an inner city high school in the capital, Santiago, and had loved it. He described the amazing warmth of the Chilean people, their passion for living, the tradition of folk music (he was a musician himself), and the snow-covered Andes Mountains that dominated the landscape.

His words painted vivid pictures for me: friends gathered at dusk to watch an orange sunset over the Pacific coast while squeezing lemon juice on fresh clams eaten from the shell or the generosity of a humble Chilean family living in a wooden house with a dirt floor and a single lightbulb hanging from a wire, offering visitors their best food.

But there was a darker side to life in Chile. In 1973, a military junta had overthrown the elected socialist government of Salvador Allende, this in a country that until then had one of the strongest democratic traditions in Latin America. Since the coup, the police state permeated every detail of daily life. Neighbors didn't trust one another for fear that one of them might be a government spy. The military leaders shut down whole departments of Chilean universities, especially sociology, political science, and theater, because these academic studies promoted supposedly subversive behavior.

The movie *Missing* captured this dark mood, depicting an American father searching for his son shortly after a military coup in an unnamed Latin American country. *Missing* was based on the true story of Charles Horman, who had "disappeared" in Chile, but it was representative of stories in many Latin American countries with military governments. In the 1970s and early 1980s, those who disagreed with their governments, especially politicians, labor leaders, and university students, often disappeared without a trace. Sometimes, as in Horman's case, it was simply for being in the wrong place at the wrong time.

Nathan gave me a worn paperback called *Audacity to Believe* that had a big impact on my understanding of the political situation in Chile while I was still in the United States. *Audacity to Believe* was the autobiography of a young doctor, Sheila Cassidy, who had tired of practicing medicine in England and decided to travel and work for a time in Chile. She arrived in 1971, during the Unidad Popular government of Allende. Although trained as a plastic surgeon, she ended up providing basic medical care in the poorest parts of the capital and grew to love the country and its people. To me, she was a very credible

7

narrator because she admitted how little she knew and how much she had to learn once she arrived in Chile.

Cassidy was shocked and horrified by the coup of September 11, 1973, which put an end to the Unidad Popular government and sent many of her friends into prison and exile. Some months after the coup, when a priest who was a friend of hers asked her to treat a patient who had been shot in a gun battle with the Chilean secret police, she did not hesitate. As a medical doctor, she felt, quite simply, it was her obligation to treat a wounded person.

The man she treated, a leader of the armed leftist opposition group known as the Movimiento de Izquierda Revolucionaria, or MIR (Revolutionary Left Movement), was one of the figures most hunted by the military. When the secret police discovered she had treated him, she was abducted from her home and taken to the notorious Villa Grimaldi, where she was tortured brutally with electric shocks to elicit the names of people she knew. She resisted until she could endure no more. After she had given the information the secret police sought— essentially the names of her friends, including many priests and nuns working with poor people—she was imprisoned. Only after months of vigorous efforts by the British government was she expelled from the country and put on a plane to Britain.

Even though I found this story incredibly unsettling, I was also fascinated by all that I was learning about Chile and wanted to see the country for myself. I was especially amazed, time and time again, by the accounts of people who worked to support one another in the most oppressive, dangerous situations and the solidarity that developed when people united against injustice.

"If I wanted to go to Chile, what could I do to earn a living?" I asked Nathan very late that first night. "I guess the only thing I know I don't want to do is teach high school."

"Well, I know there is a small orphanage in Santiago where you might work," Nathan said. "It's got about a dozen kids and is a real hand-to-mouth operation, but they might be willing to take you on. I don't know her very well, but the woman who runs it, Olga Díaz, seems amazing."

Together we drafted a letter in Spanish to Olga offering my services. About a month later, I received a three-page, handwritten letter from Olga, which a Spanish-speaking friend helped me translate. In a careful, cursive script, she wrote that the orphanage was called *hogar,* or "home," and that the thirteen children at the hogar formed a family, not an institution. The rest of the letter, though, was less reassuring. Most of the children there had been abandoned or physically abused. Some had lived on the streets. "The process of adjustment," she wrote, "is long, slow, and difficult." The letter concluded, "We are pleased you are interested in spending one year working with us. It is a good life, but difficult. You can be sure, though, that you will be a welcome member of our family."

I abandoned the idea of law school, and in September Nathan and I set off for Latin America—first Mexico, then Peru and Bolivia. In November, we arrived in Chile. Once there, a day after arriving in Santiago, I journeyed with Nathan to meet my new family.

"What's the street number again?" Nathan asked after we had walked about a half mile down a dirt road called Rosa Ester. I looked at the address on Olga's letter, now water-stained and wrinkled. I had been carrying it with me for the past three months.

"Rosa Ester 3281," I said.

"You'll probably recognize the house when you see it again," I said to Nathan.

"I've never been to this house."

"You've never been here?" I asked. I was under the impression that he had, and it made me anxious that he had no clue where it was or what it was like.

"Maybe I wasn't clear, but I only met Olga through some friends at a party," he told me. This was the thin connection on which my future hung.

When we finally arrived at a wooden gate with the numbers 3281 painted in orange, the sun was high in a clear blue sky.

"Hello," Nathan yelled over the fence.

The gate opened, and children came running from every direction. The girls and younger boys gave us a kiss on the right cheek. Some of the older boys extended their hands to shake. A chubby, dark-haired boy hung on my leg. A short, squat woman with a yellow apron introduced the children, whose names came so fast I got none of them.

"Are you Olga?" I asked the woman.

"No, no," she said giggling, her hand covering her mouth, "I'm Tía Eliana. I just help out here."

The kids asked a barrage of questions in Spanish. I only understood, "Where are you from?"

"*Estados Unidos,*" I responded, and immediately there were lots of giggles at my accent.

A woman with shoulder-length black hair came out of the thick-walled yellow adobe house. She was wearing a bright red cotton skirt and silky white blouse.

"My name is Olga Díaz," she said, simultaneously extending her hand and leaning forward to kiss me on the right cheek. She was tall and thin, with penetrating brown eyes, and looked to be in her late twenties. She was wearing high-heeled red shoes: clearly not the ma-tron I had imagined from the letter.

"I see you've met some of the children," she said in Spanish. "There are five more in the afternoon session at school."

"¿Cuánto calza? ¿Cuánto calza?" the oldest boy, Sebastián, who was twelve, repeated. I had no idea what he was asking. I turned to Nathan, who had gotten used to serving as my translator.

"He wants to know your shoe size," he said.

"It's a twelve," I told Sebastián in my best Spanish. Sebastián eyed me suspiciously.

Nathan laughed. "In Chile the shoe sizes are in centimeters—you're probably a forty-six."

"Forty-six," I told Sebastián in Spanish.

Sebastián used his hands the way fishermen do to describe the fish that got away. He couldn't seem to imagine feet so large.

"In Chile," Nathan said to me in English, "people think there is a direct correlation between the size of your feet and, well, your manhood."

Sebastián couldn't stop laughing and stepped back and tripped, landing on top of a pregnant German shepherd. The dog yelped and backed up, knocking over, like dominoes, first a little girl in a yellow dress and then a little boy. Both began to cry. Olga told Sebastián to put the dog behind the house. She picked up the two crying children, brushed them off, and sent them away to play.

Inside the house, I noticed that the slatted wood floors of the liv-ing room smelled of fresh wax. We sat in the living room on plywood furniture covered with foam cushions and a green and yellow hand-knitted afghan. Sunlight coming through the open window cut the room in half, and I sat in the shadows understanding a fraction of what was said.

Olga's room and two small bedrooms for the children were off this main room. In the boys' room there were three sets of bunk beds, con-structed of two-by-fours. There was not a shoe or a discarded sock in sight. The girls' room also had three sets of identical bunk beds on which cloth dolls and stuffed animals lay.

I wondered if this place was always so neat. I also wondered where I was supposed to sleep in this small house. Four more children, wearing school uniforms, came into the living room. The girls were in blue jumpers with white blouses, the boys in gray slacks, light-blue shirts, and navy-blue ties. On their ties was the name of their school, Forjadores del Futuro—"Trailblazers of the Future," Nathan translated for me.

Seven-year-old Alfredo had pieces of leaves in his hair and dirt on his face. The front of his shirt was gray.

"Alfredo," Olga said, "what happened to you?"

"They, at school, they, um, they needed a goalie in the soccer game . . ." he answered.

"Tomorrow morning you're going to wash your own school clothes," she said.

Another boy came into the living room. His school shirt was torn. He was not wearing a tie. He held a tissue up to his bloody nose.

"Marcelo gets into a fight every day," one of the girls volunteered.

Olga shook her head and said to me, "This is Marcelo. I promise you, before long, you will know him well." Marcelo stared at me. He said nothing. I extended my hand. Marcelo turned away and went into the bathroom.

A few minutes later, Néstor came bounding in the front door. Néstor was a twenty-three-year-old grade school teacher who lived and worked part-time at the orphanage. He talked rapidly while motioning with his hands, throwing his arms wide, then pushing back the long black bangs that hung in his eyes. His gestures suggested a frightening amount of energy. I smiled and nodded, not understanding a single word he said.

He said something to me that I didn't catch. Everyone laughed. He smiled, patted me on the back, and said something else that ended with "gringo," the only word I understood. Everyone laughed again.

"You'll be sharing the bedroom at the back of the house with Néstor," Olga told me. "Well," she added, "it's not a real bedroom, just an old shed behind the kitchen that now has two beds. I hope that will be okay."

"Wash your hands for dinner," Olga instructed the assembled crowd. Children scampered.

Eighteen of us—thirteen kids and five adults, including me—reassembled in a long room, thin as a bowling alley, that had been added onto the adobe house to serve as a dining room.

"Before we had this room," Olga explained, "we couldn't sit everyone together at one table." The room had been built from scrap lumber, donated by the neighborhood association.

Néstor asked Patricio to say grace. For the first time since I arrived, there was silence.

"We thank God for this food we are to receive, and we pray for the children begging in the streets, for the unemployed, for those in prison, and for those who do not have this glass of milk. Amen."

Plates were filled with chicken stew left over from lunch and little *marraqueta* loaves of fresh bread.

After dinner, I walked Nathan to the front gate. He and I had spent every day of the last two months together traveling through Mexico, Peru, Bolivia, and Chile, with him serving as mentor and translator. I watched him walk down the dirt road to catch a bus back to Santiago. Despite the house full of people, I felt completely alone.

When I returned, school uniforms had already been traded for pink nightgowns and striped and patterned cotton pajamas. After bickering, laughing, and cajoling, all thirteen kids were in their bunk beds. Following Olga's lead, I went from bed to bed giving each child a goodnight kiss on the cheek. When I bent down to kiss two-year-old Andrés, who was in the bottom bunk, he shot up his leg and caught me in the face with his foot. I jerked up my head and cracked it against the top bunk bed. Andrés laughed.

"I should have warned you," Olga said. "He gave me a black eye the first time I tried to change his diapers. He was about a year old then."

Néstor came into the boys' room.

"Let's go," he said. "Vamos." I followed Néstor out the back door, across a dark field, and over an irrigation ditch. A dog barked nearby. It sounded like a big dog. Néstor talked the whole time.

"Néstor, can you speak more slowly?" I asked him in Spanish.

"I espeak English," he said with a big grin on his face.

"Really?"

"My name Néstor. Dis is a pencil," he added. He laughed and resumed speaking rapidly in Spanish.

We came upon a paved road, streetlights, a group of houses, and a liquor store. We went into the liquor store and Néstor bought two large bottles of dark beer called *malta*. Néstor introduced me as *el gringo* to three rough-looking men standing at the wooden counter drinking beer from the liter bottles. One had a swollen black eye and a blood-stained striped T-shirt.

Walking back, I imagine that Néstor must have told me the story of the one with the bloody T-shirt. Unfortunately, I couldn't understand any of it. Occasionally, he would pat me on the back.

Back at the hogar, Néstor poured the *malta* into a plastic pitcher. He beat an egg and sugar into the dark beer.

"Malta con huevo," Néstor explained. The kitchen light flickered and went out.

Néstor continued beating the mixture. Olga lit a candle and stuck it in the empty beer bottle. The spring breeze came through the open window and the candle flame flickered, throwing shadows on our faces. Néstor explained something about the lights or the beer and eggs—I wasn't sure which. I drank the sweet mixture and wondered if I'd ever understand.

The light in the kitchen came on again.

Olga and Néstor raised their glasses and she said, "Bienvenido a tu nuevo hogar. Welcome to your new home."

Later, I unpacked my brown L. L. Bean duffel bag and took inventory: two pairs of pants, four shirts, socks and underwear, a worn pair of Nike running shoes, a book of short stories by Gabriel García Márquez, a blue hardbound journal that chronicled my travels during the past two months, Olga's letter, and thirty-six dollars in cash. I hung up my empty duffel bag on a hook, climbed into bed, and tried to imagine this place as home.

The next thing I knew an alarm clock was blaring. It was 5:50 a.m. Néstor moved around the bedroom, the radio playing at full volume, and then he turned on the light. His black hair was wet and combed straight back. He put on a green knit tie while rattling off things in Spanish I didn't understand. He walked out of the room, leaving the radio and the light on. I turned off the radio and light and put the pillow over my head.

I woke up again a little later. The morning sun was filtering through a plastic sheet stapled over the window frame. I got out of bed and crossed the cold cement kitchen floor to go to the bathroom. Olga's voice came from the boys' room.

"Take the sheets off the bed," she told Marcelo.

The room stank of urine. Marcelo glared at Olga, not reacting. Finally, he yanked the sheets off the bed. Two-year-old Andrés ran through the living room and out the back door, a flash of dark skin and white underwear. Eight-year-old Verónica, already dressed, her hair pulled back with a blue bandana, chased after him. She pulled Andrés by the arm back into the house. He didn't resist.

Another two-year-old was waiting with me in front of the single bathroom which seventeen of us now shared. He was wearing one-piece blue pajamas with a zipper down the front and saying things in Spanish that I didn't understand. I knocked on the bathroom door.

He crossed his legs and started to cry. I knocked again. Jackie, the German shepherd, came barreling through the living room—in the back door and out the front. In the process, the dog knocked over four-year-old Karen, who started to cry.

After quite a long wait, the bathroom door opened. Ten-year-old Sonia, the oldest girl at the hogar, came out, her wet brown hair pulled back with two small combs.

"Didn't you hear me knocking?" I asked.

"I have to go to school in the morning, too, you know."

The little boy and I entered the bathroom with its cement floor, cracked mirror, and window that opened from the shower into the kitchen. I bent down to unzip his pajamas. They were wet. Standing in front of the toilet, he looked up at me.

"Tío, I don't have to go now," he said.

I got him changed just in time for breakfast. Olga served hot chocolate in mugs and toasted bread with scrambled eggs spread on top like jam. The kids ate in two shifts at the small table in the kitchen. The five older ones, in their blue school uniforms, headed out the door at 7:30 a.m. and returned at 1:00. The second group went to school from 1:30 until 6:00 in the afternoon. Like most schools in poorer neighborhoods in Chile, Trailblazers of the Future didn't have enough classrooms and desks for all the students to attend at one session.

After breakfast, everyone at home did chores. I attempted to help Verónica, who was already cleaning the living room. Verónica had a round face and freckles, her eyes brown with a speck of green. She pushed all the furniture to one side of the room and began rubbing a large steel-wool pad called a *virutilla* with her foot across the floor to take off the old wax.

I tried to imitate her.

"No, Tío!" she said. "Don't you know how to do this?"

She was amazed that I was so ignorant of something so simple. She demonstrated that the *virutilla* had to be rubbed the same way as the wood slats on the floor—not across them, as I was doing. We rubbed off the old wax and swept up the remains. Then, on hands and knees, we put down a new coat of red wax squirted from a plastic tube. We moved all the furniture to the other side of the room and repeated the process. It took about half an hour, and the floor didn't look substantially different from when we started. It may have been a little shinier.

Once chores were finished, Olga asked me if I could help the three first graders—Marcelo, Yoana, and Alfredo—with their homework.

All three were sitting at the long dinner table when I arrived. Yoana sat up straight and smiled. Alfredo, who was soaking wet, having just washed his school uniform, slouched. Marcelo stared at the wall.

Before Marcelo came to the orphanage two months earlier, I learned, he had been living in a one-room shack with his grandfather, who was blind. Marcelo was eight or nine—his grandfather wasn't sure. Marcelo had started first grade once, maybe twice, but he didn't like it so he quit. During his first two weeks at the orphanage, he would climb a tree in the backyard every day and curse at anyone who got near him.

"Take out your notebooks," I told the three. Yoana giggled at my accent in Spanish, Alfredo smiled, Marcelo didn't move. He didn't have a notebook in his school bag, so I gave him a sheet of paper.

"Do you have any homework?" I asked.

"No, Tío," Yoana answered.

"Are you sure? Tía Olga said you had homework."

"Oh, yeah, maybe we're supposed to practice writing our names," Yoana said.

"Okay, now write your names on the top of the sheet."

"I don't know how," Yoana said. Her almond-shaped eyes made her look almost Asian.

"Copy these letters," I said, spelling out YOANA in big letters at the top of the page.

"Sure, Tío," said Yoana. She immediately filled the page with a wavy script that looked like a four-year-old's doodles.

I wrote ALFREDO. He copied it, holding his pencil so tightly that his knuckles turned white. He wrote in a tiny, tight print that filled half a line on the page.

Marcelo stared straight ahead, hardly blinking. I wrote MARCELO at the top of the page.

"Marcelo, you want to try?" I said, sliding the sheet in front of him. He didn't move.

I gave Yoana another sheet of paper. Sweat beaded on her nose as she wrote.

"Come on, Marcelo, pick up your pencil. Alfredo and Yoana are going to beat you." He stared at me. I picked up his hand and put the pencil between his fingers. He made a fist around the pencil and pushed down until the lead point broke. I found another pencil and took his hand through the motions of writing his name. He resisted, but we came out with a wobbly "MORCOLO."

"Now, that wasn't bad, was it?"

Yoana handed me a page covered with intersecting lines that looked nothing like letters. She smiled and asked, "Is it good now, Tío?"

The corrugated aluminum roof intensified the heat in the room. My shirt was wet. Marcelo broke off the pencil point a second time.

"Can I go now?" he asked.

"We'll try again tomorrow," I told them. Marcelo slammed the plywood door as he left.

That evening, after everyone had gone to bed, I was alone in my room at the back of the house. Néstor was spending the night at his brother's house. There was a muffled knock at the door. Sebastián, the oldest of the group, stuck his head in, smiled, and pulled the door shut behind him, as if he had just committed a crime.

"Is Néstor here?" he whispered.

"No," I whispered in reply.

He then pointed to the small black-and-white portable TV set on the top shelf. It was 9:30 on a school night. I let him turn on the set. When the fuzz cleared, a soccer match was on the TV screen. Sebastián sat mesmerized at the end of my bed, hunched over, his elbows on his knees, fingers at his mouth.

"Okay," he said as his team, Colo-Colo, took the ball down the field. He bit his fingernails.

"Estúpido," he yelled as a referee made a call against Colo-Colo and then covered his mouth, afraid he'd made too much noise.

"Okay, okay," he whispered, whether things looked good or bad, "Okay, okay." His legs never stopped shaking.

In the final seconds, Colo-Colo beat Cobreloa 4-3. Sebastián held his right hand over his mouth, waving his left hand up and down, sweating as though he had been playing himself. He took a deep breath, turned off the television, and put it back up on the shelf.

"This is our secret," he said to me, as he pulled the door shut behind him.

That weekend, Sebastián made it his personal challenge to teach me to play soccer, Chilean-style. The other boys except Marcelo joined us on the field. He climbed a tree next to the field and watched.

I had played soccer twice before in my life. These boys had been playing since they were three. Nor did it help that my running shoes were falling apart, the right sole of my shoe flapping freely every time I ran. I got the ball and immediately kicked it over the fence and into the bushes. Sebastián pulled me aside.

"Don't kick the ball so hard. Relax," he told me. Patricio climbed the fence and brought back the ball.

"Come on, let's play," Carlos yelled. I got the ball again. Carlos stuck his feet between mine. I kicked him in the shins, but it didn't stop him from stealing the ball. He laughed as he went down field, dribbling, to score a goal. I tried to relax the next time Sebastián kicked me the ball. Carlos took it away from me again. He was eight years old. This happened a couple more times, until it was apparent I would be a marginal player in this game. There was a pause in the action while we got a drink of water from the hose.

"I'm just going for a short jog," I told the soccer players. "You guys keep playing."

But Sebastián and Patricio said they wanted to run, and then Carlos and Alfredo decided they also wanted to go. Marcelo continued watching from his perch in the tree. We did exercises on the grass next to the dirt soccer field. Three of the girls joined us for jumping jacks. As we headed out the gate, the two youngest girls stood at the gate and cried until we agreed to let them go with us. And thus the neighbors got their first glimpse of the new gringo, tall and skinny, white legs and knobby knees flying in all directions, running down the dusty Rosa Ester Road followed by a pack of nine kids.

THREE

ᔓ

SPANISH LESSONS

ᔓ

My Spanish was so important only because it was so bad.

"Yo quiero comprar fósforos," I told the old man behind the counter at the store at the end of the dirt road.

"What?"

I tried again. "I want to buy matches."

"I don't understand you," he said.

"Fósforos," I said, trying to articulate the critical word. The old man nodded his head and smiled. He was missing two teeth. He reached to the shelf behind him and took down a bottle of vegetable oil.

"Fósforos!"

He reached for toilet paper.

"Fuego," I said. "Fire," making a motion like the striking of a match. "Bueno," he said as he went through a curtain to the back room. He returned with a brown paper bag full of charcoal.

"He wants cigarettes," a woman with a mesh bag full of potatoes told the man behind the counter.

"No, he wants skin lotion," another woman volunteered. I made the motion of striking a match again.

"Fósforos," I begged. I wanted to shout, "I'm really not as stupid as you think I am."

Carlos walked into the store.

"He wants fósforos," Carlos said.

"Oh, fósforos!" said the old man. "Fósforos!" both of the women repeated.

I shook my head yes, yes, *fósforos*. The two women giggled. I gave him the twenty pesos and he gave me a package of matches. The old man shook his head.

"Fósforos," he said, "why didn't you say fósforos?"

Incidents like this were common. Each morning I'd wake up hoping that today my Spanish would be better: that I would get off this plateau where I'd been stuck for the last month—understanding just enough to get me in trouble.

I tired of always stopping conversations with "What?" or "I don't understand," so I'd taken to nodding and agreeing even when I had no idea what was being said. The situation was worst with Néstor, who seemed to talk faster every day.

"Where were you, gringo?" Néstor demanded when he walked in the door one night.

"When?"

"I waited for two hours with twenty kilos of fish that someone from school gave me. Fresh fish in the hot sun. Great. I finally gave most of it away and came home on the bus with six fish. Why didn't you pick me up?"

"From where?"

"Yesterday, you said you would meet me at 4:00 in the downtown fish market."

"I'm sorry. I thought you were talking about something next week."

"Gringo, you're hanging just like a light bulb," Néstor told me.

Olga translated this into Spanish I could understand. "He's saying you're having a hard time understanding—like a light bulb just hanging on a wire in the air."

"Don't worry, gringo, I'm just pulling your hair," Néstor said.

Again Olga. "He says he's just teasing you."

"In English, we say 'pulling your leg,'" I offered.

"Pulling your leg!" Néstor said, laughing. He reached down and pulled on my blue jeans. "You gringos really are crazy!"

Although Néstor's rapid-fire Spanish continued to confuse me, I eventually developed a strategy to deal with uncomprehending shopkeepers. I would take along one of the kids whenever I went shopping.

Although only slightly taller than knee-high, Andrés was a particularly good translator, and together we went one morning to buy eggs for lunch. Andrés, in addition to his linguistic skills, was fascinated with anatomy. As we walked to buy the eggs, he asked, "Why don't you have bones in your eyes?" and "How does your tongue carry food all the way down to your feet?"

"Which house sells the eggs?" I asked Andrés.

"The egg lady lives there," he said, pointing to a white adobe house. A few steps closer and the smell was a dead giveaway.

"Good morning," I said to the egg lady in Spanish, "I want three trays of eggs."

The egg lady peered out from behind her thick, nearly opaque glasses. She neither moved nor said a word. I repeated the phrase, trying to articulate each word in Spanish. The woman shrugged.

"My tío is a gringo," Andrés said to her by way of explanation. "He wants three trays of eggs."

The woman returned with three cardboard trays of brown eggs that she wrapped in newspaper and tied with twine. Walking home, Andrés, the answer-giver, became curious about his own answer.

"Tío, what's a gringo?"

In many parts of Latin America, *gringo* was a derogatory term. In Mexico, for example, *gringo* often carried much the same meaning that "whitey" or "honkey" did in the United States. One legend maintained that during the Mexican-American War, in which Mexico lost significant territory to the United States, the Yankees wore green, and Mexicans could be heard shouting across the border, "Green-go, Green-go." In Chile, however, gringo was used much more benignly and referred to most any light-skinned foreigner—European, North American, or Australian. Not particularly wanting to explain all this to Andrés, I said, "Gringos are people who come from other countries."

"Oh," Andrés said.

"So you are a gringo?"

"Yes."

"Is Tío Nathan a gringo?" Andrés said, referring to my American friend, to whom Andrés had taken a particular liking.

"Yes."

"Is Tía Olga a gringa?" he asked.

"No," I said laughing, "she is very Chilean."

"And Tía Eliana? Is she a gringa?" he asked again.

"No, no," I said, smiling at the idea of short, dark-haired, and square-featured Eliana being mistaken for a *gringa*.

Andrés was silent the rest of the way home. He walked in the dry drainage ditch, looking straight ahead. The sun beat down on the dirt road, and bees swarmed round the rose and honeysuckle bushes. As we neared the house, Andrés rejoined me on the road and broke the silence.

"All gringos have a penis," he said.

I stopped. I tried to explain to Andrés that a gringo was a foreigner and it was just a coincidence that all the men he named were gringos and women were not. Yes, I explained, there were women gringos, okay, but they are called "gringas." This explanation only seemed to confuse him. Shortly before lunch, I heard Patricio taunting my egg-buying companion.

"Andrés says he is a gringo! Andrés says he is a gringo!" Andrés stared furiously at Patricio, unable to understand the breach of such a confidence.

Patricio was thin and had a thin face, high cheekbones, and a delicate nose. Patricio's brother Carlos had similar features. Everyone called Patricio by the nickname "Pato," which struck me as funny because *pato*, I had learned in the first-grade Spanish reader, meant "duck." Pato did not find my revelation funny. At ten, Pato was probably the smartest kid in his fourth-grade class, and most things seemed to come to him easily, especially school and sports.

One day I noticed that Pato's sneakers had broken shoelaces that were only long enough to go through two of the five loops.

"Pato, put some new shoestrings in your shoes," I told him.

"Tío, I don't have any."

"Okay, I'll pick some up tomorrow."

"Really, you'd do that for me?"

"It's not a big deal."

The next day I handed him a new pair of white shoestrings.

"Nobody ever bought anything like this for me before, ever." He had tears in his eyes.

"Pato is really a special kid," I told Olga later that evening.

"Yeah, he is," she said.

I told her the story about the shoestrings. She paused. "Pato has been here almost two years. He's been given new things—new clothes, a new soccer ball, new things for school. Pato and Carlos were the first two I ever took responsibility for, and they're both very special to me. But don't get too taken in. Pato sometimes takes advantage of people, especially people who don't know him very well."

After a while I did begin to see a more troubled side to Pato. He was the only one of the kids who would say he didn't want to be at the hogar and sometimes raised the issue with the other kids. He told them he had a family he could return to, while they did not.

"This is just temporary," I overheard him telling Sebastián. "My mom is going to come and get me as soon as she works out everything with my dad."

"Don't be stupid," Carlos once told his older brother Pato on hearing that Pato was planning to go home soon. "Dad's in jail and Mom doesn't care about us. You're never going to live with her." Pato was hard-nosed about everything but his family, whereas Carlos was hard-nosed about nothing except his family.

If Pato needed new shoestrings, I desperately needed new shoes. The soles of the Nike running shoes that had taken me across two continents developed holes the size of silver dollars. The sole of the left one had been glued but wouldn't stick for more than a day or two, and I usually smelled of the rubber cement that was holding my shoe together. I set out to buy new shoes, flapping as I walked.

Vicuña McKenna Avenue, a major retail district, had two full blocks of stores selling nothing but shoes. I got off the bus when the first shoe shop came into sight. It was an adobe building with a high ceiling. There was only one kind of sneaker, with a cheap plastic sole.

"Let me try on a size 46."

"We don't have them in size 46," the saleswoman responded.

Well, at least she understood me, I thought.

"OK, the brown shoes."

"We don't have them in size 46 either."

"What do you have in size 46?"

"I'm sorry," she said, "we don't sell them that big."

I went to the next store. Smiles, but no size 46.

I entered a third store.

"Do you have size 46?"

"No, sorry, sir."

There were eight shoe stores on the block. I went to all of them. Same story. The final store was larger than the others, with chairs and knee-high mirrors. It was air conditioned.

"Do you have size 46?" I asked the owner.

"Espera, espera, por favor. Wait just one minute, wait, please," he said before disappearing behind a red velvet curtain at the back of the store.

I tried to imagine the ugliest shoes possible. Maybe yellow leather ones, like bowling shoes. Whatever he had, I would buy. The owner came back with his wife, a heavy woman with no teeth. She was wearing a dirty red apron and smelled of fish and garlic. He did not have a pair of shoes in his hands. The two of them stood in front of me without saying a word.

"Size 46," he finally said, pointing to my feet.

His wife burst out laughing, a big toothless laugh. She laughed so hard that the rolls of fat on her arms shook.

"I'm sorry," the owner said. "I don't have shoes that big. Nobody has ever asked for them so big, and my wife has never seen feet that big. I just had to show her."

FOUR

OLGA AND THE HOGAR

I began to piece together Olga's story and that of the Hogar Domingo Savio. Olga grew up in the coastal town of Viña del Mar in a working-class family with two sisters and one brother. Her father worked in the navy and traveled a great deal. As in many Chilean families, women were the strong figures, and Olga's mother was no exception. She taught all four of her children the importance of hard work, and those values played a big part in Olga's worldview.

After finishing a university degree in education, Olga taught grade school, then worked at two different large orphanages, the second one with over three hundred children. She was responsible for about sixty young girls who lived, ate, and went to school together. They rarely interacted with anyone outside the orphanage.

"When the girls were eighteen," Olga explained, "they were put out on their own. About the only thing they were qualified to do was to become maids." She found the conditions oppressive, including a priest there who required the older girls to give him baths. "Is it any surprise that very shortly after these girls left the orphanage their babies end up back in the same orphanage?" she asked.

Olga became increasingly frustrated with what she called "the warehousing of children," and so when an eccentric French priest, Padre Louis, in what was at that time considered a subversive act, conspired with her about starting something different and smaller, modeled after a family, she jumped at the chance. People laughed at her naïveté. A young, single woman in Chile, with almost no resources and no institutional sponsor except a crazy priest, was launching a well-intentioned project that was destined to fail. But Olga was determined.

Padre Louis paid the rent for the first few months, and the project was born.

Abandoned and abused children were brought by relatives, teachers, or social workers who knew Olga, and more seemed to arrive every week. Children with incredible and tragic stories: a badly malnourished baby and his three-year-old sister who were living on the street with their mentally ill mother, a young boy who was physically and sexually abused, a little girl whose mother was a drug addict. After two months, Padre Louis and Olga were responsible for ten children under twelve years old. She approached social service and church organizations for financial support. Padre Louis grew frustrated by the challenges of raising money every month and wanted to give it up, but Olga said, "As long as there is one child remaining here, I will make this work."

She went from door to door, literally, looking for support. On one occasion, she was required to fill out a form, and the first line required the "name of the institution." At that time the orphanage had no name. Olga knew that simply writing *hogar*—"home"—wouldn't work. Olga looked up from the desk where she was sitting and saw a framed picture of a saint, Domingo Savio. She knew he had a special relationship with children and thought that he was the patron saint of orphans. She filled in the blank line with Hogar Domingo Savio, and the orphanage had a name. Only later did she learn that the pious Italian boy Domingo Savio, who died in 1857 at the age of fourteen, was actually the patron saint of choirboys.

Olga applied for funds from the government agency that dealt with orphanages. When it became apparent that the government would have control over which children could live at the hogar, she declined its assistance.

"Better to live hand to mouth than to be told, 'Oh, by the way, we're going to take this child and give you a different one tomorrow'," she said. "The reason I started the hogar was to get away from warehousing children."

Olga, Néstor, and I drove to Las Condes, a wealthy suburb of Santiago, where we matched the address on the scrap of paper Olga was carrying to a two-story, white brick house. We peered through a high, black metal fence into a rose garden and manicured lawn. We were there to see the nineteen-year-old maid who opened the house's gate. She invited us into a living room that was furnished with a leather couch, a marble coffee table, and walnut paneling. She was wearing a pink polyester uniform and was obviously ill at ease playing hostess in the family's living room.

"I don't know what to do," she said and began crying before she could say anything else. The story came out in pieces. She had a fourteen-month-old son named Héctor who had been staying with relatives. Because of her job, she could only see Héctor on Sundays.

"They treated him real bad . . . he couldn't stay," the woman said.

"What do you mean?" Olga asked.

The woman left the room and returned with a little boy dressed in blue cotton shorts and a white T-shirt. He had light brown hair, hollow cheeks, a pasty complexion, and enormous brown eyes. The mother pulled up Héctor's T-shirt and pointed to small circular scabs on his stomach.

"They burned him with cigarettes," she said and started to cry again. "When I saw this, I brought Héctor to this house with me . . . but the owner of the house told me either the child goes or I do."

Héctor clung to his mother's leg. "I don't know what to do. I have nowhere to go if I lose this job. You have to take him. I have nowhere else to turn."

There was a pause.

"You are his mother," Olga said, "and you have to take responsibility for your baby . . . but we can help you out until you work it out with the owner or find a new job. You must understand this is a temporary situation." The woman nodded her head vigorously, as she left the room to get the boy's things.

"Her boss must be a real witch," Olga whispered to Néstor and me. The mother returned with a white plastic bag full of Héctor's clothes. She pushed the child toward me. Immediately Héctor started crying. Olga moved toward him. She lifted him up, jostled him, and talked to him softly.

"Héctor, everything is going to be just fine," she told him. He continued to cry. His mother stood at the gate. Olga, Néstor, Héctor, and I climbed into the car, as it was beginning to get dark. Héctor sat on Olga's lap, and she let him play with the car's interior light, turning it on and off.

As we drove back, Olga said, "I have to pick up something at the store. I'll just be a minute." We stopped, and Héctor stayed in the car with Néstor and me. I held him, but he cried the entire time Olga was in the store.

"What do you want to bet it was a man who burned Héctor's stomach?" Néstor asked.

When Olga returned, she held Héctor, and he quieted. She had bought a container of apple juice with a straw and a small stuffed brown bear. She gave the bear to Héctor.

"This is a friend you can sleep with tonight," she told him.

The hogar was quiet when we returned. Eliana had already put all the children to bed. Since there were no extra beds, Olga turned down the sheets at the foot of Andrés's bed and tucked in Héctor and his brown bear.

Although the economic situation at the time in Chile was terrible, Olga always managed to pay the rent and keep food on the table. She was an incredible entrepreneur.

"The way I approach people when asking for help is to make them part of a dream. What dream is more compelling than creating a better world for a child who has been abandoned or abused?" She organized a group of individuals to bring fresh vegetables and fish to the hogar each week. She went to kindergartens and grade schools and encouraged them to conduct campaigns to collect used clothing and powdered milk. Olga was never afraid to ask. If the hogar was down to its last kilo of powdered milk, she would "hit the streets." This might mean having tea with a group of women from Los Leones Country Club in one of Santiago's wealthy neighborhoods or going back to one of the schools on her list.

"Just think of little Héctor," she would say, having poignantly told the story of how he arrived at the hogar. "Right now, what that little boy needs are three things: love, a stable environment, and healthy food. Two of those things we can provide, no problem. But right now we only have one package of powdered milk for all those growing children!"

Inevitably, the next day someone would arrive with a big sack of powdered milk. Olga once struck a deal with one of Santiago's best hotels to give the hogar all its old towels and chipped china. In fact, the hotel donated so much that Olga distributed the extras throughout the barrio. As a result, families in La Granja, some of whom didn't have indoor plumbing, were regularly dining off fine china from the five-star Hotel Carrera.

"God will provide," Olga always said. Occasionally she added, "And the harder we work, the better He provides."

Néstor and others like me lived and worked at the orphanage for various periods of time, but it was clear that Olga was the person who was responsible for this home. She was the stable element in the lives of these children. The younger children all called her *mamá*.

I learned many things from Olga, including the art of shopping in Santiago's outdoor markets. She would walk through the entire market once—past oranges and apples piled high in wooden crates and carrots and purple beets tied together in bunches on plastic sheets, past pink fish hung from rusty metal hooks and chicken claws in plastic tubs sold by the dozen for soup, past ropes of braided garlic cloves and brown cinnamon sticks lined up on wooden tables, past the olives sold out of barrels, the little green almond-shaped ones at thirty pesos a kilo and the dark, fat, shiny ones at fifty pesos a kilo. The first trip was to check out the prices, and then on the return passage she would start making purchases.

"This lettuce is so scraggly, aren't you embarrassed to be selling it at fifteen pesos a bunch?" she would ask. Fifteen pesos was about fifty cents. This was part of a ritual between buyer and seller that had probably been transpiring for centuries. Olga was masterful.

"How much is the cod?" Olga asked.

"One hundred pesos a kilo," said the fish seller in his dirty gray apron.

"You've got at least five kilos there," Olga said. "It's already late, and I know you won't be able to sell all of that today. Also I know that you wouldn't sell fish that wasn't fresh—so you'll have to throw out what you don't sell today. You know how the kids at the hogar love your fish. I'll buy all five kilos for three hundred pesos." Inevitably, a deal would be struck.

Sometimes Olga drove me crazy. She was strong-willed and, at times, bullheaded, a description I don't think she would argue with. Incredibly, she believed the same things to be true of me. She was also convinced that when I wanted to be alone, even to get away from the noise, then something was wrong.

"Don't you want to watch TV with us?" she would ask me if I was reading in my room at the back of the house.

"No, thanks," I said.

"Is everything okay?"

"Yes, it's just nice to have a few minutes of quiet time."

"You're sure everything is okay?"

"Positive."

Chileans typically believed that if you didn't want to be in a room full of people, something was amiss, and the remedy was, obviously, to pull you, physically if necessary, back into the room full of people. After I had lived for a few months at the hogar, Olga grew convinced that gringos had more than a few quirks of their own. These included having no sense of how to dress properly (I never ironed my clothes), being rigid, abrupt, impatient, and obsessed with time.

On the issue of time, the language itself conveyed a central difference of perspective: *una visita gringa*—"a gringo visit"—meant a rushed visit, whereas *hora Chilena*—"Chilean time"—meant that an event was likely to start anytime from twenty minutes to some hours later than scheduled.

"Olga, it's already 7:20," I said, holding the wedding invitation in my hand, which announced that the ceremonies would begin at 7 p.m. It was my first chance to attend a wedding in Chile, and it was at least a twenty-minute walk to the church.

"Don't be so impatient, gringo," Olga said. I had always believed that telling someone emphatically not to be impatient did not help matters but decided not to comment.

We arrived at 8:00 and were among the first in the church. The service started around 9 p.m.

While at times she may have been impatient with me, she had an incredible way with children. She loved these kids enormously but also demanded much from them.

"I learned when I was teaching that you have to set high expectations. Kids internalize what they see all around them. You have to strive for excellence. I'm stubborn and hardheaded, but I think you need to be tough to make something like this hogar work," she said.

Olga's personal life had not worked out as she had hoped it would. "Maybe one day I'll get lucky and meet my *media naranja,* my better half," or literally the "other half of the orange."

Olga almost never talked about one important man who had touched her life. Actually, it was eight-year-old Verónica who first told me about Nino. He had been a novice monk at the Trappist monastery in the countryside east of Santiago. Nino had decided that life in the monastery was not his vocation and that he needed to make a transition to whatever he would do next.

Padre Louis knew Nino and told Olga that this former monk would be a great help and wonderful with the children, and he was. From the way Verónica and others talked about Nino, he was a terrific man—patient and fun-loving. Nino built the wooden floor in the shed behind the kitchen that I was now using as a bedroom. He helped out with everything, including cooking and cleaning—not typical behavior for a Chilean man. What Verónica remembered most was how he made Olga laugh. There were games with buckets of water and treasure hunts. All the kids were counting on Nino to develop a permanent relationship at the hogar. From a few kids, there were less than subtle hints about the future of Olga's relationship with Nino. Verónica and Yoana bickered over who would be the flower girl at the wedding.

After working and living for some months at the hogar, Nino traveled to his hometown in Temuco about seven hundred miles south of Santiago. Some weeks later, Olga received a terse letter from Nino explaining that he would not be returning to Santiago. He had reconnected with a woman in Temuco whom he had known before entering the monastery, and they had gotten married.

NOT AS IMAGINED

Walking toward the hogar, usually even before I'd smell the honeysuckle bush that had pushed through the unpainted wooden fence, I'd hear the kids playing. Carlos's voice, as usual, rose above the rest. He saw me approaching and ran to meet me at the gate.

"Tío, did you know the *pacos* killed a girl in my class?" Carlos asked.

Pacos was a derogatory name for the Chilean police, the *carabineros*.

"They shot a girl and she died," Carlos repeated. "Pacos culiados," he said under his breath, "fucking pigs."

Olga filled in the details of the shooting. About a week earlier, the girl, a nine-year-old classmate of Carlos, had been staying at her grandmother's house in La Legua, one of Santiago's poorest neighborhoods. That night, a man had been abducted from his home in the neighborhood by agents of the Centro Nacional de Información, the CNI secret police. The next morning the community erupted in protest, blocking streets and burning old tires. To break up the protest, the *carabineros* arrived in full riot gear, with giant water cannons mounted on their military vehicles. They wielded nightsticks brutally against men and women who were in the street. One *carabinero* shot into the crowd and hit Carlos's classmate in the arm. Her gunshot wound became infected, and she died a few days later in the hospital.

There was a pattern to the story—the person had done nothing wrong but simply was in the wrong place at the wrong time.

"We don't have to go to classes tomorrow because of the funeral!" Carlos added. I wasn't sure if Carlos was anxious or excited by the news.

I wondered if he felt overwhelmed living in a country under military rule surrounded by *carabineros* with machine guns at every bus stop who could kill a nine-year-old girl with impunity. I certainly did.

Of Chile's four official military units—the army, the air force, the navy, and the *carabineros* police—the olive green-clad *carabineros* were Chile's most visible face of repression. That said, it was the quasi-military CNI thugs, operating under the cover of night and with no uniforms except the dark sunglasses they usually wore, who were the most feared.

Not knowing what else to do with this information, I found my journal, sat on a concrete block in the shade on the side of the house, and began to write, an almost instinctual response to try to process information beyond my control.

I had kept a journal for as long as I could remember. In grade school, I wrote on scraps of paper that I hid in a shoe box under my bed. I don't recall all the important things I wrote and kept in the box, which had "PRIVATE" scrawled in big black letters on the top, but I distinctly remember in eighth grade being so terrified someone would find what I had written that I took all the papers, folded them in half, and wound thick, gray electrical tape around the paper until it looked like a lead plate. I then hid the package in the basement. Even there, I was afraid someone might find it, so I stuck the package under some newspapers in the garbage can. The trash went out, to my great relief, as it always did on Mondays, and my secrets were safe.

Years later, my instincts to write had changed little. If I didn't have my journal, I wrote on scraps of paper and on napkins, in a process that was enormously private. I guess writing my private thoughts helped me keep things in perspective. Sometimes I would now read things I'd written six months before about the crisis of the moment but realize that the details seemed foggy, the crisis nearly forgotten. It was good to think that six months from now, the current crisis might similarly be a murky memory.

Sometimes I'd write about things because I just didn't know what else to do with them, like "Tío, did you know the police killed a girl in my class?" and I'd play out my fears in writing about something similar happening to one of the kids here, one of *my* kids.

But some journal themes were repeated year after year: trying to figure out who I was and what was most important; trying to make sense of conflicting versions of truth; the sense of being on a journey, a pilgrimage, a great adventure; the need to learn to live with the constant gap between expectation and reality and the fear of disappointing those I loved.

I knew I had disappointed my parents by coming to Chile. A few weeks before I was to leave, my hometown's local morning paper, the *Fort Wayne Journal Gazette,* had an article about General Augusto Pinochet's violent efforts to crush the opposition in Chile. There was a picture of tanks in the streets of downtown Santiago. I knew these images were unlikely to help my case with my parents.

The summer before I left, I read a little about contemporary Chilean history and politics. There seemed to be at least two competing versions of "the truth."

Version one. Salvador Allende's socialist government took power in the early 1970s, with only about a third of the vote. The government, once in power, encouraged violent takeovers of factories by workers, widespread grabs at private property, and reckless printing of money that resulted in incredible inflation. Allende's ties with Fidel Castro in Cuba grew increasingly strong. There were shortages of food, and in their frustration middle-class Chilean housewives organized, banging together pots and pans in the streets in protest. As has happened at other moments in Chilean history, the military stepped in to return order. An article in *Reader's Digest* I saw that summer by the Georgetown political science professor Jeane Kirkpatrick justified U.S. support for military governments such as that in Chile. She argued that there were totalitarian regimes linked to communist states that were repressive by nature, would never become more democratic, and should not be supported. On the other hand, authoritarian regimes— pro-Western, anticommunist—had a tendency historically to develop into democracies or, in the case of Chile, return to their democratic roots, and needed to be supported. By early 1973, even some democratically minded Chileans argued that it was sensible for the military to step in to end the chaos and return order.

Version two. In 1970, Chileans freely elected a socialist president. Although the votes were divided among three candidates, Allende was elected in a fair process. There were new policies to help the poor and redress historic injustices, as well as a flourishing of cultural expression, of art, music, and poetry. Not surprisingly, these government policies directly threatened the Chilean upper class. Furthermore, the

United States was terrified by the idea that a freely elected socialist government in Latin America might be successful. The United States did everything within its power, short of invading, to bring down the Allende government. The CIA financed efforts to undermine the government, including a massive media campaign against Allende and payments to Chilean truckers not to bring food into major Chilean cities. These efforts made the food shortages worse and heightened the sense of crisis and chaos.

The two versions agreed that on September 11, 1973, after months of protests and food shortages, the Chilean armed forces, led by the army's General Pinochet and the military heads of the navy, air force, and police, launched an attack against the government. President Allende died the same day in the presidential palace. Version one says he shot himself, rather than face the consequences of the chaos he had brought on Chile. Version two says he died a martyr, at the hands of the military.

About a week before I was to leave for Chile, I found myself groping for words to assuage my parents' fears.

"Chile sounds like a really dangerous place with all those political problems," my mother said, raising the subject that we avoided talking about most of the summer before my departure.

"I'll be careful, and I'm sure I won't have any problems."

"Tell us more about where you'll be working," my father said. He had worked for IBM since graduating from college and wasn't much impressed by my plans to "explore different options."

"It's an orphanage run by a Chilean woman, Olga Díaz. My friend Nathan Stone wrote her a letter, and she said it's fine that I come."

"So what are you going to do there?" my father asked.

"Just help out in any way I can."

"And they're going to pay you a salary?"

"I don't think so, but I'm not sure. But I'll live there so I won't have any expenses."

"So what if this orphanage job doesn't work out?"

"I guess I could teach English to businessmen or something like that."

There was a long pause. "Sounds like you really haven't thought this out very well," he said. I looked down at my hands resting on the table and didn't say anything.

When I was about eight or nine, my father and I began a communication ritual at the dinner table that continued for three or four years and became highly developed. I would sit down at the opposite end of the table from him. As I was considered to have the worst table manners and the worst attitude of the five kids in our family, my father would direct me to sit next to him. I'd sigh dramatically at the injustice of being singled out again and would move to the chair next to him and start eating.

"Don't gulp your food down with milk," my father would say.

Another sigh.

"Steve, please, don't put your elbows on the table."

I would roll my eyes.

"Don't roll your eyes at me, young man."

"I'm not rolling my eyes at you," I'd say. In my mind I was rolling my eyes at the unfair situation. That subtle distinction was lost on my father, and within two minutes the sequence would end with me being sent to my bedroom, where I would stew about the injustices I had to endure daily. At the time, I could never understand why my three brothers and sister rarely seemed to get sent away from the dinner table, and that only deepened the sense of unfairness. Ironically, more than anything in the world I wanted my father's approval, while I probably did exactly the things that made him think I didn't give a damn about what he thought.

My mother was often the mediator in the family. After I'd been sent away from the dinner table, she'd come to my bedroom with the meal's last piece of apple pie.

"Why don't you go and apologize to your father?" she'd ask me. She'd also ask my father to talk with me. So I would search out my father and mumble an apology or he would come to my room and tell me he was sorry, all in preparation for a repetition of the scene the next night.

Even though I had graduated from college, when discussing my plans to go to Chile with my parents, I felt we were back at the dinner table and I had just rolled my eyes and been sent to my room.

"There sure are plenty of needs here in the United States. If you're interested in helping, you don't need to go all the way to South America," my father said.

I knew there were many needs in the United States and that I didn't have another plan if the orphanage job didn't work. I didn't have much money either. With the nine hundred dollars I saved from my first year of teaching, I imagined I had enough to travel for two months overland to Chile. I'd figure out how I'd earn enough money to get back once I got down there.

Although I truly wanted to help people, I also wanted to backpack through the Andes Mountains and visit Machu Picchu in Peru; to walk the white beaches of the Pacific coast of South America and experience the solidarity that people feel living under military rule; to drink Chilean red wine and eat clams out of the shells; to study the stars of the Southern Hemisphere; and to learn about another culture and to speak Spanish well. What I wanted was an adventure. I had little interest in going to law school, but I didn't want to tell my parents all this.

"We don't want to tell you what to do, Steve, but it's just that law school seems like such a good fit for you," said my mother. "You could really help people if you became a lawyer."

"I'll be able to get a one-year deferment to law school and come back, and everything will be on course," I responded. They were trying to protect me, just as I was trying to protect them.

Later, as I was packing, my father came into my bedroom and said, "I might not agree with your decision, but I'm proud of you for making your own decisions."

I appreciated the gesture, but he was clearly not as proud of me as he would have been had I made the *right* decision, that is, the one he wanted me to make.

SUMMER

I didn't doubt I had made the right decision as I watched the end of the school year award ceremonies a month after I'd arrived in Santiago. Standing in the dirt patio of the Trailblazers of the Future School, I felt like a proud parent.

Verónica was the top student in her second-grade class of forty-five students. As she confidently strode up the stacked wooden crates that served as the stage, I had to remind myself that this mature little girl was only eight years old. Verónica's mother dropped her off one day with Olga and said she would return "as soon as she sorted out a few things." That was three years ago. In Verónica's mind, the situation was clear: she called Olga *mamá*.

December was the beginning of summer in the Southern Hemisphere, and everything did seem turned upside down. In addition to hot, dusty days, December brought innumerable social events at the orphanage. Through Olga's entrepreneurial outreach efforts, at least a half dozen school groups had "social service projects" putting together seemingly identical Christmas parties for "the orphans," as did employees from the telephone company and an insurance company. The kids never seemed to tire of ice cream and paper hats and a house full of strangers. I found it difficult to be around the house with so many people, feeling like a spectator, unnecessary, superfluous.

"I'm so glad we can help out the orphans," a woman from the telephone company told me. "They seem just like normal children." I ate my ice cream off the paper plate in silence.

The week before Christmas there was a heat wave, with temperatures in the nineties. It was strange to hang tinsel and Christmas decorations on a Christmas tree (a sickly one right out of "Charlie Brown's

Christmas") while wearing shorts and a T-shirt, stranger yet to hear "Jingle Bells" and "White Christmas" in Spanish. What could these songs mean to Chileans as they packed picnic baskets, towels, and suntan lotion and went to the beach with their families on the days around Christmas?

Olga made sure that Christmas was something more than just an abundance of food, toys, and Christmas parties organized by the telephone company. In the weeks leading up to Christmas, she organized evening sessions at which she would read stories from the New Testament and ask the kids their thoughts on the stories.

"Why do we celebrate Christmas?" Olga asked.

"Because it's the birthday of baby Jesus," Sonia responded.

"What are you going to pray for this Christmas?"

"That my mother and sister have enough food," Sonia said.

For Christmas Eve Olga invited the French priest, Padre Louis, to celebrate a mass in the back patio. He had been one of the few people who had believed in her when she began the hogar. Although Padre Louis had not been much help on the economic front, he stayed engaged on the spiritual one. After mass, there was a celebration unlike any I'd ever experienced at Christmas.

The children's handmade paper ornaments and a green paper tablecloth adorned the dining room. Olga and Eliana had been cooking all day, and there were four baked chickens, french fries (a great delicacy in the house), tomato and avocado salad, and strawberry ice cream. After the feast, while the table was being cleared of chicken bones and ice cream dishes, the youngest ones stood around, nervously asking what could be in the dozens of brightly wrapped packages under the Christmas tree. In their excitement, Andrés and Juanito both wet their pants.

After dinner, Olga read off the names on the different packages wrapped in green or red tissue paper. Each child came forward and took back their presents. Andrés plopped down next to the tree and immediately ripped open the packages. Verónica carefully removed and folded the wrapping paper so she could save it and use it again.

Looking at the assortment of new trucks and dolls, dresses and pants, shoes and underwear for the kids, I felt less hostile toward the gift-bearing groups who had invaded the house over the past weeks. There was a bright red fire engine for Marcelo. After he opened it, he looked up and asked, "Is this for me?" Olga nodded. He smiled and said, "Before this, the best Christmas present I ever got was a *pan de Pascua*." Pan de Pascua was a Chilean fruitcake.

Most of the kids had made gifts for Olga, Néstor, Eliana, and me—drawings and painted pine cones, crocheted doilies, and hand-painted Christmas cards. Sebastián gave me a pair of new white athletic socks he had bought with his own money.

"I bet these will help you play soccer better," he told me.

After the last present was opened and all the wrapping paper was cleared away (with Verónica carefully picking through the pile for ribbons and bows), Néstor inserted a tape in the cassette player that produced tinny salsa music.

"Time to dance," he yelled, and with that every adult and child danced on the patio under the stars, first to salsa, then to funky versions of Christmas tunes, and then to the soundtrack from *Saturday Night Fever*. Olga and I dipped and discoed, and the kids just kept dancing.

At about one in the morning, feeling exhausted, I asked Olga, "Don't you think we should put the kids to bed?"

"Gringo, they're enjoying themselves," she told me. "Tonight and New Year's are the only times we let them stay up like this. It makes them feel grown up. It also means that they will be so tired that they'll sleep in tomorrow morning, so we can sleep too."

She smiled the most wonderful smile, her eyes sparkling. I was twenty-three, and she was thirty-one. She seemed so much older than I and much more worldly. I smelled her perfume as we danced a slow dance. I would have held her closer, but I was intimidated and in awe. Olga was one of the strongest women I'd ever met.

At about two in the morning, as I said good night to everyone and went to drop in a heap on my bed, Néstor flipped over the salsa cassette for probably the tenth time and yelled, "Let's dance."

A few weeks after Christmas, a box arrived in the mail from my family. It contained saline solution for my contacts (an expensive and almost impossible to find item in Santiago), one pair of Nike running shoes and one pair of brown leather shoes, both in beautiful size twelve, and a matted five-by-seven-inch photo of the family. In the picture, my mother, father, three brothers, sister, sister-in-law, and two dogs were lined up in front of my parents' white marble fireplace. A pine cone wreath with a red bow hung over the fireplace and in the picture Mom held up a sign that read "Feliz Navidad, Esteban, y Próspero Año Nuevo a Olga y los niños"—"Merry Christmas, Steve, and a Happy New Year to Olga and the children." In her accompanying letter, she explained that the translation was courtesy of the local high school Spanish teacher. Mom's letter concluded, "We really will miss you this Christmas, but we're all so looking forward to seeing you in September."

The letter made me more than a little uncomfortable. I'd avoided telling my parents that I had recently decided I wouldn't accept my deferred admission to Indiana University Law School and that I wouldn't be back in September as we had originally discussed.

I procrastinated writing to tell them I wanted to stay longer in Chile for reasons that were extremely hard to articulate to myself, much less to someone else. Although it was only January, I was confident that come September I wouldn't be ready to return. There was just too much left undone, too much yet to learn.

SEVEN

MORE SPANISH AND OTHER
LESSONS ABOUT CHILE

If you ask Chileans about the things of which they are most proud, their country's poets would certainly be near the top of the list. Gabriela Mistral, a schoolteacher from northern Chile, won the country's first Nobel Prize for Literature in 1945, but it was Pablo Neruda, who received the Nobel Prize in 1971, who won their hearts.

Neruda, born in 1904, had working-class roots, and he even changed his original name, Neftalí Reyes Basualto, so that his father, a railroad worker, would not learn that his son was a poet. I fell in love with Neruda's poetry on first reading. I learned quite a bit of Spanish by reading and rereading my *Pablo Neruda: Selected Poems, A Bilingual Edition*, edited by Nathaniel Tarn. I read through that yellowing volume of more than five hundred pages—Spanish poetry on the left, English translation on the right—so many times that the pages fell out of the bindings, and I had to put a rubber band around it.

Neruda's poetry often deals with concrete objects and concrete emotions, of history and foreign lands, and reading a little makes you want to read more. His works are infused with joy and passion, humor and energy. In life, he was an eccentric and eclectic collector of toy ships and shells, foreign coins and bottles, Russian dolls and mismatched plates—and his poetry demonstrates the same kind of enthusiasm, curiosity, and spontaneity. Even when his writings turn dark, you see a human being struggling to make sense of big, difficult, and painful questions. Maybe I liked him so much because his was the first poetry I could really understand in Spanish, as so much of his language is very tangible, such as this piece of a poem from "Night on the Island" from *The Captain's Verses*.

Pan, vino, amor, y rabia
pongo en ti
porque eres la copa
que esperaba el regalo de mi vida

Bread, wine, love, and anger
I heap upon you
because you are the cup
that was waiting for the gift of my life.

Neruda joined the Communist Party of Chile in 1945 and became a senator the same year. He traveled the world, especially in Europe and Asia, where at different times he served as a diplomat, but he loved Chile and always considered it his home. We shared a birthday—July 12—and for some reason that seemed an important connection. As is true of many national icons, everyone tried to make Neruda into whatever it was they wanted him to be. He was held up by different groups as representing their views, whether as romantic or political leader, rebel or artist, communist or statesman.

I also learned a lot of Spanish in attempting to teach the first graders their ABC's. Classes with Yoana, Alfredo, and Marcelo were a circus. Initially, I tried to teach the three of them together for an hour a day. Yoana couldn't follow what was going on, Alfredo fidgeted, and Marcelo hit, pinched, and did anything he could to annoy the other two. Taking them on one at a time at the black desk in my bedroom worked much better. How many hundreds of times did I repeat *a-e-i-o-u* in Spanish? Probably just enough for me to stop confusing the sounds in English and Spanish. I learned much of my Spanish the way a child does—not by memorizing conjugations of verbs, but by putting sounds together with objects, especially the pictures in the first grade reader—*pelota y araña, muñeca y cachorro*—ball and spider, doll and puppy.

Yoana always wanted to be first to sit at the desk for class. She brought me dandelions, marbles, and her drawings, cocking her head and smiling in a way that was frighteningly seductive for an eight-year-old. These were mannerisms she had learned in begging for money.

"I always gave a person a flower before I asked for money," she once told me. She wrote her "b's" and "p's" backwards, inverted her vowels, and could never remember what we had done the class before.

She smiled, her almond eyes shining. "I'm learning real good, no?" After about twenty minutes she said in a grown-up voice, "Are we done, professor?" I nodded. "Fine," she said before scampering off to rejoin the youngest girls playing with their dolls.

Alfredo always arrived filthy, the dirt ground into his shirt and face and hands, a twig or leaf adorning his mussed brown hair. He lived to play soccer, especially goalie, since it provided an excuse to leap into the dirt on a regular basis. He had grown up in the countryside, in Santa Mónica, a farming community where there were woods to explore, streams to swim in, and trees to climb. Alfredo's mother, Olivia, raised him, his frizzy-haired older sister Sonia, and his two younger sisters in a one-room shack with a dirt floor. Olivia tried to keep the children clean by hauling water in buckets from a nearby stream. Every day she would sweep the dirt floor of the shack. But there was simply not enough food for the five of them to eat—they survived by drinking tea and eating white bread, the staples of the Chilean poor. From a country priest, Olivia learned of the hogar. She brought the two oldest children, Sonia and Alfredo, and asked if they could stay. They would be able to go to school, and the two little girls remaining at home would have more food. Olga agreed. Alfredo and Sonia were the only children who were at the orphanage for purely economic reasons. At least once a month, Olivia made the three-hour bus trip from Santa Mónica to Santiago to visit her children. She always contributed something from her garden, a canvas bag of celery or a box of tomatoes.

Carlos loved to tell the story of Alfredo's arrival at the hogar. "The first time farm-boy Alfredo saw the toilet flush, he went tearing out of the bathroom, sure he would be pulled into the toilet along with everything else in the room!"

Alfredo had an aversion to soap. His passion for dirt, however, was not matched by a similar passion for reading and writing. Studying was tolerable, but soccer was better. At my desk, he wrote in a minuscule script using a tiny red pencil stub.

"Alfredo, where's the new pencil I gave you yesterday?"

He shrugged and continued writing, gripping the stub tightly. Alfredo, who had just turned seven, was intelligent in a straightforward, honest way, and by the end of the summer we had worked through the entire first grade reader. While he learned to write the words in Spanish—"horse," "boat," and "ball"—I was learning too; by the end of the summer we were both tackling words like "penguin," "umbrella," and "diamond."

After class with Alfredo, I tracked down Marcelo. He usually hid in a ditch or up in a tree. I brought him, sometimes physically carrying him, to my bedroom.

"Marcelo," I told him, "I know you really, truly want to study with me," as I physically maneuvered him into the chair at the desk. The situation with Marcelo reminded me of when I was ten years old. I spent part of the summer at my grandmother's farm in Ohio trying to tame a wild barn cat. I would corner the cat, grab it, and take it, sitting on a porch swing, talking softly, convinced that my attention would transform the cat into a loyal pet. Within five minutes, though, the cat would manage to get a fang or claw loose and in the process regain its freedom. I never did tame it, and on my return home my mother exclaimed, "What happened to your hands?"

I had equal luck that summer with Marcelo.

"*CA-CE-CI-CO-CU*," I said, pointing to the page with the letter "C" in the reader.

"*CA-CA, CA-CA,*" Marcelo said, defiantly staring at me. *Caca* in Spanish means "shit." I tried coaxing, joking, and disciplining, but nothing worked. His reaction was the same day after day: a cold, angry stare and then after a while, "Can I go now?"

Marcelo did love listening to stories and watching TV. I overheard him repeating stories he'd seen on TV almost word for word to the little boys. Marcelo's obvious intelligence made my unsuccessful efforts with him all the more frustrating.

From Olga and Néstor I learned about Chile, life, children, and more than a modicum of Spanish. Shortly after I arrived, we stayed up late one night and drank *pisco,* a strong brandylike liquor made from grapes that was served with lemon and sugar to create a *pisco sour.* That evening had specifically been set aside so Olga and Néstor could teach me Chilean slang, especially all the words I shouldn't be asking about in front of the kids. I duly wrote two pages of columns of words. My journal that night began with a diverse list of *garabatos:*

> *marica*—queer
> *puta*—whore (but also used as an exclamation for something really good or really bad)
> > *hijo de puta*—son of a bitch (note: *putear* means to yell at someone)
> > *cafiche*—pimp

The worst *garabatos* are, not surprisingly, related to people's mothers. In Chile, a *concha* is a shell and *concha su madre* is probably one of the ugliest expressions you can utter about someone's mother's private parts.

"*Huevón,* now that's an important one," said Néstor. "In Chile, guys use it, on one hand, when they're talking about their best friend, *huevón,* and on the other hand, their absolute worst enemy, is, yes, *huevón.*"

"A bad *huevón* is an 'asshole'", Olga added helpfully.

"So how do you know when it's the good *huevón* and when it is the bad *huevón?*" I asked.

"It's all context, gringo," he said. "For example, if I say to you, 'Todos los pacos son huevones . . . All the cops are *huevones* . . .' are we talking about good or bad *huevones?*" Néstor asked.

"Más que huevones, los pacos son hijos de putas," I suggested. "Even worse than *huevones,* the *pacos* are sons of bitches."

"*Puta,* gringo, I didn't think you would ever learn to speak Chilean, but, *huevón,* I think it's going to work," said Néstor proudly, sounding a little like an enthusiastic Professor Henry Higgins speaking to Eliza Doolittle.

We assembled the children for dinner, but there were only twelve. The vacancy was at four-year-old Karen's place. I had yet to hear the fair-skinned, timid little girl utter a complete sentence. Typically, Karen stared out through her sad brown eyes, frightened and seeming to understand nothing. Before coming to the hogar, she had lived the first three years of her life with her epileptic mother, constantly moving from place to place.

Carlos complained at the dinner delay: "Stupid girl, she climbs under things and falls asleep and you can never find her when it's time to eat." Carlos's prediction proved true: we found Karen curled up under a bed in the girls' room.

The next morning Karen had a slight fever, and by six that evening her temperature had climbed to nearly 104 degrees. For medical and dental care, we usually took the kids to CORDAM, the government-run medical clinic for children in orphanages. CORDAM provided surprisingly good medical care, but unfortunately it was open only from nine to five on weekdays. At all other times, we had to utilize Santiago's public clinics, notorious for overcrowding, long waits, and arrogant doctors.

Karen and I went to the Sotero del Río Public Hospital, which was only about ten minutes by car from the hogar. In the waiting room, we sat on hard orange plastic chairs. We were surrounded by mothers with crying babies. Across from us was a boy with a burnt arm that oozed pus and a little girl with a forehead wound that bled through the gauze patch.

"Karen, how do you feel?" She was pale, her forehead hot.

She didn't respond: it was hard to believe she was the sister of Andrés, who never shut up. Olga called Andrés *el preguntón*—"the one who questions." Carlos called Karen *la gata*—"the cat."

Karen and I continued waiting in silence. I probably spent about ten hours a week waiting in doctors' and dentists' offices. I was not able to speak Spanish very well, but I could drive and I could sit in waiting rooms with sick children.

To pass the time, I had started carrying around a book called *Donde no hay doctor—Where There Is No Doctor*. It was the size of a telephone book and printed on telephone book paper. A guidebook written primarily for people in Latin America who lived far from medical centers, it was also enormously useful for someone as ignorant as I was about medicine. The book emphatically stated that ordinary people, if provided with clear information, could prevent and treat most common health problems in their homes more easily, cheaply, and effectively than in faraway expensive clinics and hospitals. Simple drawings illustrated much of the text. It had no-nonsense directions for how to reduce fevers, deal with contagious infections, and tend cuts and burns, as well as how to recognize when it was imperative to seek professional medical help. From the book, I learned that bacterial infections required penicillin and viral infections did not. The book validated many home remedies that Chileans had used for generations but were thought to be old-fashioned and unscientific, such as cinnamon tea for diarrhea, aloe juice for cuts, and cough syrup made by boiling the acornlike seeds of a eucalyptus tree.

The book also spurred me to ask questions: Why was penicillin sold over the counter in Santiago and given for the slightest cold? Why were expensive vitamin injections, especially for vitamin C, used here so widely, when the money could so much better be spent on fresh fruits and vegetables? Why did so many clinics give so little attention to the human side of the healing process?

It was probably a combination of reading that book, worrying about the kids' health, and spending as much time as I did at medical clinics, coupled with my own frustration at my lack of any concrete professional skills, that got me thinking about the possibility of becoming a doctor. I was increasingly confident I would never study law, but medicine, that might be something useful. If I wanted to apply to medical school, I'd need a year, maybe two, doing the basic science courses I hadn't taken as a philosophy major.

I was playing with mental timetables when the nurse called out, "Karen Carmona Díaz."

It was now almost nine o'clock. We walked down a dark corridor into a brightly lit linoleum-tiled room that smelled of rubbing alcohol. There were three metallic tables in the room. The nurse instructed me to lift Karen onto one.

A heavyset doctor in a white jacket arrived. She felt Karen's glands and asked Karen to open her mouth.

"Say *ahhh*," the doctor said.

The doctor moved a wooden tongue depressor around in Karen's mouth. She grunted something I didn't understand, turned her back to us, wrote something on a pad, handed me a pink slip with illegible words, and turned to the next table and began attending the boy with the burnt arm. I imagined she would say something else. She didn't. Already the nurse was ushering in another woman with her sick child to sit on our table.

"What does this mean?" I asked the nurse, showing her the pink slip I had been given.

"You need to take it to the pharmacy."

"But what does Karen have?"

I must have said it loudly because the doctor turned around and said, "The little girl will be fine. Keep her in bed for a few days and give her the medicine I prescribed." She was gone before I had a chance to ask anything else.

∽

POLITICS

∽

O ne thing I learned in Chile was
that politics intruded into people's lives, whether they were interested
in politics or not. On a rainy summer evening, a rare occurrence as
summers are usually incredibly dry, I was walking past Santa Rosa
church. The lights were on inside the church that night, something I
had never seen before.

On a fence, a poster explained there was a special mass as part of
"Defend Life Week." I wasn't sure if I wanted to get out of the rain or
if I was just curious, but I pushed open the church's heavy oak doors.
Only the front half of the church was lit. A mass had already begun,
with about sixty people gathered near the altar in the light. I had never
been in this church at night; I had only entered it on Sunday mornings, when organ music droned and flies and dust were everywhere,
with fidgeting children whom we obligated to attend mass every few
Sundays against their better judgment. I remembered summer Sundays
when old women in white shawls sprinkled water from liter Coke bottles on the front steps of the church to keep the dust down.

Candles flickered about a statue of Saint Rosa in a corner niche.
Around the feet of the plaster statue, dozens of handwritten notes and
homemade wooden plaques lay draped like fallen leaves. One plaque
began "Most Holy Saint Rosa, thank you for your intercession on behalf of my son, Juan, who had lost his way . . ."

I sat down in the dark at the back of the church. In place of the
usual homily, the priest asked two visitors to speak to the congregation about "Defend Life Week."

A young bearded man about my age climbed the pulpit steps.

"My name is Pablo. Three years ago, I was detained," he began. Although I did not understand every word he said, I certainly followed the narrative.

He had been part of a student organization promoting human rights at the Catholic University. At two in the morning, an unmarked police car came to his parents' home, where he lived. Men broke into the house and took him to a detention center for about two weeks. He was questioned about his political activities, friends, and professors. He was beaten, and electric charges were placed on sensitive parts of his body, including his testicles.

His account was clinical, as if he had been some outsider observing what had happened to Pablo, and not Pablo himself.

"And then in the middle of the night, I was blindfolded and taken out of the building and made to lie on the floor of a car. One of the men sat with his feet on top of me. I was sure they were going to kill me. We drove for a long time and then the car stopped. I was pulled out of the car and dumped on the ground. I could smell the garbage and I was sure that this is where they'd pull the trigger. But then, I heard the car pull away. I took off the blindfold and made my way back to Santiago. The next day I continued with the struggle."

Pablo stepped down and returned to his pew. No one said anything. A young woman with long, dark brown hair, wearing a red and blue wool sweater, climbed the steps to the pulpit.

"My name is Ana and I . . ." She hesitated. She looked dwarfed by the large pulpit, and her face barely reached the microphone. "I have never talked to a group of people before about the terrible things that happened to me. This is very difficult for me, but I think it is important that others know what is happening here in Chile. I was detained on my way home from the university one afternoon. I was beaten and given electrical shock before these men asked me a single question, before they even asked my name. I kept thinking, you have the wrong person, you don't want me. I work with teenagers in our church group and I go to school. I'm not active in any political organization. What do I know about anything?

"I told the man, 'You have the wrong person,' and I told him my full name. He said to me, 'We know who you are, you communist slut,' and hit me. That evening two men came to the room where I was tied up and they raped me. The next day I was raped again. They kept asking for names of partners, but never told me what they wanted with me or why they had done these things to me. I never told them anything that was of any use to them, but after three days they let me go. This all happened over a year ago, and this is the first time I have been able to talk about it like this."

She acted as if she wanted to say something else but, not quite knowing what to do, looked at the priest. He nodded, and she stepped down from the pulpit. The priest stood, and the mass continued. I let my head rest against the wooden pew for a few minutes and then I got up, squeezed through the big wooden doors, and walked home in a light drizzle.

I knew that nothing of Pablo's or Ana's story would ever appear in a newspaper, for if it did, it would be dangerous for them and for the journalist who wrote the story. The stories of abuses were often written anonymously by family and friends and sent out of the country to be published. Occasionally, local papers in Chile reprinted stories that had been published abroad.

When confronted with evidence of disappearances from national and international human rights organizations, government officials discounted most accounts as communist propaganda. When a prominent and respected human rights critic disappeared, the public relations office of the government gave press statements that he had secretly run off with a woman, abandoning his wife and family, and, too embarrassed to show his face again in this country, had faked his own disappearance.

One story, however, received widespread attention both in Chile and around the world. Orlando Letelier was one of the best-known figures in the Allende government, having served as the foreign minister and ambassador to the United States. After the coup, the military government imprisoned Letelier for a year on the brutally frigid Dawson Island, off the southern tip of Chile. Letelier was then sent into exile, and he went to Washington, D.C., where he worked at the Institute for Policy Studies. In his two years in Washington, he became one of Pinochet's most outspoken and influential critics.

On September 26, 1976, a rainy morning in Washington, Letelier was driving to work in his Chevrolet with his assistant, the U.S. citizen Ronni Moffitt, and her husband, Michael. As the car passed through Sheridan Circle in the middle of the embassy district, a remote control bomb that had been placed under Letelier's seat exploded, killing both him and Ronni Moffit. Michael, who survived the attack, cried out something that probably no passerby understood: "La DINA! La DINA!"

After nearly two years of investigation in the United States, the FBI pieced together evidence that led to several indictments, including those of members of Pinochet's Dirección de Inteligencia Nacional secret police, commonly known as DINA. The U.S. government even requested the extradition of the sinister head of the DINA, Manuel Contreras. Chilean newspapers printed the allegations that had been lodged by the U.S. government and human rights organizations around the world. The international outrage was so great, and the DINA's name so discredited, that Pinochet dissolved the agency and replaced it with a new one, more innocuously called the Centro Nacional de Informaciones, or CNI, whose mission was nearly identical to that of the DINA. At the same time, Contreras was removed from his senior DINA post, but he was promoted to general and continued to be influential in the military government and the secret police.

Through Nathan, I met people in the Familiares de Detenidos y Desaparecidos, the support group for family members of the detained and disappeared ones. Nathan told me about his friend Inelia, who had become an active member of the group after her son disappeared. The secret police had barged into her apartment in the middle of the night and dragged away her only son, who was seventeen at the time. She never saw him again.

I first saw Inelia, a short, heavyset woman with premature white hair, at a folk concert organized to raise money for *familiares*. Six musicians sat in a half circle with guitars and drums, while couples performed Chilean dances. In the traditional *la cueca* dance, a man and woman, each waving a handkerchief, performed a ritualized dance of flirting and courting, with intricate footwork.

In the final performance of the evening, the lights were turned down. As the guitar began strumming, Inelia walked alone into the half circle of chairs and danced *la cueca sola*. Wearing a simple gray dress, she moved with incredible grace across the floor. She waved her handkerchief, bowed, and moved in unison with an invisible partner. The haunting presence of the missing person was palpable.

A few days later, Inelia invited me to her small third-story apartment in a public housing project. Over tea, bread, and jam, she talked about her life working as a waitress and searching for her son, Héctor. Even though his disappearance had happened over nine years ago, she was convinced he was still alive, and not a day passed that her energy was not focused on finding him or, in the worst of cases, finding out what had happened to him.

Like other wives and mothers who had lost their loved ones, she stitched together scraps of cloth to leave a record of the harrowing tales of those who had been detained and disappeared. The backing was typically made of burlap, and hence the Spanish word for burlap, *arpilleras,* was used for these clandestine tapestries.

She left the room and then came back with a folded *arpillera* that she opened on the table. Héctor's story was stitched on a cloth the size of a placemat. In the *arpillera,* the single largest piece of fabric was the sky, made from a silky piece of dark blue fabric, with embroidered white stars. Her son, Héctor, was wearing light blue garments made from what looked like someone's old pajamas. He was escorted with his head down toward a car, surrounded by three men made from dark brown cloth that could have come from an old pair of corduroy pants. A woman in a yellow housecoat represented Inelia, and above her head, in a stitched voice bubble like you would see in a cartoon, were the words "Mi Hijo, NO—My son, NO."

"He will be twenty-six years old next month," she told me.

I didn't know what to say.

"This is for you," she said, pushing the *arpillera* across the table toward me.

"Oh, I don't think I could take it," I said, uncertain how to respond to this gift.

"The reason I make these is so that others know his story and can help find him," she said. "Please take it. I have something else for you, but you can read it when you get home," she added, handing me an envelope.

"The worst of all is that I never even learned why they took him away. After all these years, no one has given me a reason. You will try to help me, won't you?" Inelia asked me at the end of our tea. I nodded and put the *arpillera* and envelope in my backpack.

Once back at the hogar, I opened the envelope. There was a grainy photocopied picture of Héctor in a crewneck T-shirt, looking like he was about thirteen years old, even though he was seventeen when he was detained. There were copies of letters from Inelia to the Organization of American States' Human Rights Commission and to the Chilean Ministry of Foreign Affairs and of Interior. A final letter was to the president of the Republic, Augusto Pinochet Ugarte, and in it she requested an investigation into the disappearance of her son. In the letter to General Pinochet, she described Héctor as the "only son of a widow" and she concluded, "Altamente agradecida anticipadamente de Ud. por la favorable acogida a la presente, lo que comprometerá mi eterna gratitud hacia Ud.—With enormous thanks in advance for your favorable consideration of my request, I promise you my eternal gratitude."

With this package in my possession, I now felt somehow implicated. What if someone found these subversive materials and it caused problems for the hogar? What could I do? I didn't know anyone with real influence in the United States. Should I write my congressman in Indiana? Should I write a letter to the *Fort Wayne Journal Gazette*? What if I did, and they opened my mail going out of the country, as I knew was often the case?

I put the *arpillera* and envelope in my bottom drawer at the hogar, hidden under a pair of blue jeans.

NINE

ᔥ

THE PACIFIC COAST

ᔥ

Near the end of the summer, with only two weeks left in February, a friend of a friend of Olga's offered us a summer beach house for ten days in the working-class Pacific seaside town of El Quisco, two hours from Santiago.

"Everyone, *everyone,* in Chile goes to the beach in February," Olga told me. "You may stay in elegant homes or in cabins or in tents, but you have to go to the beach. It wouldn't be summer vacation if you didn't."

"We're leaving early in the morning," Olga told the assembled group that evening. "You need to have everything ready tonight. In the morning, you will make your beds, we'll eat breakfast, and then we're going."

The girls laid out all their clothes, neatly folded, on their beds. Verónica ironed Karen's red sun dress. As I often had before, I had to stop myself and remember that Verónica was only eight years old. She looked after the little kids—and me—as if she were a mother. The boys spent more time talking than preparing.

"It's like a huge pool that moves," Carlos told those who had never seen the ocean.

"The waves are so big they are huge. They crash down and they eat little boys alive," Carlos told Juanito, who was three and afraid of a long list of things real and imaginary, among them loud noises, the bogeyman, insects, and the dark.

"But the waves don't chew little boys, they swallow them whole," Carlos concluded.

Juanito ran away crying. Olga stood in the doorway to the boys' room.

"Carlos," Olga threatened, "if Juanito wets his bed, you're washing his sheets."

The next morning, four of the kids' beds had to be stripped of wet sheets—a sure sign that anxiety levels were high.

"This isn't fair," Carlos said, as he yanked off Juanito's sheets and took them outside to be washed. "This isn't fair at all. Juanito's a little baby, and I have to clean it up."

Néstor pulled the white two-door Suzuki car out of the driveway. Sebastián and Pato shared the front seat with Néstor; the back of the car was stacked with enough clothes and food for ten days. Néstor, Sebastián, and Pato were to get everything ready in El Quisco before the rest of us arrived by bus.

Olga and I walked to the bus stop with the remaining twelve kids, who were carrying the towels, blankets, balls, dolls, bears, and buckets that didn't fit in the car. Verónica carried a large aluminum tea-kettle. The boys all had their bathing suits on under their clothes. We walked a quarter of a mile to the bus stop and waited.

"Is this stupid bus ever going to come?" Carlos asked after about three minutes. As if upon his bidding, the blue-and-white La Granja bus #37 appeared with its familiar white rusting sideboards. Olga negotiated with the bus driver, who let the fourteen of us ride for the price of six fares.

We endured the hour-long ride downtown to the Santiago bus terminal. The terminal offered expeditions to faraway cities such as Lima, Buenos Aires, and Rio de Janeiro, but most people waited for buses that went to Chile's nearby coast. Even so, Olga's purchase of fourteen tickets for El Quisco invited a double take from the ticket vendor.

At exactly noon, the air-conditioned Pullman bus with plush, red-upholstered seats pulled out of the terminal, followed a series of one-way streets past Santiago's prison, over the River Mapocho, and headed west. Vicki and Tanya, the two dark-haired sisters, sat next to each other holding hands. It had taken awhile, but I could finally tell them apart: Tanya had a thinner face and more freckles than Vicki. Tanya also had a wonderful, melodious laugh.

After an hour and a half, the bus climbed over a ridge and descended the winding road to the rocky coast. The bus stopped in front of a small grocery store next to the beach. There was no bus terminal at Quisco.

We reassembled children, towels, blankets, balls, dolls, bears, and buckets, thrilled that nothing seemed to be missing.

"Tía, let's go to the beach now," Carlos said to Olga.

"No, let's put away these things in the cabin first and then we'll go for a swim," Olga said.

The cabin, on the map, was five blocks away from the beach. We followed the ascending dirt road. The afternoon sun beat down. The blocks were long, and the rutted road ever steeper. The little ones kept falling behind. I carried Héctor piggyback. Karen started to cry.

"Save me, save me. Water, give me water," Carlos said dramatically as if crossing Chile's Atacama Desert. "I'm dying of thirst," he said, falling on the dirt road. "I'm dead."

"You're a moron," Verónica said, stepping over Carlos.

"Isn't it great to be on vacation?" Olga asked of no one in particular. We finally arrived at the fifth block and spotted the orphanage's white car parked in front of a row of scrubby bushes. Behind the bushes was an unpainted wooden shack.

Néstor stood in the doorway.

"Welcome to El Quisco!"

Inside the shack were five sets of triple bunk beds, the top bunk about twenty inches below the ceiling. The only running water was a hose out back, located near the outhouse. It was hard to fit everyone and the gear in the cabin at the same time.

"Let's go swimming," Néstor yelled, and the eight youngest kids crammed into the car. The rest jogged behind.

Néstor drove slowly down the hill.

"Let's keep those feet moving," he yelled back to the joggers. When the car reached the beach, Andrés was the first out.

"WOOOO," he yelled as he dashed down the beach. He didn't stop until he hit the water. A wave crashed down on top of him. Néstor dove in after Andrés and fished him out of the ocean. Andrés, who was as fearless as he was foolhardy, just beamed. Juanito, who was neither fearless nor foolhardy, stood by the car, not moving. "Will the waves really eat me?" he asked. By the late afternoon, Juanito would let the water wash over his knees before he would run away.

In the evening, we all went to the Quisco Carnival—sand and saw-dust, cotton candy and fried dough, games in which a wooden ring tossed around a bottleneck wins you a canned ham. There were three rides: a merry-go-round with pink and yellow blinking lights, white spinning teacups, and a roller coaster with three humps.

Each kid received a ticket for one ride. Each had to make a long, painful decision. The older boys and Sonia opted for the roller coaster, the other girls for the spinning teacups, and the younger boys, except for Andrés, for the merry-go-round.

"I want to go on the roller coaster," Andrés said.

"I don't think you're big enough," I replied.

"Yes I am," he told me, standing at his tallest.

"Let's ask the man at the roller coaster."

A teenager in a white T-shirt said Andrés could go if he was with one of the older boys.

Andrés sat with Sebastián. They put on seat belts. The cars started slowly up the first ramp, then whooshed up and down the three humps. They circled maybe a half dozen times and came back to the start.

"That was great," Sebastián said.

Andrés's face was flushed.

"I want to go on that one again," Andrés said.

"Sorry, everyone only gets one ticket," Olga reminded him.

"I want to go again."

"No, sorry," Olga said.

Andrés was quiet at first, then hurled himself, white shorts and striped red and white T-shirt, onto the dirt. He threw an incredible howling tantrum, screaming so loudly he had difficulty breathing. A crowd gathered. Most, I imagined, had never heard a child scream so loud or so long. Even having grown up in a family where my brothers, sister, and I were constantly breaking limbs and needing to be stitched up, not to mention throwing our own tantrums for necessities denied, I could not remember ever hearing such anguished, painful wailing.

The teenager running the roller coaster walked over to us and said, "He can go again for free."

"No, thanks," Olga told him. "He'll think this is what he should do to get what he wants."

Olga grabbed Andrés by the arm and stood him up.

"Andrés, are you done embarrassing yourself?"

Andrés cried for a few more minutes. The crowd dispersed. His clothes were covered with sawdust and sand. He whimpered. Finally, he stopped. He brushed off his front and looked at Olga, got his breath and then, as if nothing had happened, remarked, "Thank you, mamá, for letting me go on the ride. Can I go on that ride again, please?"

"No," said Olga, with a smile.

The days blurred one into another, as we prepared and packed food and spent long hours at the beach, where I prayed every day that no one would drown. While Néstor and Olga packed for the beach one morning, I volunteered to stay behind with four-year-old Karen, who was badly sunburned from the day before. I'd spent too much time with too many children and needed some space.

Karen had recovered from the illness that had taken us to the hospital some weeks earlier, although I never did learn what she had. Even when healthy, Karen was typically pale and rather sickly looking. After a couple of hours in the sun, she had turned a purplish-red.

Spending the afternoon with "never-says-anything" Karen promised to be quiet. The two of us sat at the little wooden table, her with a drawing pad, me with a stack of blank paper. First, I wrote to the dean of Indiana University Law School that I wouldn't be enrolling next September. Next, I composed a letter to my parents that I knew they would not like. I informed them that I'd decided to drop the law school idea and that I would be staying longer in Chile than I had originally planned. Fortunately, the letter would take about two weeks to get to Indiana, and since we didn't have a phone it would be another two weeks before I heard back on the issue.

Across the table, Karen drew pictures with yellow and blue crayons. In one, the sun was blue and the mountains yellow. She put down her crayons and spoke the first full sentence I had ever heard her utter.

"Tío, why do boys have one crack in back and girls have two cracks?"

The next morning, I planned to sneak out of the beach house early while everyone slept. I found my shoes, jeans, and a sweatshirt in the dark room. I tried not to make noise, but Verónica heard me.

"Tío, where are you going?" she inquired.

"I'm just going down to the beach. I'll be back in a little bit. It's early, go back to sleep." She rolled over, and I shut the door behind me.

Down the dirt road I went, past beach houses and tents; the fog hovered near the ground. The beach was deserted. This morning the Pacific was gray-green, somber. In the distance, waves crashed against gray rock cliffs. The early morning sun filtered through the remaining wisps of clouds, a shaft of light glistened on green strands of seaweed. I carried my journal and my tattered copy of *Pablo Neruda: Selected Poems*. I found a dry rock to sit on near the crashing waves and read. Neruda had a beach house at Isla Negra, only a few miles from where I sat. He wrote,

> ¿Cuánto vive el hombre, por fin?
> ¿Vive mil días o uno solo?

¿Una semana o varios siglos?
¿Por cuánto tiempo muere el hombre?
¿Qué quiere decir 'Para Siempre'?

Preocupado por este asunto
me dediqué a aclarar las cosas.

How long does a man live, after all?
Does he live a thousand days, or one only?
For a week, or for several centuries?
How long does a man spend dying?
What does it mean to say 'for ever'?

Lost in this preoccupation,
I set myself to clear things up.

So did I. I desperately needed to make some sense of my time in Chile and where it was taking me. Since coming to Chile four months earlier, I was acutely aware of how few real skills I had to offer to anyone. Not being able to speak the language well only intensified the feelings of inadequacy. I desperately wanted to help but felt awkward, not knowing even where to begin. The internal debates about going to medical school had begun about a month earlier while I sat with sick children in public hospital waiting rooms. Couldn't I offer something here if I became a doctor? But was it worth the sacrifice: five or six years in school and the rest of my life tied to the medical profession? Was this something important I should pay attention to, or just another one of those passing whims?

As I sat on the rock, the salty breeze on my skin, the fog began to disperse, and as the surrounding view became clearer, so did a picture of my life. I'd stay in Chile another year, living and learning. I'd begin exploring how I could take the science courses I needed to enter medical school. If I was going to be a good doctor, I'd need to learn to be more methodical and organized. The waves of the incoming tide crashed against the rocks and began to spray me—a sure signal that it was time to return to the cabin. But sitting on the rock, I felt I'd made a decision to study medicine and become a doctor. No small accomplishment for a ten-day vacation.

That afternoon, we had planned to catch a bus back to Santiago at five o'clock. At six, Néstor was still at the beach with the kids.

When would I learn that nothing in Chile ever happened on time or as planned? We finally left about eight o'clock. I had a walloping headache. Sitting on the bus back to Santiago, I wrote on the back of an envelope.

> Return to Santiago
> a strange sense of vertigo,
> depressing,
> wounds festering,
> fields of dry weeds,
> produce nothing but worthless seeds.
>
> We need money.
> I need a job. So many things to do.
> So many doubts.
> No poetry in that.

The first day back in Santiago, Vicki's and Tanya's mother visited the hogar.

"Mamá, mamá," the little girls screamed as they ran to greet her.

"Hola, María," Olga added coolly.

María was accompanied by a man with slicked-back black hair, yellow polyester pants, a yellow print silk shirt, and silver chains around his neck, as if he came right from Hollywood central casting for the movie *Latin Thugs*. He even had a single gold tooth and diamond stud earring.

"This is my partner, Alejandro," María said.

Vicki's and Tanya's eyes grew wide. Tanya, the younger of the two, stepped back a little.

"I want to take my girls home with me," María told Olga.

"María, you're not going to yank them around like you did last time. Last time you said you were taking them for good and a month later they were back here."

"This is different," María said.

"Fine, María, if you take them out, they are not coming back. It's just not fair to them."

"I know."

There was a long silence.

"Girls, get your things," María told Tanya and Vicki. They looked at Olga. She nodded.

The sisters went to their bedroom and stuffed all their clothes into two white plastic garbage bags. They hastily kissed everyone goodbye.

The orange wooden gate shut behind María, Alejandro, Tanya, and Vicki.

Later, on the porch, I husked corn on the cob, while Olga rasped the ears of corn across a handheld grater to make corn mush for a Chilean dish called *pastel de choclo*. She was unusually quiet.

"It's really hot out here," I said, making conversation.

"You know what really gets me?" Olga asked, one who rarely just made conversation. "María visited, what, maybe three times this last year, and now, one day, she shows up with some man who will pay the rent for the next month and then says to me, 'Oh yeah, I want my girls now. I want to be a mother again.' Just think what will happen to those girls living in that pig sty. It's just not fair."

She paused grating the corn as her tears fell into the mush.

ᔎ

THE END OF SUMMER

ᔎ

It was a late Sunday afternoon in early March, still summer but cool, cooler than I had expected. I needed to put on a sweatshirt. The light was diffuse, a white-gray haze glowing behind stark, gray-green mountains. The leaves on the poplars were still green, except for a single branch on one tree that was already sporting a row of yellow. The air was tinged with autumn. Olga was visiting some friends in town, Néstor was visiting his brother, and Eliana was on her day off, which left me alone with all the kids. I sat on the back porch, trying to darn my tattered socks.

"Tío," Verónica observed, "you shouldn't use dark thread to fix your white socks."

"I don't think anyone will notice."

"Tío," she said, laughing, shaking her head, "do you want me to do it?"

"No, thanks, Verónica."

"I just finished ironing my clothes and giving the little boys a bath. Do you want me to iron your shirt so it will be ready when you go to work on Monday?"

"Sure, thanks, that would be great."

On that Monday, five months after arriving in Chile, I was to begin a job teaching English to adults at the Chilean-North American Institute in downtown Santiago. The pay was only four dollars an hour, but it was a start. We needed the money at the orphanage, and I needed a break from changing diapers, cleaning, and cooking.

As I darned my socks, the kids played, laughed, and fought. The past few days I'd felt disengaged, almost as if I was watching a movie, floating on the breeze. The life decisions I'd recently made had done little to draw me back to the kids. Perhaps my mind was still at the medical school I would attend, and all the things that had to happen to get me there.

Héctor came over to where I was sitting. He was less afraid of me now and no longer cried when I picked him up. He tentatively took one of my socks from the pile, then more obviously taunted me, pulling at the sock in my hand, wanting to play. I chased after him, caught him, lifted him up, put him down. I grabbed my sock from him and ran. He chased me and grabbed my leg and reached for the sock. I lifted him up again and he laughed. He never seemed to tire. "Do it again, Tío," he said, holding his arms up. "Tío, do it again."

On a Monday evening I began teaching a beginning-level English class on the second-floor classroom at the Chilean-North American Institute. What a revelation to be in front of a classroom of adults who hungered to know what I knew. Ever since I had arrived in Chile, I had felt as though I was not in control of anything in my life and had little to offer anyone. But now, in front of thirty-six English students, I was perceived as the expert.

I gave all my students English names I could pronounce without having to roll my "rr's." María became Mary, and Geraldo became Harry.

"Mary, can you introduce yourself to Harry?"

"Por Dios, tengo que hablar en inglés!" María responded in Spanish—"Oh my God, I have to speak in English!"

I nodded. There was a long pause. "My name is Mary," she said slowly, her hand in front of her mouth. "Good to meet you, Harry."

"Okay, Harry, your turn. Introduce yourself to Mary."

Harry visibly perspired. He stood up and said very loudly, "Mary I Arry. Good meet you."

There were a number of giggles. Harry bowed and smiled.

The class turned to me expectantly, waiting to see what the professor wanted to do next.

I'd had a year's experience teaching, but it had been nothing like this. After graduating from college with a philosophy major, I taught high school for one year. I was optimistic about what I could accomplish in that one year, teaching at a Catholic high school in a small town in Colorado: I had planned to share with my students the best of my college literature, philosophy, and theology classes. There would be stimulating debates on social issues and literature. My mantra was that you had to "think for yourself."

My first sophomore literature class set the tone for the year. The first day of class, I began by writing my name, "Mr. Reifenberg," on the blackboard, then spent the next forty-five minutes walking them, step by step, through a four-page syllabus. I explained how much I thought they would enjoy Fyodor Dostoyevsky's six-hundred-page *Crime and Punishment*, a book I had added to the reading list. I gave them a speech about plagiarism. At the end, with a few minutes left in the period, I asked if there were any questions.

Silence. Finally, sophomore Eddie Hanson in the back row raised his hand. "Yeah, I have a question," he said.

"Go ahead," I said.

"Steve, hmm, yeah, Steve," he said, "are you old enough to buy us beer?"

There was laughter on their part, awkwardness on mine.

After fumbling around with a response, I finally said, "Yes, and I'm also old enough to get you thrown out of my class."

That interaction and many others like it made me overly determined not to lose control of the class. My strategy was to work the boys so hard and keep them so busy that they wouldn't have time to get into trouble. I had regular pop quizzes and weekly papers. My maintain-control-at-all-costs strategy with the boys was only reinforced the October afternoon when the French teacher across the hall ran out of her classroom crying, "Those animals set my wastebasket on fire!"

Before I would go to school in the morning, I practiced making mean faces in the mirror. My lowest moment came one afternoon in the school's restroom. There were no separate restrooms for the teachers. As I reached for the toilet paper, I looked up and read, "Mr. Reifenberg sucks the big one." Having graded all those quizzes and papers, I recognized the handwriting. It belonged to one of my better students; one of the boys who I hoped was getting something out of my class.

Now, by contrast, my students at the Chilean-North American Institute were textbook models—adults who were paying for classes because they wanted to learn. They laughed at my jokes and wrote down every word I wrote on the blackboard. They were attentive and slightly intimidated by the professor, but not too intimidated. After the first class, as I was walking out streaked with white chalk dust, two different students asked me over to their homes for dinner with their families.

The teaching euphoria, however, did not carry over to the next morning. I woke up feeling like I had a terrible hangover, although I hadn't been drinking at all.

"I told you not to eat that meat pie before you went to bed," Olga said the next morning as I exited the bathroom for the third time in about an hour. She could find the direct causal link to any mental or physical problem: a stomach problem was the result of combining something hot such as coffee with something cold like ice cream; a back or neck problem was the result of not properly protecting yourself from a cool breeze.

"You're not going to take a shower just after eating!" she once exclaimed, horrified, as I walked to the bathroom with a towel around my neck after breakfast.

"I couldn't get in the bathroom earlier," I responded.

"Don't you know that will give you stomach cramps?"

Sitting on the toilet, I counted the number of cream-colored tiles on the floor. I stood up but immediately had to sit back down. I counted the black and white tiles on the bathroom wall. There were 148. The white plaster wall above the tiles had turned a brownish green and desperately needed to be painted. The shower curtain was torn.

I was mobile long enough to get a copy of the novel I was reading, *Hijo de ladrón—Son of a Thief*—before I made my way back, quickly, to the bathroom. I kicked out Verónica, who was fixing her hair. I sat down again and finished the last ten pages of my novel.

There was a knock on the door.

"Tío, por favor."

"I'm almost done," I called out.

I stood up, my legs numb from sitting so long. I was half proud that I had finally finished the book, half sad that the book was over. I opened the bathroom door. Karen, Héctor, and Carlos were in line to get into the bathroom.

"Tío, some of us have to go to the bathroom sometimes too, you know," Carlos said.

I started to walk back to my room, but didn't make it far before I was waiting in line behind Carlos to get back inside.

I taught a second class, but by the end was so dizzy I could hardly stand up. The bus ride home was interminable. When I got there, I fell into bed at 8 p.m. and didn't wake up until the next morning, still dressed. I took my temperature. I was disappointed that I felt this bad yet had almost no fever. I convinced myself that I was fine, got up, only to have my body convince me to get back in bed later that afternoon. By then, I was somehow reassured when I did have a 102 fever—at least it wasn't all in my head. I felt worse as the day progressed, and my fever rose to 104.

I found my copy of *Where There Is No Doctor*. With my symptoms, I had a choice of malaria, typhus, or typhoid. Every noise, every sound, seemed amplified tenfold.

"Shut up," Verónica screamed outside my window, "don't you know that Tío Steve is sick and needs quiet!"

I buried my head in a pillow sandwich. My tangled sheets were soaked in sweat. Being sick in bed reminded me of my childhood. I had all the usual onetime childhood diseases—measles, mumps, chicken pox. I had my adenoids out twice and my tonsils out once (or was it the other way around?). I also had pneumonia and constant respiratory infections, including regular bouts of croup. One of my earliest memories is of my father holding me over a sink with hot running water and a towel over my head. Then he would lean me over a footstool and pat my back gently and I would cough up phlegm onto a newspaper.

Sick in Santiago, I floated in and out of consciousness. When I was awake, childhood memories flooded back. I remember being just tall enough to push our big green Lawnboy mower across our backyard in Terre Haute, Indiana. In my mind, our yard was the size of a football field, and it seemed I was always pushing uphill. Every Saturday morning, unless it rained, my father told my two brothers and me to cut the lawn. My brother Mike, who was one year older, did everything he was asked without complaining. My brother Phil, who was a year younger than I, would tell my father, "I'm going to do this job faster and better than anyone's ever done it."

I was less enthusiastic. Having finished second grade, I wanted to become an environmentalist and suggested we let the grass grow.

"We'll just have to cut it again next Saturday. Why don't we grow a field?" I asked my father who, not surprisingly, did not respond well to that suggestion.

One sunny Saturday morning the grass-cutting routine was broken. The lawn mower did not come out of the garage. Instead, my father called Mike, who was nine, into my parents' bedroom.

I shuddered to think what Mike could have done. You never got called into my parents' room, with the door shut, unless it was something very serious. About fifteen minutes later, Mike walked out looking pale.

My father called me. My stomach sank. I tried to figure out what an eight-year-old could have done that was so serious as to interrupt the grass-cutting routine and require that I sit on my father's bed with the door shut.

"I want to talk to you about how babies are born," my father said. He took out a book. I was confused and still trying to figure out what I had done wrong.

He opened the book. There were pictures in the book; first a dog on top of another dog, and then one horse trying to climb on the back of another horse.

My father turned the page, and there was a picture of two big, ugly bullfrogs, one on top of the other. My father was talking the whole time he was turning the pages. It was all a blur, except the picture of the two frogs frozen in my mind.

"And that's how babies are made," he concluded.

The connections weren't clear, but I concluded making babies had something to do with my father putting frogs inside my mother. I began to cry.

"Do you have any questions you want to ask me about this?" he asked. He looked pale in the bright sunlight that came through the window.

"How many times have you done that frog-thing to my mother?" I demanded. It was one of the few times in my life I had seen my father at a loss for words. He crossed and then uncrossed his legs.

"Five times," he said, as there were five of us kids.

The tears ran down my cheeks, and we sat in silence.

"Do you have any more questions?"

I whimpered a little and then shook my head.

"Well, then," he said, indicating it was over.

My father cut the grass on that Saturday afternoon, and we didn't have any more conversations about the frog-thing.

A visiting neighbor wanted to give me vitamin C shots. I was too weak to question whether vitamin C shots were what I needed. I was rolled on my stomach, my shorts were pulled down, and I was given a shot. Another older woman distributed free "cures"—green pills, blue pills, and red pills—all from one jar. I refused them all, graciously. After a week in bed, Olga took me to see a licensed doctor, Dr. Jorge Vivanco.

After a series of exams, a stool sample, and a blood test, Dr. Vivanco told me, "You have a form of typhoid. It's called paratyphoid. It's not as serious as regular typhoid, that can be deadly, but it's still pretty serious. You probably picked it up from some salmonella bacteria, probably in the water. You'll need to stay in bed a minimum of two weeks. This shouldn't be difficult, because I imagine you won't have much energy to get up and move around. Do you have any good books?"

"Not really," I said.

Dr. Vivanco went to the back room and came out with two books by a Peruvian novelist, Mario Vargas Llosa.

"Being sick doesn't have to be all bad," he said, handing me the books.

So in addition to taking care of twelve kids, Olga now had to take care of me. Olga called the Chilean-North American Institute to keep them apprised of my situation.

"Sorry, Steve," she said on returning from making the phone call next door. "They already hired a new teacher for your classes." If mental attitude was the key to wellness, my typhus became terminal.

I was sleeping about eighteen hours a day. One afternoon, when I was momentarily feeling better, I remember sitting up and watching the boys play soccer through my window. They dribbled the soccer ball with such grace on the dusty soccer field. Marcelo was the only boy who would never play soccer. He'd most often climb up in a tree and watch the game from his perch. I identified with Marcelo, watching from the sidelines. Soccer wasn't popular where I was growing up, but football, basketball, and baseball were. I don't know whether I didn't like these sports because I was terrible at them, or I was terrible because I didn't like them. The only sports I really liked were gymnastics and swimming, which, in my neighborhood, were considered sissy sports for girls.

My older brother Mike was amazingly good at sports, especially baseball. He was always the captain who picked the baseball team. I was usually the last one picked, and if he got stuck with me, he'd say, "Put Steve in right field."

The good part was that the balls rarely got hit to right field. The bad part was the one time a ball was hit to me in a two-hour-plus game, more likely than not I'd be practicing handstands and the ball would fly over my feet sticking up in the air. This improved neither my ball-playing reputation nor my liking for the game.

I wondered if Marcelo had similar feelings about soccer and motioned him to come over to my window. He climbed down from the tree, walked over to the window and stared at me.

"How are you doing, Marcelo?"

No response.

"So you don't feel like playing soccer, huh?"

He shrugged his shoulders and walked away.

I lay down and didn't wake up until the next morning.

Most of the time when I was awake, I stared at the ceiling because my head hurt too much to read or even to sit at the window.

"Do you think you should call your parents and tell them you are sick?" Olga asked.

I simply shook my head no.

I took my medicine and drank lots of liquids. I planned my bathroom trips to conserve energy and maybe, partially and very grudgingly, came to accept the idea that there are simply some things you cannot control, and that the best I could do was learn to be patient and wait until I got better.

ⷶ

ELEVEN

A NEW SCHOOL YEAR

ⷶ

The school year in Chile began in March, and the kids got off to a less than stellar start. Marcelo came home with a bloody nose and torn shirt the first week of class. Yoana's second-grade teacher wrote *flojita*, "lazy," on Yoana's papers and sent home a note stating that Yoana did nothing but play at school.

I lectured Yoana from my sick bed.

"Yoana, you studied so hard this summer. Why don't you work now?" I demanded. She shrugged. I sent her to her bed to think about it.

"If things don't improve with Yoana, we should have her repeat first grade," Olga said. "She's just not mature enough."

"I don't think that's a good idea," I said, having invested considerable time working Yoana through the first grade reader so she would be prepared for second grade. My concern was probably as much about my success as a tutor as Yoana's as a student.

Many mornings I had the illusion that I was better, but in the afternoon my temperature would rise and I would feel worse. As the cycle repeated each day, I'd feel more useless, and I began to wonder if I would ever get well, doubting it had been a good idea to come to Chile. I apologized to Olga about being such a burden.

"I really did come to help, you know," I said one afternoon, so frustrated I was on the verge of tears.

"Sometimes it's good to realize you need other people's help, even though you don't want it," Olga said. "I think independent people really learn a lot when they realize that there are times they should just accept someone else's help."

She came back about an hour later.

"Look what just came for you," Olga said, handing me a letter bearing my father's distinctive print. "This should cheer you up."

It had been a month since I had sent my parents the letter from the beach in which I had written so confidently that I was not going to law school and that I was staying in Chile because of all the important things I was doing. My father wrote:

Dear Steve:

It's been 24 hours since your letter arrived and I've had a chance to gather my thoughts and feelings. My feelings are strong (like yours) and like yours are not easily explainable. I have feelings of *sadness, rejection,* and *pride.*

The feeling of *sadness* is a natural one that comes with the knowledge that you will be missing from family and friends who are experiencing various events in their lives. I guess it's really a very selfish reaction to this separation in distance and time.

Rejection: Your decision to spend two years out of the country seems to be a rejection of a way of life that shaped you into what you are. That "way of life" demanded that parents love and nourish their children spiritually and provide for their educational and material needs. We felt these very real needs could be best fulfilled by your mother staying in the home and by me working in the world of business. That world of business (that you are quick to put down) has provided you with 16 years of the best private education money can buy. The same business will allow me to pay off college loans over the next 10 years. If all followed your direction—business, industry, and institutions as we know them would collapse and we would revert back to an agrarian economy based on a barter system—hardly a system equipped to support, endow, and pay tuition to prestigious institutions like Notre Dame. The good, caring, providing people of the world would have no money to support worthwhile causes like Notre Dame, Holy Cross priests, or Olga. You seem to bite the hand that feeds you!

It's unlikely that my words on this paper will change your mind. However, I think it most likely you will change your own mind as you better understand what motivates man—self interest (sounds like capitalism) as their self interest is served and their basic needs are met, good men go on to take care of others. There will always be others. Hopefully there will also be good men of means.

Pride: I'm proud of the way my children have grown and become the individuals they are. I'm especially proud of your dedication to what you are doing and of your courage to do what you think is right. I'm most proud to call you my son.

Dad

I wrote a postcard note back to both my parents. It spoke of trivial things, mostly about the weather in Santiago in March. It seemed easier than admitting I was sick, that I was a burden to others, that I wondered if I should have come, that I missed them, and that I didn't have a clue how to reply to my father's letter.

I watched the days grow cooler, and at night I would need a blanket on the bed. As I started to feel a little better, I would lie in bed and alternate between visions of being a doctor and being a writer. I read short stories by Mario Vargas Llosa, a Peruvian author I quickly came to respect enormously. In the author's preface to *The Cubs and Other Stories* Vargas Llosa recalled writing these stories early in his career:

> I have a certain fondness for them, because they remind me of those difficult years when, even though literature mattered more to me than anything else in the world, it never entered my mind that one day I would be a writer—in the real sense of that word.

I had always written for myself, and I was sure I would continue to write. Like Vargas Llosa, I asked myself, as I filled these blue hardbound journals with my scribbles, if I would ever be a writer—in the real sense of the word?

I thought about being a doctor in a different way than I thought about writing. Medicine both excited and scared me. Medicine would give me a set of skills so that I could better serve others, do something useful with my life, and justify my existence. But I knew it would also be a long ordeal. Was this the right path for someone who never liked high school biology and chemistry? I played with mental timetables again. If I went back to the States in December, I could begin taking the college-level chemistry, biology, and physics I'd need. Could I take the MCAT exam and apply to medical schools the following year? Or would it take two years of science courses before I could apply?

While still recuperating, I received a letter from my sister, Karla, describing the tremors my last letter had caused on the home front. Nonetheless, she encouraged me to stay the course. She concluded the letter by writing that Rick, my youngest brother, who had just turned seventeen, was not particularly helping matters.

"Anytime anyone mentions your name," she wrote, "Rick bows his head and says *God rest his soul*. In fact, he has stopped using your name altogether, and just says *God rest his soul* in its place. As you can imagine, Mom's not real happy with your new name."

∽

PROFESSIONAL CONVERSATIONS

∽

The paratyphoid made it difficult for me to walk, even to the bathroom. But one evening, after more than three weeks in bed, I was able to shuffle to the kitchen and sit at the table with Olga. Although I was only drinking orange juice, it was a heady feeling being upright again. Andrés, hearing the noise in the kitchen, joined us. Uninvited, he pulled up a chair to the table. He smiled.

"Where's my glass?" he asked.

"Shouldn't you be in bed, young man?" Olga asked.

A few minutes later, Sonia stood in the doorway to the kitchen.

"Pretty soon we'll have all twelve in the kitchen," Olga commented.

"Tía, why is everyone talking about banging pots and pans?" Sonia asked Olga.

"It's part of a protest against General Pinochet."

"Is he a dictator?" Sonia asked.

"Where did you hear that?" Olga said.

"My friend at school said that Pinochet is an assassin and that he is a dictator. What's a dictator?"

"A dictator is a person . . ." Olga began and then paused. "Let me give you an example. If someone walked into your class at school with a gun and said to the teacher, 'I'm in charge,' and made the teacher leave, and then tried to teach the class, that would be a dictator."

"In this case the teacher has a big gun, and students are very unhappy and they want to let him know," Néstor added. "The only way they know how to show him how unhappy they are is by banging together pots and pans."

Sonia was always asking questions.

"So, why do they always call God a He?" Sonia asked at lunch the next day.

"Me da rabia," she added, which means "It makes me so mad" but translates literally as "It gives me rabies."

Sonia's face was expressive and wide, made to look even wider by her wild spray of light brown curly hair, which she would try, unsuccessfully, to discipline with bobby pins.

"People just get the pronouns mixed up," Olga told Sonia. "Everybody knows that God is really a She."

"But people say God always existed. How can God have always existed? Who knew God was there in the first place?" Sonia asked. She was relentless. "If God is so powerful that God can do anything, how do we know God won't decide to end or go away?" To any response from around the table, Sonia responded, "I just can't understand that."

"Sonia, have you ever had a good thing happen in your life?" Olga asked.

"Yes."

"Have you ever felt loved?" Olga asked.

"Yes."

"Well, that's the presence of God in your life."

This quieted Sonia for a good three or four minutes.

I spent the next month recuperating from paratyphoid. As soon as I was able to walk around without getting dizzy, I decided to visit the Chilean-North American Institute to lobby for my job. The director didn't even apologize for letting me go.

"There are a lot of people in Santiago who can teach English and need the job," she said. "It's too bad you got sick. I heard your students liked you."

So, resume in hand, in the midst of a recession, still prone to get dizzy when I stood up or walked too fast, I pounded the pavement, as many other Chileans were doing, in search of a paying job. My sense of self-worth also got very tied up with the notion of getting a job outside the orphanage.

"So, Tío, what is your profession?" Sonia asked at lunch a few days later. She had a particular knack for asking questions at the wrong time.

"I don't think I have a profession right now. I'm unemployed."

"But when you're not unemployed, what are you? Like some people are farmers, and some people are doctors, and some people are policemen, and some people are teachers or engineers. So what's your profession?"

"That's a hard one to answer."

"Well, what did you study?"

"I studied philosophy."

"What's that?"

"Philosophy is a study of all kinds of important questions, about the meaning of life, and about the existence of God, and about all kinds of questions that science can't answer."

"Did you learn all the answers to all those questions?"

"Well, no, but at least it helped me understand the right questions."

"And that's what you studied all those years to learn?"

"Yes."

"Now, I understand why you don't have a profession," she said, and then she laughed and laughed.

That night, I couldn't sleep. I felt queasy thinking about medical school. Just the idea of returning to school to take all the science classes (chemistry, organic chemistry, biology, and physics) I would need to take even to apply to medical school made me nervous. But this was the only route to becoming a doctor. If I could contribute something like Dr. Vivanco, if I had something concrete to offer, if I could help make someone well, it would be worth the effort. Sometimes I knew for sure I didn't want to go to medical school, but I still thought I should be a doctor. Undecided, I committed myself to help all I could around the orphanage and to see if my efforts couldn't make a difference somewhere.

The next morning, Sonia asked very seriously, "Tío, what will my profession be?"

"What do you want to do?"

"I want to make money so I can help my mom and my two sisters. I want to buy my mom a house and I need to make a lot of money so my sisters can get a good education," Sonia said.

"Those are good goals."

"Yes, but what will my profession be?"

"What kind of profession do you want to have?"

"I don't have any idea!" she said. "That's why I'm asking you."

"Well, you could be a teacher."

"And have to deal with all those little brats, no way."

"A nurse?"

"I don't want to carry bedpans for any doctor."

"A doctor?"

"I don't like the sight of blood."

"President?"

"You have to be a soldier to be president in this country. I also heard someone say you have to be a fool to be president of this country."

"Bueno, then, what about being a psychiatrist?"

"What's a psychiatrist?"

"Someone who's trained as a doctor but helps people with problems that they're having, mostly by talking with them."

"You don't have to see any blood?"

I shook my head.

"Hey, that's interesting, psychiatrist. I'll have to think about that one," she said as she departed.

THIRTEEN

၈

ON BEING A TEACHER

၈

Nathan Stone, who had originally put me in touch with Olga, helped me find my way to a profession, or at a minimum to a way of earning some much-needed money, for myself and for the hogar. Since his return to Chile, Nathan had begun teaching high school English at St. George's College, a private Catholic school with over a thousand students in kindergarten through high school. With his help, I landed a job as an English instructor for preschool and grade school teachers. It was a better job than I had at the Chilean-North American Institute: the pay was higher and the classes smaller.

St. George's grassy campus edged right up to the foothills of the Andes. Between the chapel and library were rows of orange trees. Having about a dozen buildings and large sports fields, it looked more like a U.S. college campus than a grade school and high school. The only downside for me was St. George's location. It was in the suburban Vitacura neighborhood on the east side of town, about fifteen miles from La Granja on the far south end of Santiago. With traffic, it could take up to two hours to get there on the dilapidated city buses called *micros*. Riding a bike, I could get to St. George's in a little over an hour. I began to do so regularly.

"Gringo," Olga said, employing the name she always used when she thought I was doing something particularly ridiculous, "there is a reason no sane human being rides a bike in Santiago traffic—it's called survival."

Bike helmets were not very common, and it never even occurred to me to get one. The truth was, even though I had to compete with the aggressive *micro* drivers, it was fantastic to be on my bike, riding on the Américo Vespucio loop across Santiago, past the simple wooden houses and concrete housing projects of the poor *poblaciones* of La Granja and La Florida, past the vineyards and open fields of Peñalolén, through the middle-class neighborhoods of Ñuñoa and La Reina to the well-manicured parks and elegant gated houses of Las Condes and Vitacura. I loved the feeling that through the power of my own legs in a little more than an hour I could travel from where I lived to a completely different world.

In Spanish they call improving a skill *perfeccionamiento,* and so I was assigned to teach "English perfection classes" to teachers at St. George's, who were being required to use more English in their classrooms. With my four kindergarten teachers, it was English of the most basic kind—simple greetings, vocabulary, songs, and nursery rhymes. With the six teachers in the intermediate group, there was a mix of conversation and grammar.

In the advanced group, there were five sophisticated women teachers who really didn't need me to teach them English. But they enjoyed getting together twice a week, drinking coffee, and talking in English. My English class was the vehicle for that get-together. For appearance's sake we would do a little grammar each class, but most of the ninety-minute class was conversation. The rule was we could talk about anything, as long as we did it all in English.

Initially, we talked about what they were doing in their classroom, about their families, and favorite travel sites. It didn't take long to realize how different their worlds were from mine in La Granja.

"Steve, you must use my summer house in Tongoy. It's about five hours north of Santiago. The house is right on the beach," first-grade teacher Isabel told me enthusiastically. "The house is painted a blue color and you can't miss it because it is the only house with a roof made of . . . what do you call it?" She grabbed her long blond hair. "It's just this color," she said, waving her hair. "It hangs over the side of the roof just like this," demonstrating with her blond hair flowing over her hand. "Do you say straw roof?"

"I think you want to say 'thatched roof' and that's an incredibly generous offer," I said.

"Perfect, yes, you must come and stay in our Tongoy house with its thatched roof."

I learned a lot about another side of Chile in my English conversations with these five teachers, including the unique role of St. George's in Chilean society.

St. George's College was originally founded as a Catholic boys' school in 1936 by the archdiocese of Santiago. Don Carlos Hamilton was the headmaster of the school, and his son was one of the school's priests. Almost from the beginning, St. George's was a lightning rod for controversy among the elite of Chilean society. In the early 1940s, at a St. George's mass that was attended by the parents of students, including some of the country's most influential citizens, Father Hamilton (the son) spoke out against the genocide that was occurring in Europe, and in the process implicitly criticized the neutrality that Chile had maintained up to that point in World War II. A priest meddling in national politics was too much for local authorities, and the school was censured, Father Hamilton reassigned, and Don Carlos resigned as headmaster.

At the time, there were many Catholic schools in Santiago and even a few English-language schools, but there were no Catholic English language schools except St. George's. The Santiago archdiocese desperately needed someone else to run the school and to do it in English.

The archdiocese, through contacts with Cardinal John O'Hara in the United States, asked for assistance in running the school. In 1943, the first three Holy Cross religious, two priests and a brother, arrived in Santiago. The Holy Cross were a "missionary congregation of educators" that ran not only the University of Notre Dame and University of Portland, but also missionary schools in Bangladesh and throughout Africa.

Little did Santiago's conservative elite who had pushed for the censure of Father Hamilton realize what they had bargained for with the arrival of the Holy Cross. Although there were certainly a variety of views within the Holy Cross congregation, by the 1960s the Holy Cross in Chile, and particularly those associated with St. George's, had taken a decidedly progressive bent to educating the country's elite. Discussions of liberation theology that stressed the gospels' call for a more just society, here and now, became common in the school corridors.

An emblematic figure during this time was St. George's principal, American Holy Cross Father Gerald Whalen, who in the early 1970s introduced a series of progressive reforms at the school, including full tuition scholarship for some boys who lived in the local shantytowns near the school in Vitacura. The incorporation of these poor boys was a revolutionary move for an elite private school in Chile.

After the coup in September 1973, the military government acted quickly to take over key universities and shut down certain departments that had been politically active. While the new regime controlled universities closely, for the most part it did not directly intervene in the management of private grade school and high school education.

St. George's was the notable exception. The military government sent an Air Force officer to run the school in 1973, and for the next four years there were incredible tensions, both within the St. George's community and between the church and the regime. In 1977, in a compromise move, the church and military government agreed that the well-respected Chilean educator and poet Don Hugo Montes would serve as St. George's rector. Independent minded and a devout Catholic, Montes worked under the government's watchful eye.

"So that's how Don Hugo got his job," said Isabel, who had provided much of the history of St. George's. "He's really a wonderful man and terrific teacher . . . but can you imagine a tougher job than trying to keep both sides happy?"

"We're never going to get to a situation where both sides are happy," said Carmen, "because Chileans aren't willing to talk about trades-ups."

"Do you mean trade-offs?" I asked.

"Yes, that's it," said Carmen. "I don't think we even have a word in Spanish that means that, trade-off . . . the idea that one side gets some of what they want and the other side gets some of what they want, but not everyone gets everything."

"I think the military pretty much gets everything it wants right now," said Isabel.

"Things are a lot more complex than some people want to admit," said Carmen, looking pointedly at Isabel. "You have to remember the chaos we lived through in the early 1970s, and even though some things this government does are, well, not nice, do we really want to go back to that chaos again?"

"For the last ten years, most people are afraid to talk about politics . . . and to talk about different ideas," Isabel said.

"So why are you willing to talk about politics?" I asked.

"Oh, we only talk about politics with each other, I think," said Carmen. "Most of us have known each other for more than twenty years. We grew up together and have all taught here for years. We do see things different, though. Isabel's our radical, and they consider me the most, well, more traditional."

"What's so interesting is all of a sudden people are sure beginning to talk publicly about politics again," Isabel responded. "Rodolfo Seguel, the leader of the copper miners' union, has called for a national strike on May eleventh."

"You don't think the government will just sit back and take that, do you?" asked Carmen.

"Steve, do you know why he chose the eleventh?" Isabel, the teacher, redirected the question at me.

"The eleventh is significant because September 11, 1973, was the day of the coup that brought General Pinochet to power, and so the eleventh is very important symbolically, both for the government and for the opposition," I said.

"Exactly right, and if Seguel pulls off this national strike, it will be the first time there has been an organized national protest since the military took over ten years ago," Isabel said.

"So what's happening in La Granja with all this talk of protests?" Elena asked me.

The women were intrigued that I was working in La Granja, one of the most politically active sections of Santiago.

"Graffiti promoting May eleventh are everywhere in La Granja," I said, relating stories of a police roundup of those who were suspected of producing mimeographed pamphlets about the strike.

"Things are different here in *barrio alto,* do you say, 'high town'?" Elena asked.

"I think you probably want to say 'uptown,'" I suggested. *Barrio alto,* in Santiago, meant the wealthier sections of town, Vitacura, Las Condes, or Providencia, where all these teachers lived.

"We almost never see things like police roundups. We live where there are mostly people who are, I guess you say, in English, 'mommies,'" Isabel said.

"Mommies?"

"Yes, that's the word, right? You know, the dead people that the Egyptians wound up in cloth, covering every part of their body, before they buried them."

"Oh, mummies."

"Yes, mummies. In Spanish we call them *momios.* That's what they call uptown people who don't believe there is repression in this country, whose eyes are tied with cloth and don't see anything that is happening in the country."

Magdalena was a music teacher at St. George's. Since she was on a different schedule than the other teachers, she couldn't join any of my regular English classes. Occasionally, though, we would meet and sit under the shade trees in St. George's courtyard between classes and talk in English. She liked to practice, and from her I learned a lot about Latin American music and literature. She was younger than most of the teachers in my classes, probably in her midtwenties.

"Come to our concert tonight," Magdalena said, one day between classes. She was singing with a group of musicians connected with the National Symphony at the huge century-old Gothic church downtown called Gratitud Nacional, "National Gratitude." I accepted.

I had never been in the downtown church on Alameda Avenue. I arrived early and wandered around, coming upon a large niche where hundreds of flickering white candles illuminated a plaster statue of the Virgin Mary. As I sat down in a pew, the orchestra and singers assembled on risers in front of the altar. I spotted Magdalena in a black dress, with her long, wavy black hair. The conductor approached the pulpit and introduced the music.

"Johann Sebastian Bach wrote his music over two hundred and fifty years ago and tonight you are going to hear excerpts from a number of his most important religious masterpieces, including his incredible *Mass in B minor*, which is also known as his *Great Mass*. These works are still enormously powerful and relevant today. There are parts where the music then becomes somber and sad as we approach that gray Friday afternoon when Jesus was crucified—and the very earth mourns the injustice of the act. Yet there are *Glorias*—*Gloria in excelsis*, and it is magnificent, with trumpets booming and bells resounding. Until Bach, it had been thought that no composer could ever capture the greatness of the words *Sanctus, Sanctus, Sanctus*. I think you'll agree with me that Bach succeeded," he said.

And with that, the wonderful music began.

After the last *Alleluia* was sung, the conductor returned to the pulpit.

"As many of you know, it has been a difficult enterprise to get all of our singers and orchestra members together given the current political situation. I want to thank the performers, each and every one of you. You can see," he said, pointing to the musicians, "in their faces their pleasure when they sing and play—and that it gives pleasure to God."

He paused, as if considering whether he should say anything else.

"In these very difficult times," he continued, "under the current climate, it is so important to have music. This music transcends the pain we live. It transcends as well as makes real those most significant moments in life. The music on paper is dead, is nothing, until it is played and sung and shared, until it is lived and experienced by us, as God's children. What I hope is that Bach's wonderful music gives us a small measure of peace in these troubled times. Finally, what I pray is that there be peace in the land . . . that there be peace, that there be peace," finally, almost inaudibly, he said, "that there be peace."

I waited around after the concert, and when Magdalena came outside she introduced me to a few of her fellow singers and briefly to the conductor.

"Do you want to go and get something to eat?" Magdalena asked me after she had said goodbye to everyone.

"Sure."

Neither of us had any ideas where. We finally found a Chinese restaurant that was still open in the basement of a shopping gallery. The sign outside had one name for the restaurant, the menus another. The food took a long time to arrive.

"I guess I'm now kind of glad it's so dark in here," she said, pointing to a chicken that was a color of orange not found in nature.

"I have a feeling the food is not going to be the highlight of the evening . . . but that concert was amazing . . . the music was just great and the conductor really put it all in perspective."

She smiled.

"So you really liked it."

I nodded my head as I chewed, reluctant to pass up a piece of Chinese chicken, even a fluorescent orange one.

"Did you know the conductor is my father?"

"No. Why didn't you tell me?"

"I wanted to get your honest reaction."

"He's really impressive, both as a conductor and as a speaker."

"Dad doesn't have many opportunities to conduct these days. He was once director of Santiago's symphony and a full professor at the university. That all changed when the military came to power. At first he was left alone because of his professional reputation. But he was critical of life under military rule and outspoken about his hopes for a return to democracy. He lost his job as conductor and then as professor. Now, the only stage where he is allowed to conduct—or rather where they cannot forbid him to conduct—is the altar of a Catholic Church."

FOURTEEN

NOISY AND COMPLICATED

The long line of unemployed people trying to get into the government's minimum employment program was one of the most dramatic testaments to the worsening economic situation. Riding my bike along Santa Rosa Street in La Granja, I passed people (were there five hundred in line?) hoping to get into the program, which gave heads of households the equivalent of thirty dollars a month for cutting weeds, picking up trash, or digging holes. Passing those haggard, resigned faces, I felt as though I was looking at a Depression-era black-and-white photo.

The military government had relied on the "Chicago boys"—Chilean economists trained at the University of Chicago and other U.S. universities—who were enamored of the wonders of a free and open economy. While the Chicago boys had been successful in opening the Chilean economy to the world, not everything had gone as planned.

The newspapers wrote about the "international debt crisis" and how all the easy money loaned to Latin America during the 1960s and 1970s had come due, with little new money in the pipeline. While the economic crisis of the early 1980s was worldwide, Latin American countries were bearing the heaviest load, shipping out much more money to U.S. banks (just to pay the interest on old debts, not even touching the principal) than was coming into the region.

Furthermore, almost a decade after the initial "shock therapy" that opened the Chilean economy to the world, and precisely because it had successfully lowered all import tariffs while most other countries had not, Chile was particularly hard hit by the economic crisis. Products from other countries could enter Chile cheaply, while Chilean products had few places to go. In the worldwide crisis, Chilean banks collapsed and factories were shut at a higher rate than in most other countries, and there were simply no jobs to be found.

There was a certain irony that in 1983 these same Chicago boys, the true believers in unbridled capitalism, were required to intervene in big ways in the economy, taking over failing banks and creating the kinds of massive public employment programs that President Roosevelt had created in the United States during the Great Depression. I imagined it was done with the calculation that if they did not, there might well be mass uprisings of the unemployed.

The month of May brought a series of thunderstorms, and the rain pounded on the corrugated metal roof over the kitchen, so loudly that at times it was hard to hear.

"Steve, can I talk to you for a minute?" Olga asked over the pounding of the rain, as we were clearing the dishes after dinner.

"Sure," I said.

"Steve, what's wrong?" she asked.

"Nothing, what do you mean?"

"You've been so distant ever since you got sick. You don't laugh as much any more."

"No, I'm fine. Just still a little tired from being sick."

"Steve, you act like an employee here, as though you always have to be working and serious."

"I'm sorry." It seemed my concerns with future plans and medical school, feelings of uselessness and of being overwhelmed by all the political violence and the economic crisis, were not as well disguised as I had thought.

"I'm sorry," I said again.

Andrés stood in his pajamas in the doorway.

"Tío, will you tell us a story?" he asked.

I kept the nighttime bedtime stories short, and after turning off the light in the boys' room I watched the kids settle into sleep for a few moments. The house was quiet. Olga was standing in the doorway to the boys' room.

"Steve, I want to ask you something. Why don't we sit down in my room?"

I followed her into her bedroom. "Forget it," she said, "it was just something silly."

We talked about the kids, Marcelo's cold and Andrés's bed-wetting. There was a pause.

"Steve, what do you think of me?"

"What do you mean?"

"I mean what do you think of me?"

"I admire you a lot and think you're one of the best friends I've ever had."

"But what do you think of me as a woman?"

"I think you're incredible.

"Are you in love with me?"

"No," I said, "I don't think so."

"Well, that's good."

"But sometimes," I added, "I look at you and think you are so beautiful, and the only thing in the world I want to do is hold you. Sometimes I feel very alone," and with that, I reached out and wrapped my arms around her. Suddenly all the reasons that had stopped me before from kissing her didn't seem important. I kissed her first on the forehead and then on the lips, then more kissing.

"Now I understand why you have to go running everyday," she said, laughing. "All that pent-up energy."

She kissed my forehead.

"It's late, and I think it is probably time for both of us to go to sleep," she said.

I left her room and stood in the kitchen, staring out the window for the longest time.

The next morning over breakfast, Olga and I avoided looking at each other directly. Later, while cleaning the house, she approached me and said, "I think things will really get confusing if we get in a romantic relationship."

I nodded in agreement, and our discussions turned to politics. The day of the May 11 national protest called for by the copper miners' union had arrived. The date had been spray-painted on brick walls in every neighborhood in Santiago. I spent the day wondering: Should we stay inside? go outside? But things were quiet all day long in our neighborhood. That evening, about 8 p.m., we put the kids to bed. As the Andes grew blue black against the darkening sky, Olga and I stood on the back porch.

"Listen," Olga said.

There was the tinny sound of someone banging a pot in the distance. The noise grew and intensified. There was banging across the street. It was a conversation neighbors had not had for more than a decade, and now they were clearly hearing what each other thought about the military government and the current economic and political crisis, and in the process they were finding a voice. A chorus of the most incredible racket came from next door. Don Alvaro was banging an iron bar against a huge cast-iron pot.

"What the hell," said Olga, running back to the house. She came back with three pans and wooden spoons. We banged away. Sonia joined us in her nightshirt. She had the lids from two pots and played them like cymbals, as the neighborhood's rough, tinny music filled the evening sky.

THE FARM REVISITED

When are you going to plant seeds for more chickens?" Andrés asked. There was no need for more chickens; the ones we had were headache enough.

Olga and I bought fifty four-week-old chicks from the egg lady. We brought them home in a large, brown cardboard box with round holes for air. The kids crowded around to look into the box. The bottom was covered with bouncing, pecking, two-inch yellow balls of feathers.

"Can we play with them?" Andrés asked.

"No, you can't even touch them. These are not toys. Do you understand me?" I said, closing the top of the box. Andrés was not in particularly good standing with me. After breakfast, I had chanced upon him and three-year-old Juanito in the bathroom. They were squirting my contact solution from the new bottle just arrived from the States at full force into the toilet.

"What are you doing with that!" I yelled.

Juanito immediately began crying.

"We're playing," Andrés answered calmly. I retrieved the half-empty bottle and gave both an extended lecture on respecting others' property.

We had acquired a book on how to raise poultry. That afternoon Néstor, Olga, and I turned the toolshed into a chicken coop in a single afternoon. We made roosting nests, installed rods for the birds to rest on, and cut a window in the shed to ensure sufficient light.

We purchased the special, expensive feed that the young chicks required. We tried to create a habitat that was, according to our book, "well-ventilated, cool but not damp." "Dampness breeds disease," the poultry bible warned.

But poultry raising, even by the book, was not a perfect science. Almost every morning we would find the limp body of another chick on the dirt floor of the coop. Fifteen chickens died during the first two weeks. We followed the instructions in the poultry book even more carefully: fresh water twice a day and exact measurements of the poultry feed. Unfortunately, on an almost daily basis some small hand would undo the latch to the chicken coop. The ensuing roundup sent the squawking chicks into neurotic fits.

"Don't run after them," I yelled at Yoana who was chasing the chicks at full speed. "Just move toward them slowly, pick them up, and put them back in the coop." There was almost no stopping the little boys, though, and more than a few chicks died shortly after hot pursuit by a three-year-old. I was convinced that when the birds finally reached egg-bearing age they would be so high-strung that they would not be able to lay eggs.

These concerns proved premature. Four months later, when the twenty or so chickens that had survived the ordeals of living at the hogar were nearing the age when they would lay eggs, someone sneaked into the henhouse at night and stole all but the four scrawniest hens while Jackie, our watchdog, slept.

Confident that these four traumatized chickens would never lay an egg, we decided to use them for a different end. In the process, I learned how to kill a chicken.

Eliana, our four-foot, ten-inch cook, picked up one of the skinny white hens. She took the chicken firmly in her small hands, put one hand on the head and one on the neck and with a single twist broke its neck. The bird, after a little movement, went limp. Eliana gave it to Verónica to drop in a pot of boiling water to make removal of the feathers easier.

I tried to imitate Eliana. I picked up the squawking chicken. I squeezed the neck and twisted the head, just as Eliana had done. Nothing happened except that the hen made sick clucking sounds. I pulled and pushed the chicken's neck to no avail.

"Tío, it's still alive," said Verónica.

"I can see that."

All the girls gathered round to watch. I used all my grip strength to try and break the neck. There was still no crack. The hen scratched desperately at the air.

After about two more minutes, the hen finally went limp, I think from lack of oxygen.

"Do you think we're going to have to eat it?" Sonia asked.

"And he used to get so mad at us when we just chased the chickens," Yoana said to the other girls as they walked back to the house.

The meat was tough, and the four hens barely provided one meal. With that, my aspirations of creating a poultry empire abated. Chickens were messy, sickly birds, certainly not worth the work.

We needed to think big. After all, we had over an acre of land. We could hire someone to cultivate the land professionally. It would also be more effective if we didn't involve the kids so directly. The water authority had been paid, so we knew water would flow through the irrigation ditches.

Olga helped reframe the project: "If we had a plow horse, the planting would go more quickly, more smoothly. With a winter crop, we could have at least two plantings a year. We could rent out the plow horse when we weren't using it." By comparison, this idea made the poultry business look like chicken feed.

I relished tearing out the shelves that had served the chickens to turn the shed into a stable. We paid three hundred dollars, the equivalent of three months' rent, for *la yegua*, a mare. The expense cleaned out all our savings.

She was a big, golden animal with a proud, white mane. We bought her from a large farm not far from the orphanage and walked her home down the dirt road. There was a celebration when she arrived. Neighbors brought hot wine spiced with cinnamon and Chilean meat pies called *empanadas*. Someone placed a garland of flowers around the horse's neck. The neighbors also inspected the horse, looking at her teeth and feeling her calves, as if kicking the tires on a used car.

That afternoon, the kids couldn't get enough of their new pet, but the yegua was getting testy with all the attention. Finally, when she had tolerated enough petting, poking, and probing, the yegua snorted and took a nip at the nearest object. It happened to be Andrés's arm. Andrés took off screaming. When I caught up with him, he was out of breath. Although the skin on his arm was not broken, he was shaking. It was the first time I had ever seen fear in his eyes.

To take care of the horse and plow the field, we hired Osvaldo, a farmer from the south of Chile. We agreed that he would plow for us three times a week for about ten dollars. He spoke very slowly, and not at all when he drank too much, which was often. It only took four visits to plow and plant the entire field. After that, we went into business. Verónica made a sign, "Yegua for Rent," which was posted on the front gate. Neighbors who rented the horse paid us in bags of lettuce and celery. Not exactly the hard cash we had imagined.

One day, after Osvaldo had been working for us for about three weeks, he knocked on the door of the orphanage. It was raining outside, and I imagined he wanted a dry place to wait out the storm. His wet hair was plastered to his forehead, and his eyes were bloodshot.

"There is something wrong with the yegua," he said slowly.

We walked somberly to the stable. The yegua was lying on the straw, her stomach heaving as she tried to breathe. We stood her up. I thought she was wet from the rain, but her body was covered with sweat. Osvaldo walked her around the fields in the rain. She stopped again and lay down in the wet grass. We couldn't get her up.

Olga went to a neighbor's house and called a veterinarian from the university. The kids gathered around the horse in the rain. The yegua's stomach was bloated and swollen.

"The yegua is pregnant," Carlos pronounced in his high-pitched voice.

"Carlos, she is not pregnant," I said.

"I saw a pregnant horse once. This horse is pregnant," Carlos said definitively.

"Her stomach started to swell just this morning . . ."

"I bet you she's pregnant."

"Carlos, you're crazy," I told him.

"You're afraid to bet me because you know I'm right."

"Right."

"Really, I'll bet you a hundred pesos that the veterinarian says the yegua is pregnant," Carlos said.

"Fine, Carlos, a hundred pesos." We shook hands.

"Carlos and Tío Steve are betting!" Verónica cried, running to tell Olga.

Throughout the afternoon, the horse had more and more difficulty breathing as white saliva foamed around her mouth.

"See, I told you," Carlos said knowingly, pointing to her belly that continued to swell. The veterinarian came just in time to pronounce the horse dead.

"It was probably a blocked intestine," he said.

He cut off a small piece of skin and flesh and put it in a plastic bag. We covered up the horse with a big black plastic sheet. The next morning the veterinarian came back.

"The horse meat is safe to eat," he told Olga.

Three neighbors who had been present for the yegua's arrival festivities only a few weeks earlier returned. Don Alvaro brought his chain saw.

"They're going to chop up the yegua," Yoana yelled, running into the house. All the children in the house scampered outside into the rain to see the action. The drizzle turned into a downpour. Olga herded the kids back into the house. Néstor and I fashioned a tent out of large pieces of canvas to protect horse and workers from the rain and to keep the horse out of the kids' view. Inside the tent, the roaring chain saw made the close quarters reek of gasoline. The saw sputtered and got stuck in a leg bone as rivers of blood wound their way through the wet grass. Don Alvaro piled up the four legs.

He shut off the chain saw and pulled an eight-inch hunting knife from his bag. There was the flash of the silver edge of the knife against the yegua's yellow belly, as Alvaro skillfully sliced the stomach open. The white intestines spilled out. Néstor snapped photos, one with Alvaro holding up the huge snakelike intestines. There were dozens of empty pots and pans, a twenty-kilo bag of salt, and buckets of hot water to rinse the organs.

Don Alvaro carved the meat into manageable chunks, and the three neighbors who had helped butcher the yegua took all the meat they could carry. A great deal of meat and intestines remained. Olga, Néstor, and I removed the empty cartons and assorted junk from a shed adjoining the house to make room for the salted horse meat. We hung the meat from the rafters with pieces of wire. Néstor and I buried the horse head and the hooves in the wet soil. By early evening, Jackie had dug up one of the hooves and paraded in the rain with her trophy.

Before the horse died, the kids at the orphanage had eaten meat about once a week. Meat was expensive, and Chileans, except for the wealthiest, generally did not eat much of it. In the weeks following the horse's passing, we ate horse sausage for breakfast, horse steaks for lunch, and ground horse chuck in the evening. After their usual diet of bread, pasta, beans, fish, and vegetables, the kids loved the meat, and a number of them gained weight. All except Andrés.

"I don't want to eat the yegua," Andrés declared the first time horse flesh was put on a plate in front of him. He refused to touch any meat in any form that was offered in the coming weeks. At about the same time Andrés became a vegetarian, I abandoned my visions of the family farm.

SIXTEEN

DONORS, DEMONS, AND DENTISTS

Olga had invited Sister Gertrudis, a stern nun in a traditional black habit not often seen in Santiago, to discuss the possibility that a foundation she represented assist the orphanage. Sister Gertrudis sat rigidly, her face expressionless, in the living room on the plywood couch with foam padding. A rosary with large, rough-hewn wooden beads hung from her leather belt. She was the type of nun who had terrified me as a kid.

Olga did most of the talking, explaining the history and the philosophy of the orphanage, peppering her talk with moving descriptions of the kids' backgrounds. She spoke mostly about four-year-old Keli, who had just arrived a few days earlier.

"Just last Friday we learned about Keli from a group of Italian nuns who live near here," Olga began. "About a month ago, one of the nuns was returning home about eleven o'clock on a cold night. There was a little girl wandering the streets. 'Where do you live?' the nun asked her. The little girl pointed to a one-room wooden shack. The sister knocked on the door. There was no answer, and the door was locked. Not knowing what else to do, the nun took the little girl, Keli, home that evening. Keli's arms and stomach were covered with a rash, and her hair was full of lice. The nun bathed her, and the next morning returned Keli to her mother. About a week later, the same scene was repeated, except this time it was raining and the door to the shack was unlocked. Inside, the mother was drunk, and it was obvious she was using the shack to work as a prostitute. She didn't want to see Keli and screamed at the nun to get out of her house. The nuns spent weeks trying to talk with the mother about her responsibilities concerning Keli. The woman wasn't interested in these 'busybodies.' Keli was locked out of the house and regularly came over to stay with the nuns. Unfortunately, the nuns were in no position to care permanently for a four-year-old.

"We decided a few months ago that twelve children was the ideal number in this small house with only two bedrooms for the children. But after hearing a story like that, what could we do? So we've decided that thirteen children is the limit."

As if it were staged, Keli, who was wearing Karen's yellow dress, walked into the living room and stood in the doorway. She had short-cropped dark hair and a square, dark face. Her arms were covered with little scabs from a rash, but a shampoo called *lindano*, we hoped, had taken care of the lice. Keli looked on apprehensively.

"Come here, Keli," Olga said. Cautiously, Keli moved toward Olga and sat with her on the couch.

"We very much hope the foundation will be able to assist the children at the hogar," Olga concluded. I thought I saw a glimmer of a tear in Sister Gertrudis's stern eyes.

Andrés joined us in the living room.

"This is Andrés," Olga said to the nun. She nodded imperially. Andrés walked over and stood in front of her and stared intently at her pasty white face until we all felt a little uncomfortable.

"Andrés, why don't you come sit with me?" I suggested.

He continued to stare at the nun.

"Why don't you shave your mustache?" Andrés asked Sister Gertrudis.

"Andrés, don't you want to go out and play?" Olga choked out. He left the room.

"I need to be going," Sister Gertrudis said abruptly.

A few weeks later, the foundation notified us via a registered letter that it had decided not to assist Hogar Domingo Savio "due to the large number of important demands on our limited resources."

That news had little impact on Andrés, Juanito, and Héctor, who spent their days chasing after each other, climbing trees, and wandering out into the street. One afternoon, I caught them knee deep in mud in the irrigation ditch that ran behind the house.

"Get out of there," I yelled.

Juanito and Héctor scampered out of the ditch and took the long way around to the house to avoid me. Andrés stepped out of the ditch slowly and deliberately. His pants were completely covered with mud. He took the direct route to the house, walking right in front of me, not at all intimidated by my arrival.

I had another run-in with three-year-old Andrés later that afternoon. "Andrés, go clean up the mess you made," I ordered after he had intentionally ripped a comic book apart in the living room. He stared back defiantly.

"I'm mad at you," he declared. "I'm going to poop on the table." His dark brown eyes didn't blink.

"Young man, you'll be sorry if you do that," I warned, unable to believe I was having this conversation with a three-year-old.

Andrés hopped on the table and pulled down his blue cotton gym shorts. He paused to glare at me one more time and then calmly pooped.

Furious, I grabbed him off the table and walloped his bottom. Then I made him clean the mess on the table and sent him to bed. After that, we began to get along much better. He knew my limits, and I knew his.

Néstor spent less and less time at the orphanage. He was teaching religion classes at two grade schools, giving guitar lessons, and running two youth programs at churches. Finally, he decided to move out and live with his brother, who was closer to downtown Santiago.

To fill the gap, a nineteen-year-old college student, Margot, began to volunteer part-time at the hogar. She was studying to be a preschool teacher, and we put her in charge of the five preschoolers who were constantly wreaking havoc.

Margot was petite and whispered when she talked. She seemed to get along well with the younger children, all except Andrés.

"Tío, Andrés is a very aggressive little boy," she told me in hushed tones.

"Tío Steve, she's lying," he yelled from across the room. Andrés also had radar ears.

Later that afternoon, as I came through the front gate, Margot was standing under the elm tree. "Andrés," she said, "please come down."

The tree was full of leaves, and I could not see Andrés, but I could hear him giggling.

"Andrés, please," she pleaded again. There was no movement except the leaves fluttering in the breeze.

"Andrés, get out of that tree this instant," I barked.

He came down out of the tree like a firefighter sliding down a pole.

"Thank you, Tío," Margot whispered.

"I want to talk with this one," I said, pointing to Andrés.

Margot went inside.

"Why do you act so badly around her?" I asked.

"Ella no sabe controlarme," Andrés, the three-year-old, responded. "She doesn't know how to control me."

As my Spanish improved, I began to tell regular bedtime stories to the kids. The stories were strange mixes of fables I remembered from my childhood, tales I made up, and things I had read. The book *Watership Down,* about a migrating warren of rabbits, provided fodder for an almost infinite number of tales. My rabbit stories were told in continuing segments, with each character taking on a personality, like a character in a soap opera. I often got in trouble because I didn't remember as well as the kids what was happening to the different characters. In recounting the story that involved the wicked foxes Juana and Sandra, who were constantly plotting to trap and roast the rabbits for supper, I said ". . . and then Juana said that . . ."

"Tío, Juana got run over by a tractor and died," Verónica pointed out.

"Oh, I meant to say, the ghost of the wicked fox Juana said that . . ."

Storytelling became very important when, in three days' time, six children came down with chicken pox. We quarantined all the sick ones in the same room, hoping to contain the plague. The room looked like a war hospital. Marcelo scratched himself until he bled. Carlos had the worst case, the dreaded disease appearing around his eyes and in his mouth. Five-year-old Karen, her hair pulled back with a rubber band and her face covered with the rash, looked like a shriveled old lady. Karen, who had always been so quiet, had begun talking with a vengeance. She would constantly interrupt my stories with side comments.

"Tío, I like your stories even if they are boring," she confided at the conclusion of what I thought was a particularly rousing tale.

"Thanks, Karen." I turned off the light in the hospital ward, and I told the sick ones, "If you start feeling bad, let me know."

Two minutes later I heard sounds from the bedroom across the hall, the room with all those who didn't have chicken pox. Cough, cough. Pause. Cough, cough. It was Andrés.

"Tío, I feel bad. Can you tell me a story?"

I spent the week of the chicken pox scourge telling stories, many of them shamelessly plagiarized from *Watership Down.* The rabbits, in search of a safe place to build a new warren, had survived pestilence, wolves, floods, and highways. I augmented their achievements to include battles with evil cannibals, flying saucers, and Martians. Fiver was the runt of the litter but also the most clever, and he always managed to get the rabbits out of these dicey situations.

That week we initiated what was to become a tradition. I would begin a story and then the kids would add to it. Each new story had to begin where the last one left off. Our story found the rabbits trapped in a cornfield as a huge tractor with spinning metal plates moved toward them.

"And Fiver, who is the smartest, stood up on his hind legs and thought about how he could save all the rabbits from the huge tractor . . ." My voice trailed off.

"Karen, your turn."

"The farmer was driving the tractor," she began.

"What kind of tractor was it?" Andrés, who had also come down with the plague, asked.

"Shut up," Karen said, insistent that no one interrupt her. "The farmer stopped the tractor. It was red. The farmer saw the rabbits and took out his gun and killed them all and that's the end of the story."

There was a pause. Everyone was stunned, including me.

"All the rabbits died and Fiver too?" two-year-old Héctor asked, big tears running down his cheeks.

"Yes," Karen said, "and that's the end of the story."

If Karen wanted to end the stories definitively, Andrés wanted them repeated over and over.

"Tell the story about the selfish giant," Andrés said. There was moaning and booing from the six older boys who shared the room with Andrés.

"Tío, we have to listen to that stupid story every night," Alfredo said.

"If I hear that story again I'm going to vomit," Carlos added diplomatically.

The selfish giant story had to be told in exactly the same way every time or Andrés complained. The story went like this: There was a giant who had a castle with a garden. In this garden, there were flowers and birds and horses and chickens. Every day, all the children from the village came to play in the garden of the giant, but one day . . .

At this point I stopped and asked Andrés, "Do you know what happened?"

Andrés continued the story. "A boy was playing in the giant's garden and he threw a rock and broke the window. The giant got mad and threw out all the children and said that they could never come back."

"And what did the smallest boy say to the giant?" I asked Andrés.

"The littlest boy said to the giant, 'You are very selfish,' and he left." Then Andrés asked me, "Do you know what happened next?" I shook my head no.

Andrés the storyteller was content and continued: "All the flowers and trees died, and the birds and horses and mice all left, then the giant was very, very unhappy, and he did not know why his garden was so ugly, and one day he went to the village and asked the littlest boy why his garden was so ugly now and why all the animals had gone away. And do you know what the little boy said?" Andrés asked me. I shook my head again.

"The little boy said, 'Your garden is ugly because there are no children playing in the garden and all the flowers and animals were very sad and they died and that's why.'"

Andrés said it very slowly so that I could catch the full significance of what the boy had said.

"He is a very smart little boy," I said. Andrés replied with a nod.

"Then what happened?" I asked.

"The giant invited all the children to play in the garden of the giant, but only the little boy went because all the others were scared. And the very first day all the flowers grew just a little. [Andrés indicated "just a little" between his thumb and forefinger.] The second day the boy went with his brother, and the flowers grew a little more. . . . After that, all the children went to play in the garden of the giant, and the flowers grew huge, and the cows and horses and birds and mice all returned."

"Did the giant ever throw out the children again?" I asked.

Andrés, very sure of himself, shaking his head said, "No!"

The story did not change, not a single word, and Andrés saw to that. It gave one faith in an oral literary tradition.

All the kids, sometimes in groups of three or four, sometimes individually, went to the dentists at CORDAM. Knowing Andrés, I imagined there might be a scene on his first visit. So I was not completely surprised when, sitting in the waiting room, I heard Andrés's familiar blood-curdling scream from inside the dentist's office. I went to see if

I could help. The dentist and the nurse were ushering Andrés out. The dentist was holding a cloth to his finger.

"That child bit my finger." He was none too pleased. After a fair amount of discussion, the dentist told me I could bring "that child" again only if someone talked with him and promised that he would not behave in the same manner on the next visit. Rather naively, I promised the doctor that I could handle everything, and I made an appointment for a week later.

So every day for a week Andrés and I played "going to the dentist." I sat at my desk, and Andrés knocked on my bedroom door.

"Come in, Señor Retamales." Andrés would sit in my desk chair. "Open wide." I probed around a little in his mouth with a toothbrush and made drilling noises. We practiced going to the dentist with what I considered great success.

On the appointed morning in the car on the way to the dentist's office, I said, "Open wide," and Andrés looked at me with his mouth gaping open. I promised him a yogurt after the dentist visit if he behaved himself.

We sat quietly in the waiting room. I complimented myself on the effectiveness of positive reinforcement and the use of role playing.

"Andrés Retamales Díaz," the nurse said.

Andrés and I walked toward the dentist's office. But when Andrés saw the dentist, he let out one of his famous banshee screams and threw his hands and legs against the door frame. It reminded me of when my cousin used to hold our cat over the rim of the toilet and then flush.

The dentist tried to assist me, but Andrés threw a flying kick to his leg. The dentist, in the least helpful manner possible, told me to "do something with this animal."

"Andrés and I will take a walk and then we will try again in half an hour," I suggested.

As soon as we left the office, Andrés calmed down, and we walked around the courtyard, now practicing both opening his mouth and walking through doorways. We returned to the office. When Andrés saw the dentist, he staged a repeat performance. I picked Andrés up by the arm and not so gently sent him outside to wait.

"That child is too excitable even to put under anesthesia," the dentist told me. "Maybe we should wait a couple of years."

"And if his teeth rot in the meantime?" I asked. The dentist didn't respond. I convinced the nurse to give Andrés one last appointment in a week. In the car, I asked Andrés why he acted so badly.

"The dentist is a bad man," he replied.

For one week, rather than relying on positive reinforcement and role-playing, I invoked a less savory tactic—fear.

As far as I knew, Andrés seemed to have only one real fear in the world—horses—going back to the time *la yegua* had nipped him. I honed in on this. Andrés had lived in fear the weeks we had la yegua at the hogar. I think it was one of his happiest days when the horse "went away," even though he never consumed the horse meat that all the other kids ate with such relish. But even scarier for Andrés than the now-deceased mare was a black horse that lived down the road. To go to the vegetable market, we had to walk past the black horse's pasture. Andrés designed alternative routes so we would not have to pass near it.

That evening, in place of the usual bedtime story, I began, "Andrés, did you know that the farmer up the road with the horse is looking for a little boy to live with him?"

This deviated from the standard way a bedtime story should begin, and Andrés complained. I continued all the same.

"It is the farmer with the black horse on the corner, and he is looking for a little boy because the horse is lonely."

Andrés's eyes widened.

"But the farmer only wants a little boy with bad teeth. The horse has bad teeth," I explained, "and he wants a little boy who also has bad teeth to sleep with the horse." Andrés was completely silent.

All the other children had finished up their visits to the dentist, and Andrés knew this, but just for emphasis I went around the room and one by one the other boys told me they had gone to the dentist and that they all had good teeth.

Sebastián, the oldest boy and aspiring actor, wiped his brow and said, "Boy, I'm glad I went to the dentist and got my teeth fixed, I sure wouldn't want to live with *that* horse!"

Andrés stared at me, all big brown eyes, hardly blinking.

"Do you have bad teeth?" I asked Andrés.

He shook his head no.

I nodded my head yes. Tears began to form in Andrés's eyes, and I wondered if I was taking this too far.

"You know, the dentist we went to today wants to fix your teeth," I said. "If you have good teeth the farmer won't want you to come near his black horse . . . but if you don't want to have good teeth, that's not a big problem but. . . ." Andrés consented to give the dentist one more try.

For a third time, we journeyed in the car to visit the dentist. Andrés ducked down in the front seat as we passed where the black horse lived. One last time we practiced "open wide" in the car. We arrived at the dentist's office, and as we entered the nurse had an *Oh-Lord-not-this-kid-again* look on her face.

The nurse called Andrés, and he stoically marched into the office alone. For twenty-five minutes I anxiously waited, not hearing a sound. Finally, the dentist and Andrés emerged.

"Is this the same Andrés Retamales that I saw last week?" he asked.

"Yes."

"What happened?"

"Andrés decided it was important to take good care of his teeth," I suggested.

"The bad man with the horse is going to have to find another boy," Andrés blurted out. The dentist gave me a strange look and returned to his office shaking his head. We stopped on the way home and bought yogurt. When we passed the farmer's house in the car, Andrés didn't duck down. In fact, without saying a word, he sat a little taller.

MARCELO

D uring a very rainy July, I abandoned my bike and endured the rush-hour traffic among the damp and packed bodies inside the bus: returning workers, shoppers, and young students packed in the bus aisles with woolen hats and scarves, book bags and packages.

"Please move to the back," the bus driver kept repeating. I tried to move down the aisle toward the back, but I got wedged between a man, thin and gaunt with a two-day shadow on his face, and a heavy-set woman with two shopping bags full of lettuce and oranges. The woman was wearing a perfume that was overpowering. An American nun who lived five years in Chile once remarked to me, "Anyone who regularly rides the buses in Santiago at rush hour cannot legitimately be considered a virgin."

In the seat in front of me, a mother sat with a baby on her lap. Her baby was wrapped in layer after layer of white and light blue knitted yarn. I could only see the child's eyes and nose. I was sure that if the child had not been in her arms, she would have been knitting. The arrival of winter was heralded when, as if by biological instinct, Chilean women converged on bus seats and waiting room benches with two knitting needles and colored balls of yarn tucked into little plastic bags.

Sitting next to the woman and knitted baby was a high school student in his standard-issue blue blazer, gray pants, and clip-on blue tie that every Chilean male wears from first grade until he finishes high school. His fingers rhythmically moved across his doodled-on notebook as if playing a piano, while he stared blankly out the bus window.

In the final row there were three generations cramped on one bench. A gray-haired grandfather, a tired-looking father, and, on the grandfather's knee, a four- or five-year-old boy. The father was half sleeping, his head drooping, but every time his chin touched his chest he jerked his head back. The grandfather, sitting next to the window, looked sternly ahead while jostling the boy on his knee. The boy, giggling, pushed his face against his grandfather's chest and then pressed his face against the window, making steam prints with his breath.

He reminded me of Andrés, wild-eyed and mischievous, who made the same steam prints on bus windows when we rode together. We seemed to always be riding the bus together to some doctor or dentist appointment. Some days Andrés would sleep on the bus, gently laying his head against my chest, reassured and warm, and I the same. Other days, cramped in a tight bus seat, he'd throw his head back hard against my chest, playfully, intentionally, waiting to see what reaction he would get.

Someone roughly moved past me in the aisle, pushing me into the woman standing next to me, breaking my dreamy trance.

I asked myself, how much of my life had I spent on these crowded buses coming or going to work or to classes or to doctor's appointments with the kids? How many novels and magazines had I read while being jostled and trying not to read the same line twice? How many nights, like tonight, did I have to stand, too tired to even try to read, resting my forehead on the cool metal bar suspended from the roof of the bus?

By the time spring arrived in September and things were finally drying out, it seemed that Marcelo had gotten over his propensity to climb the tree in the backyard and curse when anyone came near him, as he had during his first months at the orphanage. Nonetheless, he continued to get into fights at the hogar and at school and to wet his bed at night. Any request that he help around the house would be met by a cold, defiant stare. He intentionally teased the little kids and the girls. Once he pulled the eyes off Yoana's two dolls.

We knew relatively little about Marcelo's background. Before coming to the hogar, he had been living in a one-room shack with his grandfather. A social worker brought him to the orphanage because he wasn't attending school. The social worker thought Marcelo was probably eight years old. Marcelo didn't even know the date of his birthday. One incident, however, brought Marcelo's history to light.

"Is there anything you want to talk about?" I asked Marcelo as we walked along the canal behind the house on our way to buy some vegetables for lunch.

"No."

"Well, I guess I just wanted to talk to you about what happened between you and that other boy." I had only heard the story secondhand. "Do you want to tell me about it?"

"We were doing dirty things," Marcelo said.

"What were you doing?"

"He wanted to touch between my legs and I let him. Someone saw us and told Tía Olga."

"And how do you feel about it now?"

"Bad."

"Has this happened before?"

"Not with that boy."

"Did it happen with other boys?"

"Yeah, with my cousin."

"What happened with your cousin?"

"He liked to touch my dick and do things with his."

"When did this happen?"

"Whenever he stayed with me and my grandfather."

"How old were you when this happened?"

"I don't know, maybe I was about as old as Karen." Karen had just turned five.

"Did it go on for a long time?"

"Yeah, until I moved here. We did dirty things all the time. That's why I'm so dirty."

"Marcelo, it's not your fault. Your cousin did things he shouldn't have done with you. But it wasn't your fault, and you're not dirty."

Marcelo didn't respond.

"You understand me, don't you?"

He shrugged his shoulders.

"Tell me about your cousin."

"What do you want to know?"

"How old is he?"

"He's maybe twenty years old now. I don't know. He didn't finish high school. He just always sniffed glue. He always smelled like airplane glue." Glue was the cheapest available drug in poor neighborhoods in Santiago, and sustained use led to permanent brain damage.

"Marcelo, did you sniff glue?"

"I just sniffed it when I got real hungry. You don't feel as hungry when you sniff glue. But it gave me a headache, so I didn't do it very much."

Not knowing what else to do or what words to say, I hugged him. He looked startled. "Why did you do that?" he asked.

"Because I think you're a really good person and I'm glad I know you." He had tears in his eyes, and so did I.

About a month later, we were able to get Marcelo into counseling at CORDAM, the government-run health services. The sessions seemed to help. The counselor encouraged us to deal more actively with Marcelo's bed-wetting because he felt it stemmed from Marcelo's low self-esteem.

Marcelo tried to stop. He didn't drink any liquid after 7 p.m. and would go to the bathroom right before he went to bed. A few hours later, I'd wake him up before I went to bed. I would drag him to the bathroom, his jet-black hair standing on end as if he had just put his hand in an electrical outlet. He would stand, tottering, still half asleep, in front of the toilet.

"Come on, Marcelo, take a leak." If he didn't, I'd turn on the faucet, and that suggestion usually got the job done. This system managed to reduce his bed-wetting from three times a week to about once a week.

Marcelo had good days and bad days. One day, he came home from school with a note from his teacher stating that he had been suspended for two days.

"So how did you behave at school today?"

"Bad," he replied matter-of-factly.

"Why?"

"I beat up a kid."

"Why did you do that?"

He didn't reply.

"Do you want to explain what happened?"

He was mute.

Verónica later explained what had happened. The bully of the fourth grade had been teasing and hitting a second grader. Marcelo told the fourth grader to stop. He didn't. Just as the teacher came on the scene, Marcelo punched the bully. Marcelo didn't attempt to explain what had happened, either to the teacher or to us.

Another day, as Marcelo and I were sitting at the big black desk in my bedroom, I said, "Marcelo, write your name on the sheet."

"Marcelo Contreras," he wrote clearly on his lined sheet of paper.

"That's amazing. How come you couldn't write it yesterday?"

He looked at me and finally smiled.

"Guess I didn't want to."

Over the spring, there were other changes. Marcelo enjoyed working with scraps of wood and building boxes or birdhouses. Andrés and Juanito followed him around, so he'd give them the things he made. Although he used to chase them away, he now let them work with him on projects. Gradually, they became his assistants, and he patiently taught them how to draw airplanes and how to make a moving vehicle using four jar lids and a milk carton.

For better or worse, Marcelo changed his modus operandi: instead of hitting, he began to give bear hugs to children and adults alike. Unfortunately, he hugged so hard it hurt. The little kids cried when they were the object of Marcelo's affection, and Olga got big bruises. Olga called it "Marcelo's special brand of affection."

§

EIGHTEEN

AN UNEXPECTED JOURNEY

§

Beyond the prosperous Vitacura and Las Condes areas on the east side of Santiago were rolling hills, rough and rocky, with almond orchards and a modest vineyard. Half hidden behind a spray of cypress trees, off a dirt road, was the La Dehesa Trappist Monastery. I never fully understood how Olga had enlisted the help of the Trappist monks in the hogar, especially since the monks typically avoided contact with the world, spending most of their day in prayer and silence.

What I did know was that Olga had discovered from the former Trappist monk, Nino, who had worked at the hogar that the Trappists quietly administered funds that assisted social projects in Chile, and with that information she had found her way to the monastery tucked away in these hills. Since her first visit, Olga had gotten the Trappists actively involved in the work of the hogar, and enthusiastically so.

I actually knew something about the Trappists, as one of my college roommates at Notre Dame had seriously considered becoming a Trappist monk, and some friends and I had gone with him to Trappist monasteries in Kentucky and Massachusetts.

The Trappists had begun as a monastic reform movement in the Middle Ages to protest the increasing worldliness and laxity of the Church. The autobiography of the most famous of Trappists, Thomas Merton, had become something of a spiritual classic. Merton grew up in Europe during World War I then came to the United States, where he graduated from Columbia University. By the time he was twenty-six years old, he had decided to enter the Abbey of Gethsemani monastery in northern Kentucky and to devote his life "To God Alone," as the sign over the entrance to that monastery read. Merton was a quite unusual Trappist. He not only wrote about the contemplative life and prayer but increasingly, from within the monastery, wrote on controversial issues of economic injustice, race relations, and nuclear war, which made some of the monastic hierarchy nervous. He became fascinated with Eastern spirituality and wrote about the many links between the spiritual traditions of East and West. He died accidentally in 1968 in Thailand while attending a religious conference.

La Dehesa monastery had been established outside of Santiago by some of Merton's monastic contemporaries from the United States in 1960. Olga told me that since the coup the Trappists in Chile had, very quietly, hidden and helped save the lives of individuals sought by the military. I imagined that Merton would have enthusiastically endorsed this kind of engagement in the world.

Arriving at La Dehesa monastery, a visitor first saw the simple wooden chapel with its blue stained-glass windows and a wooden sign that read *silencio*. Behind the public spaces were the private quarters of the twenty or so monks, a mix of Chileans and gringos, who still followed the rules for monastic life developed by St. Benedict in the sixth century. The monks did manual labor and prayed, beginning their days chanting Vigils at about 4:00 a.m. and finishing with the chanting of Vespers at about 8 p.m.

We would regularly go to the monastery to pick up a check for the hogar and on some occasions to meet with the abbot. With his crew cut and athletic build, the abbot of the monastery, Father Richard, looked more like a Marine than a monk. His blue eyes, though, were calm, and his voice soft. He warmly greeted us and gave Olga a kiss on the cheek.

Olga brought him up to date on all the latest developments with the children.

"I am glad that, overall, things are going so well. You are doing very important work," he said as he handed Olga the check. Through a private foundation, La Dehesa provided a four-hundred-dollar check each month for the hogar—our only regular source of income. All the rest came as piecemeal donations. The first one hundred of the four hundred dollars went immediately to pay the monthly rent for the house.

"Oh, I almost forgot. Steve Dougherty, who helps finance our social service projects, is going to be visiting Chile next month, and he'd like to visit the orphanage," Father Richard told us. I knew little more about Mr. Dougherty than that he was a Texan in the oil business.

"We'd be very pleased to have Mr. Dougherty and you visit the orphanage," Olga said, and a date and time were set.

In anticipation of the visit, at Olga's direction, we spent two days cleaning walls, washing windows, and waxing floors. "It's fine if Mr. Dougherty thinks we're poor. Actually, it's important that he think we're poor, but I don't want him thinking we're dirty," Olga stated categorically.

On the appointed afternoon in November, Mr. Dougherty and Father Richard paid a visit to the orphanage.

"Just call me Steve," was the first thing Mr. Dougherty said to me. It turned out he was only a few years older than I was. Olga introduced Father Richard and Steve to all the kids, who were as clean as the house. Pigpen Alfredo was wearing a white shirt that had just been ironed. His top button was clasped. He couldn't have looked more uncomfortable if he had been wearing a hair shirt. I gave Steve a tour and asked him how he had become interested in Chile.

"I inherited a little money from my family's oil business and wanted to do something worthwhile with it," he said. "Father Richard is somebody I trust a lot, and he came up with the idea of setting up the foundation and hooking up with social organizations here in Chile."

"I say this very sincerely," I told him. "I don't know what we'd do without the four hundred dollars a month we receive from the foundation."

"I'm glad it helps. It's a great orphanage. The kids all seem so happy," he said. "You could have a great little farm here, ya know," he said, surveying the abandoned field, standing near the ditch where the goat and horse head were buried. "Have you ever tried farming the land?" he asked innocently.

"Well," I said, trying to be diplomatic, "we've tried a few agricultural projects." I didn't mention the goat or the horse or the chickens.

"I'm sure y'all have your hands full just keeping all those kids fed and clothed. You know what is really amazing is how they all seem like part of a big family," he said.

"It really is a good group of kids, and it does feel like a family—a big, unwieldy family," I said.

Alfredo joined our walk. "Tío, can I take off this shirt? It hurts my neck."

"Go ask Tía Olga," I suggested. With a dejected look, he sighed and walked away. He knew what Olga's response to his request would be.

"What was all that about?"

"Alfredo would rather be playing in the dirt than dressed up in a white shirt," I explained.

"Well, I can certainly understand that." Steve paused and added, "I'm just glad the foundation can help this big family. Families are really important. Tell me about your family."

We talked about my parents, my three brothers and one sister, and about the fact that I hadn't seen any of them for over a year.

"Are you going home for Christmas this year?"

"Not this year. It's really expensive to fly back. But I stay in close touch with them, and I'm sure next year I'll be home for Christmas."

We went back inside and had dinner before Steve and Father Richard headed back to the monastery. During dinner, Alfredo spilled a mug of hot chocolate on his white shirt. He seemed much more comfortable sitting with a large brown stain down the front of his shirt.

About a week later, a message for me arrived via a banker friend of Steve Dougherty's. "Merry Christmas. There is a round-trip plane ticket in your name at the Pan Am ticket office in Santiago for you to go home for Christmas. You need to let the Pan Am office know your travel plans."

Once the idea was planted, I desperately wanted to go but felt guilty. A plane ticket cost seven hundred dollars. Surely, we could do something better with the money at the hogar. I told Olga my concerns.

"Gringo, are you crazy? Go spend Christmas with your family, that's what he gave you the money for." And so I did.

Since the trip was a surprise to me, I planned to surprise my family for Christmas. My flight was routed through New York City, so I got a four-day stopover and visited my college roommate and his family outside of Albany, New York. Members of his family were incredulous that I would just show up in Indiana after being gone for a year and a half.

"Nobody knows? What if they've decided to spend Christmas somewhere else?" one asked. "What if this is too big of a shock for your mom and she has a heart attack?" another queried.

I decided to call my sister, Karla, to get a reading on the situation. She said she would call Dad and see if he thought it prudent to surprise Mom. I talked again to Karla the next day from New York.

"When I got Dad on the phone, I told him we were going to have a big surprise for Christmas, a special guest, God rest his soul. And Dad said, 'No kidding, God rest his soul is back in the country!'"

I couldn't believe it. My own father calling me God rest his soul.

"Well," Karla said, "Dad thinks it would be a great surprise for Mom and that we should keep it a secret. So I'll see you on the twenty-fourth."

On December 24, I flew into Indianapolis Airport. Giant snow-plows were pushing the fresh-fallen snow off to the side of the runway. My sister picked me up, and we drove north to Fort Wayne, two hours away. Blue Christmas lights were strung across the trees in the front yard of the Reifenberg home. Karla and I got out of the car. Karla went to the front door. I hung back in the shadows. Mom met Karla at the door and gave her a hug.

"Merry Christmas, honey," she said. "Karla, who's standing out there in the driveway?"

"I think it is God rest his soul," Karla said, giggling.

I walked out of the shadows.

My mother's face went white, and she stood there dumbfounded. For an instant, I wondered if this was such a good idea. Then she walked up to me and hugged me and then hugged me again tighter and wouldn't let me go.

"What a wonderful, wonderful Christmas present," she repeated over and over. "I couldn't have had a better Christmas present." Later, my parents, brothers, sister, and I sat around talking at the kitchen ta-ble, eating Christmas cookies and homemade chocolate butter crunch. I had brought little gifts from Chile—copper bracelets, an embroidered wall hanging made by the kids at the hogar, a sweater, a leather book-mark—and my family acted as if they were great treasures.

"I feel so bad," Mom said. "I sent your presents to Chile, so we don't have anything here for you."

"See, Steve, she doesn't really love you," Rick, my youngest brother, a junior in high school, commented. "I got lots of presents. They love me a lot."

"Now, don't you two start," Mom warned.

"Fine, I won't beat him up just yet. It's still Christmas Eve," I said.

"You wish. I've been working out. You'd be dead meat if you put one finger on me," seventeen-year-old Rick retorted.

"Okay, you guys," Mom said in her most serious voice.

My father actually seemed to be enjoying the bantering. I wasn't sure if it was because I had come home safely and it was hard for him to be as angry at me in person as he was in writing, or that time had passed and he had mellowed, but neither of us mentioned his letter.

I brought out photos of the kids and the Chilean countryside, and there were lots of questions and appropriate "oohs" and "aahs" as my family looked at the pictures. That Christmas Eve we stayed up until 2 a.m. with our Christmas celebration, just as I was sure they were doing at the hogar. All we lacked was the tinny music and the dancing.

I stayed connected to Chile in different ways while I was in the United States. I spent a couple of January afternoons in the Fort Wayne downtown library reading things about Chile that I could never read in Chile. I had heard of something called the Church Committee that had investigated illegal U.S. activities in Chile, but I didn't know much more than that.

I learned that the Church Committee was established after the *New York Times* published an article in December 1973 by Seymour Hersh describing Central Intelligence Agency operations overseas that included assassination attempts against foreign leaders and covert attempts to overthrow foreign governments. These revelations convinced many members of Congress that they had been too lax in their oversight responsibilities, and the United States Senate Select Committee to Study Governmental Operations with Respect to Intelligence Activities was formed.

Chaired by Senator Frank Church of Idaho, it became known simply as the Church Committee. Among other things, the committee investigated U.S.-led attempts to assassinate leaders in the Congo, the Dominican Republic, and Vietnam as well as a plan to use the Mafia to kill Fidel Castro in Cuba.

In 1975 and 1976, the Church Committee published fourteen reports "on U.S. intelligence agencies, their operations, and the alleged abuses of law and of power." In the Fort Wayne library, I found the 94th Congress's 1st Session Committee Report, printed on December 18, 1975, titled "COVERT ACTION IN CHILE 1963–1973."

What was clear, the report began, "was that covert United States involvement in Chile in the decade between 1963 and 1973 was extensive and continuous." The CIA had spent three million dollars in an effort to influence the outcome of the Chilean presidential elections of 1964. Eight million dollars were spent, covertly, in the three years between 1970 and the military coup in September 1973. The range of activities undertaken by the CIA included "covert action, clandestine intelligence collection, liaison with local police and intelligence services, and counterintelligence." The scope of "normal" activities of the

CIA station in Santiago included, among other things, "efforts to oppose communist and left-wing influence in student, peasant and labor organization."

The CIA money, as I had heard but never seen in print in Chile, had financed everything from payments to the press to criticize the Allende government to large-scale support for opposition Chilean political parties, "from public opinion polls to direct attempts to bring about a military coup."

The report stated that in 1970, shortly after President Allende was elected to office but before he took power, "the CIA attempted to bring about a coup in Chile, at the express request of President Nixon and under the injunction not to inform the Departments of State or Defense or the Ambassador of the project." The CIA passed weapons to a group of Chilean military officers who plotted the coup. When the coup attempt failed and Allende was inaugurated as president, the CIA funded and encouraged opposition groups in Chile.

The committee report raised the question explicitly: "Was the United States directly involved, covertly, in the 1973 coup in Chile?"

"The Committee has found no evidence that it was. However, the United States sought in 1970 to foment a military coup in Chile; after 1970 it adopted a policy both overt and covert, of opposition to Allende; and it remained in intelligence contact with the Chilean military, including officers who were participating in coup plotting."

Most people in the opposition in Chile would find it hard to believe, given U.S. history, that there was not a more direct U.S. involvement in the coup, but what was striking to me was how much the U.S. government formally admitted it had done.

The summary of the report concluded, "The pattern of United States covert action in Chile is striking but not unique. It arose in the context not only of American foreign policy, but also of covert U.S. involvement in other countries within and outside Latin America. The scale of CIA involvement in Chile was unusual but by no means unprecedented."

Even though this information was probably sitting in most libraries in the United States, it was disconcerting how few people, me included, knew about the ways U.S. policies were negatively influencing other countries.

One pledge I had made to Olga before I left Santiago was to try to raise money in the United States for the hogar. I thought, if I was lucky, I could raise seven hundred dollars, the amount the plane ticket had cost.

Over the next two weeks, I spoke to grade school and high school classes in Fort Wayne about the hogar. My parents talked to their friends about the orphanage and donated money themselves. Donations came flowing in: checks for twenty, a hundred, and two hundred dollars; a second-grade class raised forty-eight dollars; a high school Spanish class raised just short of two hundred dollars.

"Buy something fun for the kids," my brother Phil told me, pushing a wad of twenty-dollar bills toward me. "You just got to promise me one thing. Don't buy something they need. Buy something fun for them."

I flew back through Houston, Texas, and met up with my friend Nathan Stone, who was also heading back to Chile. During my short visit to Houston, his father, Clayton, put me in touch with bankers, corporate lawyers, and company presidents to talk about the hogar.

"These are people with resources and their hearts in the right place," Clatyon had told me. In Houston we did far better than I would have ever imagined, and my volunteer career as an hogar fund-raiser was launched.

I flew into Santiago on a hot January afternoon. The flight from Buenos Aires, over the rugged Andes Mountains, provided an entirely different perspective from that when I had arrived by land. The first journey to Chile with Nathan was a blur of buses and trains, their aisles crammed with crates and bags of flour, dogs and live chickens, on winding dirt roads through the Andes Mountains of Peru and Bolivia. Squat women with black pigtails and bowler hats sold sweet rolls and caramels at every stop. This was followed by a two-day train ride on wooden-slatted seats from La Paz, Bolivia, into the Atacama Desert of northern Chile, where shimmering heat waves rose from the dunes. I remembered sand and grit in my hair, the sticky, sweet taste of Inca Cola—Peru's version of Coca-Cola, which was the only thing to drink on the train—and the red sunset over dunes which stretched to the horizon like waves of the sea. I finally saw water at Antofagasta, Chile, and I swam for the first time in the Pacific Ocean off the coast of South America. All too quickly we climbed back on a bus to travel a thousand miles south along the Pacific coastline. When the bus turned eastward, away from the coast, to the capital city of Santiago, the surrounding lush green valley came as a surprise.

This time the surprise was the speed of the journey. In twenty hours, I had traveled from winter in the United States to summer in Santiago.

I took a cab from the airport, since no one knew when I was arriving, and marveled at the summer sights. Outdoor stalls had watermelons and cantaloupes piled high. Children wore shorts, men and women short sleeves. The cab deposited me in front of the hogar, and I stood for a few minutes on the dirt street. I heard children's voices behind the orange wooden gate. I peered over the fence. Yoana was sitting in the dirt, playing with a doll. Andrés and Juanito were shooting marbles into a ditch. They were all a toasty brown color—a sure sign they'd been to the beach while I was gone. I didn't know how long I stood there. Finally, Yoana looked up and yelled, "Tío Esteve," and the children swarmed.

In my bag I had at least one small gift for each kid—a matchbox car or bracelet, a two-dollar plastic watch, or earrings. I also carried with me, at Olga's request, two tubs of peanut butter and three bags of now-melted chocolate chips, items not sold in Chile.

"Welcome back, gringo," Olga said, kissing me on the cheek.

When things calmed down, I called Olga aside. First, I handed her an envelope with thirteen hundred dollars in cash. It was money designated to purchase an automatic washer, a clothes dryer, and a typewriter—three things Olga had wanted since I met her. Then I told her to sit down and handed her the list of donations for the house—they totaled $14,800. Her tears started flowing.

"Okay, here's the story. The people who donated this money agreed that we could buy a house and that the only condition is that the hogar continue to help children in need."

"I don't know how to thank you."

I explained to Olga that my visit simply got the ball rolling, how so many people got involved, especially my family and friends in Fort Wayne, and Clayton Stone's help with all kinds of people in Houston and that really it was a joint effort between those two cities—Fort Wayne, Indiana, and Houston, Texas—and a testament to the great training I'd had here watching Olga ask people for money.

Olga laughed. "I have to learn English just to try to thank these people . . . but I can never thank them enough, only pray that someday they may realize what an amazing gift they have given these children, who will now have a permanent home."

༄

NINETEEN

A HOME ON TUPUNGATO STREET

༄

Once the initial shock wore off, we began the hard work of deciding where in Santiago to buy a house. Olga was interested in moving to an area with better schools and one that wasn't so far out of the city.

"We've got to do this right. Can you imagine how much work it is going to be moving all these kids and stuff? I don't want to have to pick up in a year and move again," she said.

We looked for weeks. Even though the economic situation was dire and people were desperate to sell, our $14,800 would only get us so far. With the money we had in hand, unless we wanted to go into debt, we would likely be able to buy a slightly better house than we were renting. The big advantage was that we would not have to pay monthly rent, and for the first time the hogar would have a sense of permanence.

In March, I returned to my classes with the teachers at St. George's, while Olga continued searching.

"It looks like we've found a house," Olga said to me one day when I came home from classes. "It's the nicest I've seen in our price range. The house is well built, with thick adobe walls, has a good roof and ventilation, and is in a relatively safe neighborhood. It has four bedrooms. There's some space for the kids to play, but it's not a farm."

"It sounds fine to me," I replied.

"It even has a little two-bedroom wooden structure on the same property with its own kitchen. It's still in La Granja, just a lot closer to Santiago so there will be more choices for schools. There are grapevines, and, get this, gringo, it has a swimming pool."

The swimming pool, it turned out, was made of three-foot-high cinder block walls painted turquoise. But there were two decent bathrooms and a walk-in pantry. It was definitely a step up from where we were living. We negotiated with the owner until the price exactly equaled every dollar raised in the United States for the purchase, and we bought the yellow adobe house on Tupungato Street.

For the move we rented a flatbed truck. We dismantled seven sets of bunk beds and moved crates of clothing and furniture, the stove and refrigerator. At the end of the afternoon, I stood in the empty room that had served as my bedroom for the past year and a half. Until that moment, I hadn't realized how badly the faded blue wallpaper was peeling. A few squares and rectangles on the wall were a slightly darker blue—where the kids' crayon drawings had been tacked to the wall. Void of furniture, the room looked small, almost uninhabitable, more like an empty shed than a bedroom. As pitiful as it looked, leaving it and "the farm" still tugged at my heart.

That evening, Andrés and I sat on the concrete ledge of the empty swimming pool at the new house.

"The new house is real nice," Andrés told me. With that assurance, I was satisfied that we had made a good purchase.

Andrés and Juanito began exploring the new neighborhood, and we decided it was important that they learn their new address in case they got lost.

Tupungato Street, I told them, was named for the second highest peak in South America, a volcano that formed part of the border between Chile and Argentina. Neither was particularly impressed by this trivia.

"Tupungato 8965," I repeated, our street name followed by the house number, as is the Chilean custom.

"Tupungato 8965," Juanito mimicked, catching on after a few tries.

Andrés didn't say anything but just stared intently.

"Come on Andrés, Tupungato 8-9-6-5."

"No, it's 8-9-10-11," he said.

"You're right. When you count it goes 8-9-10-11, but our street number is Tupungato 8-9-6-5."

"No, it's Tupungato 8-9-10-11," he said and stomped off angrily.

Although we had exactly enough to pay for the new house in cash, nothing was left for extras. After paying off the house, we discovered it was the same battle as always, keeping food and milk on the table and shoes on dozens of growing feet and paying gas and light bills. Our powdered milk bill was sixty dollars a month.

"Can you believe it?" Olga asked. "Right now we buy five pounds of bread every day. Five pounds! And we only have one teenager. It scares me to even think how much these kids will be eating in a few years."

Tupungato Street was a much more urban setting than was our Rosa Ester family farm. The houses were much closer together, and the details of the lives of the neighbors became much more apparent. Although a lot happened in the *patio atrás,* as Olga called it, "the back patio" or, as Americans would say, "behind closed doors," some of the most dramatic scenes—in small houses, especially some with multiple families living under one roof—made it into the street.

One evening toward the end of our first month on Tupungato Street, our neighbor Pedro, typically a mild-mannered carpenter in his mid-twenties, was roaring drunk and yelling at the top of his lungs. Binge drinking, especially at the end of each month, when men had a few pesos in their pockets, seemed to unleash all kinds of verbal and physical abuse. After only a few weeks in the neighborhood, I had heard stories that Pedro was savage with his wife and kids when drunk.

His wife, Marta, had locked him out of their small wooden house, and Pedro alternated between weeping and demanding that his wife let him in.

"Puta de mierda," he yelled before finally crumbling into a ball on the sidewalk in front of the gate.

"That's just what I told Marta to do," another neighbor watching the scene told me. "He's a bastard when he drinks, and I told her to lock the bastard out, and thank God she followed my advice."

Sebastián's thirteenth birthday occurred the same month we moved. With it came Sebastián's first real pains and the longings of adolescence, the uncertainty, the tensions. Sebastián found it increasingly difficult to share the same bedroom with seven other boys, three of whom were under five. He was tired of being treated like a little kid.

As I was no longer sharing a room with Néstor, I invited Sebastián to move into my room at the back of the new house. I laid down the rules: he would have the same responsibilities as the other kids; he would have to keep his things neat and organized; and I would allow one soccer poster and one small Michael Jackson poster on the wall.

The move worked out better than I had imagined. Living with him, I found time to give him a little extra help with his studies, and he began doing better in school. I also really enjoyed his company. When the rest of the children were in bed and the house quiet, the two of us would stay up in the room at the back of the house with the lamp lit between the two beds, reading or talking.

Sometimes I would write in my journal at night.

"What are you writing?" he asked. Although I'd kept a journal as long as I could remember, I was always uneasy about letting people know that I wrote, much less letting them read what I had written. So Sebastián's straightforward question was not an easy one to answer.

"Oh, I'm just writing about some things I'm thinking about."

"Like what? Read me something."

"Um, well." I hesitated. "Bueno, okay, here's what I wrote," I said, translating into Spanish my most recent entry:

Last night I was up until ten o'clock with Olga and the three third graders trying to finish their homework—making a picture of a boat with spaghetti noodles and paint. Marcelo covered the page with parallel rows of noodles. He painted the water brown and the sky grey and with a single ravioli noodle made a floundering boat in the middle of his linear sea. Alfredo, with Olga's help, made a striking ship with sails set against a rough, blue sea with gushing white waves. Yoana's noodles got too wet, curled up, and gooey so that nothing would stick to the paper. All my attempts to "touch up" her work could not save it. Finally Verónica, who has a lot more patience than I, started from scratch and helped Yoana make a neat and orderly noodle ship on a calm blue sea.

This morning we packed up all their art work in layers of newspaper so the noodles would not break. The younger kids and the girls, as they do every school morning, gave me a kiss goodbye. The older boys offered me their hands instead of their cheeks. Alfredo, who just turned nine, wavered between hand and cheek and today definitely extended his hand. Carlos refused to say goodbye at all because I hadn't let him stay up last night and watch T.V.

I waited for a moment as the nine of them went off to school, trotting down the street in their blue school uniforms and brown book bags. Their hair was freshly combed and still wet, under a grey sky on an autumn morning, reminiscent of Marcelo's noodle sky, only less linear. I watched their confident strides until they turned the corner. Karen always trails behind just a little and was the last one to turn the corner. Their voices faded. In a funny way, seeing them off fills me with pride and hope, and on mornings like today I ask myself how I'm ever going to leave them. Is it really true that before the end of this year I'll be leaving Chile?

When I finished reading, Sebastián frowned.

"Why did you write all that?" he asked.

"I've just written down things that I think about. I'm not sure why." I wished I could have given a better answer.

The next night when I entered the room, I saw Sebastián propped up in my bed, his face dwarfed by my glasses, which rested precariously on the end of his nose. From under the covers he pulled out one of my blue journals (written in English) and pretended to read: "I have decided to give my ten-speed bicycle to Sebastián because he is such a good, hard-working person," he began in Spanish. Then he started laughing and could not continue, throwing the covers over his head; and the blankets shook with his laughter.

TWENTY

CATHOLICS, MORMONS, AND EVANGELICALS

Remaining in Chile meant I had to renew my visa. The process was an exercise in patience and perseverance: first, a visit downtown to the immigration office, then to the internal revenue department in another part of Santiago, then to the international police. Each step required new documents with seals or signatures from different offices—one open only from 10 a.m. to 2 p.m., another from 2 to 5 p.m. With a fair amount of luck, a week of constant effort would result in a valid new visa stamp filling a page of my U.S. passport.

The international police office was closed between 1 and 3 p.m. With nothing else to do, I walked around Santiago's historic Plaza de Armas, admiring its palm trees, benches, and a bandstand and reading a mimeographed brochure about it. The central plaza was surrounded by key government buildings built during Spanish colonial rule, including the original Spanish Governor's House and the Town Hall. Some things had changed since colonial times. The prison that had once stood on the plaza had been moved to another part of town along the river.

In front of the Town Hall, an enormous black iron statue depicted Santiago's founder, the Spanish conquistador Pedro de Valdivia, sitting regally on horseback. Inside the Town Hall, there was a copy of the letter Pedro de Valdivia had written to King Charles V in 1545, a kind of sixteenth-century travel brochure extolling the virtues of Chile and particularly its new capital, Santiago:

And in order to tell the merchants and other people who wish to come and live here, to come, for this is the best country in the world to live and beget children. I say this because: the land is very pleasant and fertile. There are four months of winter, and it only rains for one or two days when the moon enters in quarter. All the other days are so fine that there is no need to crouch by the fireside. The summer is so temperate and breezy that it is possible to walk all day in the sun without inconvenience. There is the richest land . . . plenty of good quality timber . . . together with productive gold mines . . . grain, building materials, water, wood and grass for the herds, to such an extent that it would appear as if God had created this land especially for the inhabitants to have everything they need ready at hand.

Like those of other travel writers, Pedro de Valdivia's claims may have been somewhat exaggerated. The promises of gold never panned out and as for the description of raining in the winter only one or two days each month, I had to imagine others may have taken exception.

What was clear, though, for many of the Spanish colonists, was that God's presence appeared in much of what the Spanish crown did. The fact that Santiago's cathedral sat on the central plaza, next to the most important government buildings, is not coincidental. The close relationship between state and church, along with the resources of a few wealthy individuals, built the incredible cathedrals and churches that border nearly every central plaza in every colonial city throughout South America, including Santiago's enormous cathedral, which dominates one half of one side of the Plaza de Armas.

A plaque inside the cathedral told its story: the original church building on the site was built in 1551. A series of fires and earthquakes brought down that edifice and several later constructions until the current gray stone cathedral was built in 1748.

In addition to the "merchants and others" drawn to South America in the sixteenth century came the first missionaries. While a few missionary groups, including the Jesuits, took an active interest in indigenous people and the poor, many of the church's most important ties were to the economic benefactors and governing elite, and these were ties forged and strengthened over the next four hundred years.

The Catholic Church's Vatican II Council in the early 1960s "threw open the window," encouraging the use of local languages at mass (rather than Latin) and a more active role for laypeople. It also emphasized the growing differences between two divergent streams of the Catholic Church in Latin America, and particularly in Chile.

The first was a traditional and hierarchical church centered around priests, bishops, cardinals, and, ultimately, the pope. To simplify a little, this vision appealed especially to the landed elite, who supported "law and order," and to pious women who attended mass. While these Catholics acknowledged the obvious inequalities between rich and poor, the one legitimate response to these inequities was *charity*, especially toward widows and orphans. However, one's ultimate reward was in heaven, and one should not focus on any radical changes to the social order.

The second vision, especially one that emerged in the 1960s, was a church *of the people* that spoke of a new "liberation theology" and focused very much on *justice* here and now. This vision closely identified with the poor, who were the great majority of people in Latin America, and argued that the central message of Jesus required quite revolutionary changes in the unjust social order.

Santiago's cathedral was clearly constructed as part of the first vision of the Church, and the grandeur of Santiago's cathedral matched that of the other monumental government buildings on the plaza. Next to the cathedral, built on the same scale, was a building that seemed cut in two. The bottom half, the first-floor Manantial bookstore, had a modern-looking front, including neon lights, which could have been part of any shopping mall anywhere in the world built in the 1960s. In contrast, the high, graceful stone arches of the upper level harkened back to an earlier era. Although there was no sign, the second level housed the offices of the Catholic Church's human rights and social service agency, called La Vicaría de la Solidaridad.

Among those who identified with a vision of the Catholic Church committed to the poor and oppressed, the Vicaría, as it was commonly called, held legendary status. After the coup, members of the Catholic Church, along with members of Evangelical and Orthodox churches and of the Jewish community, joined to organize the Comité de Cooperación para la Paz en Chile, the Committee of Cooperation for Peace. The core of the committee was a group of lawyers who took on the cases of the families of children and spouses who had been detained or who had disappeared.

The committee's lawyers were nearly overwhelmed by people begging them to take on their cases. The government targeted the committee lawyers, accusing them of being Marxist-Leninists and traitors to the state. Chile's influential cardinal Raúl Silva Henríquez, a longtime player on the national political scene, cautiously supported the group.

Cardinal Silva Henríquez acted as a kind of bridge between the differing visions of the Church. When the military government shut down the Peace Committee in January 1976, the cardinal immediately took a courageous step by announcing that the archdiocese would create a new institution, called the Vicaría de la Solidaridad, directly under the auspices of the Church. Housed on the second-floor church offices next to the cathedral, the Vicaría was intended to continue the work of the Peace Committee.

The Vicaría attracted some of the most talented lawyers and professionals in the country. They were paid a pittance and put their own lives, and often those of their families, in danger. The Vicaría lawyers filed thousands of habeas corpus petitions on behalf of prisoners who had "disappeared" from the mid-1970s through the early 1980s. During that entire period, the Supreme Court dismissed all except about ten petitions. Even in the face of detailed witness reports of detentions and specific information about where individuals were being held, the government would deny that the individuals were in custody. Although the Vicaría's formal legal efforts may have had little impact, the dogged documentation of crimes and the lawyers' willingness to disseminate and publish their findings internationally saved many lives.

The Vicaría also provided support for victims of torture and for the family members of the detained and disappeared as well as for Chileans living in exile. The Vicaría set up soup kitchens and day care centers in poor neighborhoods throughout Santiago. With its array of social, medical, and psychological services and its careful documenting of cases of torture and disappearance, the Vicaría became one of the most respected human rights organizations in Latin America. In this country where everything was so complex, the Vicaría lawyers and professionals were my heroes, even more so because they were such underdogs in this pitched battle with the military government.

Most Latin Americans are Roman Catholics, and Chileans are no different. Only after I arrived in Santiago did I realize that there were other influential religious groups, and some, such as the Mormons and Evangelical Protestants, were growing rapidly.

The fact that Mormon missionaries from the United States were among the few gringos who ever showed up anywhere near La Granja meant that I was initially often mistaken for a Mormon. When I taught at St. George's I often wore my only dress shirt, a white one, along with a colorful tie, and combined this with my tennis shoes. My attire occasionally elicited responses from friends and fellow teachers.

"You couldn't look more like a gringo Mormon if you tried," Nathan once told me.

The irony was that growing up in Indiana, I couldn't ever remember even meeting a Mormon. The first Mormon I ever met was in Chile.

"Usted es Mormón?" I was once asked by a neighbor, shortly after I had arrived. Hearing that word for the first time, I didn't even recognize it, given the different accent in Spanish. As I often did when at a loss for the meaning of a Spanish word, I went for an English cognate. I could only imagine the person was asking me, "Are you a moron?"

"Pienso que no," I stammered, "I don't think so." Our conversation left us both scratching our heads.

Perhaps an occasional Mormon found his or her way to our neighborhood, but it was the Evangelicals who changed it. One evening while walking down Tupungato Street I heard guitar music and singing and realized we had a new neighbor.

On the gate in front of one of the nondescript wooden houses one block up the dirt road from the hogar was a hand-painted sign that read Asamblea de Dios, the Assembly of God.

This group of about fifteen people had visited the houses in our neighborhood a few times since we arrived, evangelizing with well-worn Bibles, guitars, and tambourines. I always felt uncomfortable with the enthusiasts of Asamblea de Dios because their never-subtle aim was to convert. One neighbor, Juan, was especially insistent with me. I tried to fend him off by telling him I was Catholic, thinking that would end the discussion.

"Just because you're Catholic doesn't mean you can't yet be saved," he told me reassuringly.

The Evangelical Protestant church was the fastest growing in Latin America, and churches like this one were springing up in neighborhoods like ours throughout the continent. Olga once explained that she thought the Evangelical church was so popular in some parts of Chile because it was not "too political." She said that many people, especially some poor people, considered the Catholic Church political, especially with Catholic groups fighting against the dictatorship.

Given those tense relations, Catholics were often at odds in very public ways with the government, and it was not a completely neutral act to remain Catholic. The evangelicals were, in contrast, *un refugio,* a refuge from those political tensions. Typically, these churches would either support the stable order of the dictatorship or at a minimum not criticize it. The military government in turn left them alone, or at times worked with them as an ally. Another attractive feature was that, like the Mormons, they used their member networks to help their own, especially when it came to finding jobs.

My neighbor Juan always stood too close to me as he enthusiastically explained a particular passage in the Bible or insisted, again, that I might yet be saved by joining the Asamblea de Dios. When I saw him standing out in front of his house, I would sometimes take the long way around the block. Now I had his whole church on my street.

It was another neighbor, Marta, though, who made me think about the Asamblea de Dios in a different light.

"You know Pedro used to have real problems," she told me, with her husband, Pedro, standing next to us.

"When he drinks he could spend almost everything he earned on wine. He couldn't control himself, and sometimes he would hit me and the kids." She paused. "It wasn't him doing that, it was the liquor speaking. But since he was saved, he hasn't touched a drop of liquor."

"I now renounce Satan and all his evil deeds," Pedro stated emphatically. Marta smiled.

So this in-your-face religion, with its rigid moral codes, patronizing views toward women, and uncomfortable evangelizing, was also leading men to stop drinking and turn around their lives, to get jobs, and in turn to decrease wife and child abuse and maybe even sometimes to help men be decent husbands and fathers.

The Vicaría had a small gift shop open to the public that sold articles made by political prisoners and the families of the detained and disappeared. When I was downtown and had a little time, especially while waiting for the next steps in processing my visa, I visited the shop, which sold handicrafts, including colorful wall hangings and artisan wool sweaters made from natural dyes. I was told the purple dyes were made from beets.

They also sold embroidered *arpilleras*, placemat-sized scenes like the one Inelia had given me of the detention of her son, Héctor. I examined a pile of them, arpillera after arpillera, many depicting detentions at night, the police almost always in dark clothing. In one, armed men drag away a daughter while family members stand around with their heads bowed; in another, a man with a hood over his head was tied to a metal bed frame and received electric shocks. There had to be sixty arpilleras in the stack, each with a name and date on the back.

After I looked at about ten arpilleras, my stomach tightened. Each piece of fabric represented the horrific story of detention, torture, disappearance of a father or son, daughter or sister. I turned away and almost knocked over another, even taller stack of arpilleras.

I moved to a different table and riffled through a cardboard shoebox full of small doves of peace and crosses carved out of soup bones by political prisoners.

It was there I overheard a Chilean man talking with a blond-haired woman dressed in a stylish brown suit.

"Este es un plato de cobre hecho por un preso político, y es un regalo de nuestra organización para usted," said the man, obviously trying to give the woman a copper plate made by a political prisoner. It was equally apparent that she didn't understand much Spanish. The woman tried repeatedly to give him money.

I finally intervened in English.

"I think he wants to give it to you. It's a gift," I suggested.

"I know," she said, "but I can't accept it as a gift. I should pay for it."

I translated her response. The man insisted on giving it to the woman, and she insisted on paying for it. She ultimately paid for the plate.

As I was leaving the shop, she approached me.

"Hello. Just so you understand what was going on—I work for the Australian embassy and since we have a professional relationship with the Vicaría I didn't want to accept the gift from someone who works here." She then explained that her embassy had a large program that assisted people who had suffered from political persecution. Something like twenty thousand humanitarian refugees came from around the world to Australia each year.

"Chilean refugees were the first that Australia accepted outside the Communist bloc since the end of World War II. I think we've accepted something like six thousand Chileans since the program began in 1973." She spoke very quickly and enthusiastically.

"Can I ask what you're doing here?" she asked, without a pause.

"Do you mean here in Santiago or here at the Vicaría?"

"Well, for starts, what are you doing in Santiago?"

"I'm working at a small orphanage," I replied.

"I knew it would be something interesting. What's the orphanage like?"

"Well, we have thirteen kids, in La Granja, south of Santiago."

"At my last posting in Korea," she said, "I got involved in an orphanage. It really meant a lot to me. Could I come and visit the orphanage sometime?"

"Fine," I said and that's how Judy Betts, a thirty-two-year-old immigration officer from the Australian embassy, got involved with the hogar.

TWENTY-ONE

BOYS, BABIES, AND BITERS

Judy's first visit to the hogar wasn't all roses.

"Andrés, that's his name, right?" she said, pointing to the dirtiest of the little kids.

I nodded.

"Well, Andrés came up to me and asked if I wanted to brush my teeth. I smiled and said, 'No, my teeth are clean, thank you very much.' Then Andrés handed me a toothbrush with a little piece of shit on it."

"Didn't I tell you they were wonderful children? Maybe I should have a talk with Andrés," I said.

"Well, don't yell at him. I like him. He's got spunk."

Judy began to visit the spunky kids at the hogar every weekend, and after about a month she invited Verónica and Sonia to spend the night at her apartment.

"We had tea in the most beautiful dining room," Verónica explained on her return. "And then we took bubble baths in this big bathtub, and then she let us dry our hair with a blow drier."

The other kids' eyes grew large and going to Tía Judy's for the weekend became the treasured prize for those who were well behaved during the week.

Héctor was the baby of the group and loved the attention he received as a result. His round, cherubic face, sandy brown hair, and big brown eyes did not hurt his cause.

"¡Qué amoroso!" countless visitors said on meeting him. "Such a lovely little boy," he heard over and over.

When Héctor turned three, he became insufferable. He could not get enough attention, and his vocabulary seemed to consist of two words: *quiero* and *mío*—"I want" and "mine." About this time, Héctor discovered he had teeth.

"Tía, Héctor just bit Juanito again," Verónica told Olga.

"The kid's on a rampage," Pato commented. "He bit me this morning." Two days earlier, he had left a pair of his teeth marks on Karen's arm.

Olga grabbed Héctor firmly by the arm.

"Young man, if you bite another person, I'm going to bite you right back. You won't like it. Do you understand me?"

Héctor nodded, his big brown eyes filling with tears.

At breakfast the next morning, I gave Héctor a plastic cup of strawberry yogurt. He didn't want to eat the yogurt because the red and white label was slightly ripped. The yogurt was fine, but all of the labels had imperfections—that was why we got them free from the dairy company.

"Héctor's getting too spoiled," Eliana, who helped out in the kitchen, told me.

Héctor hit his spoon against the white plastic yogurt tub.

"Héctor, just eat the yogurt," I told him.

He hammered away at the cup of yogurt with his spoon.

"Tío, you need to discipline him!" Eliana demanded. This meant she wanted me to spank him. There was a real tension in the house about spanking, which I almost never did. Olga and Eliana both considered that giving an occasional spanking was part of my job at the hogar, especially because I was the only adult male living there.

"The children have got to learn respect and they've got to learn some boundaries. It's best to do that with words. But sometimes words aren't enough, and you need to get their attention," was Olga's advice.

"These kids need *mano dura*, a firm hand," Eliana had told me on more than one occasion, making it clear that she thought my hand was not.

"Héctor, stop that, you're going to make a mess."

He continued until he broke the yogurt cup. He then proceeded to spoon the yogurt into Keli's lap. I pulled Héctor off his chair and sent him to bed.

While I remained extremely ambivalent about spanking, Olga taught me that children didn't want everything they demanded, and I imagined Héctor would have thought something strangely amiss if I had not taken some action. I grew convinced that the kids craved, unconsciously, of course, to have some well-defined boundaries so that they didn't have to constantly test, particularly these kids because their lives before coming to the hogar had been so chaotic. With relatively clear boundaries in place, they could comfortably go about the business of being kids.

Judy began to get people who worked at the embassies of other countries involved in the hogar. At Judy's suggestion, a couple from the British embassy invited all the children from the hogar to lunch at their elegant home in Vitacura.

On the appointed Sunday morning, the kids put on freshly ironed dresses, shirts, and pants. Verónica did all the girls' hair in French braids. Olga gave last-minute instructions before half the group packed into the car and the other half settled on the bus.

"You're going to someone's home, and you are their guests. I expect it will be a very nice house, and I expect you to be on your best behavior. Don't touch anything in their house without asking permission first," Olga told the group.

"Will there be any kids there?" Sonia asked.

"Yes, probably five or six little kids," Olga answered. "But I doubt if any of these kids speak Spanish."

"Great, what are we supposed to do with them if they don't speak Spanish?" Carlos asked.

"Carlos, you just have to introduce yourself and be as friendly as you can," Olga said.

"Tía, what will you do if Héctor bites one of these kids?" Verónica asked.

"Héctor knows what will happen," Olga said, looking directly at Héctor.

We arrived at a rambling, one-story, white brick house with manicured gardens and a swimming pool. There were already about a dozen adults and six kids in the backyard and on the patio. The child-to-adult ratio quickly changed when we arrived with our thirteen kids.

I tried to keep an eye on Héctor. A blond-haired boy about Héctor's age in blue Oshkosh overalls walked directly up to him. They stared at each other without saying a word. A silent face-off.

Finally, Héctor placed his hand in the middle of his chest and said, "Yo soy Héctor—I am Héctor." After that the two seemed to hit it off, and I headed for the tables with food.

There was a banquet laid out on two tables: sliced ham and turkey, four kinds of bread, potato salad, pickles, olives, deviled eggs, pies, and cakes. Our kids recognized only about half of the gringo food.

"You're crazy if you think I'm going to eat eggs that somebody else chewed. Look, somebody spit back the yellow part," Carlos said to Marcelo, pointing to the deviled eggs. There was also a tray of Chilean meat pies called *empanadas*.

"Where did you get the empanadas?" I asked Lynn, our hostess.

"Oh, just at the supermarket."

"These are good," I said as I munched on one, "but if you really want some good empanadas, the best empanadas in Santiago, you need to go to La Granja."

"Is it near the orphanage?" Judy asked.

"Not far at all," I replied.

"I'd really like to visit the orphanage, and maybe then we could all go there for lunch," Lynn said. "There are also some people at the Australian embassy who want to go out to the orphanage. Maybe I could bring them along, and we could make a day of it."

"Sure, just let me know when."

As we were talking, a blond woman I had not met went running across the backyard.

"What happened?" I asked.

"I overheard something about one of the kids biting another," Lynn said.

"Shit," I said, a little too loudly.

I joined the blond woman who was standing with Héctor and the little British boy in overalls. She was visibly upset.

"Nothing like this has ever happened before," she said to me. "I'm just so sorry. I just don't know what to say."

"What?" I asked.

"I just don't know why Johnnie bit Hector. Johnnie's never done anything like this before! Thank God, he didn't break the skin."

Héctor, with the angelic face, had tears streaming down his cheeks.

"Héctor, are you all right?" I asked.

"Sí," he said sheepishly.

"I'm just so embarrassed and sorry," the mother repeated.

"Don't worry too much. No one was hurt, and it could have just as easily been the other way around."

"You're really so kind to say that," she said. "Maybe Héctor would like to play with one of Johnnie's toys."

Héctor sniffled and then consented to play with Johnnie's fire engine.

"Héctor is such a beautiful little boy," she said, "and he's so well behaved."

Judy organized an expedition for people connected with the Australian and British embassies to visit the hogar. Six people got a tour of the new house, played with the kids, and then, as agreed, we all went afterward for empanadas at the Panadería Gabriela Mistral bakery.

Just as we were arriving at the Panadería Gabriela Mistral, a large woman with a white apron was pulling out a dozen hot empanadas from the big adobe oven with a long-handled wooden spatula like those used for pizzas. The empanadas—meat pies with ground beef and finely chopped onions, cinnamon, and sugar, half an egg, and olives—were hot, sweet, and flavorful. We sat under the grapevines, ate empanadas, and drank Chilean red wine. Everyone bought extra empanadas to take home.

"These are fantastic," Lynn said. "They really are as good as you said they'd be." Everyone, especially me, considered the outing a great success.

That diagnosis changed, however, about two weeks later as I was sitting on the bus reading *La Tercera* newspaper. A small article on page seventeen made my stomach sink. The article began, "Health inspectors moved to close down the Panadería Gabriela Mistral in La Granja. . . . The owners were found to be using dog meat in their empanadas."

Immediately, the mental calculations began. What was the likelihood that anyone whom I had taken there would read this article? It was only a small article in Spanish in the local paper on page seventeen. Ugh. But what if a group from the British or Australian embassy decided to go back on their own? Carlos soon resolved the issue of whether anyone would find out.

"Tío, did you know that they closed the empanada place?" he asked me the next day.

"I heard they did."

"Yeah, but do you know why?"

"Yeah, I guess it wasn't clean enough."

"THAT'S NOT IT! THEY WERE FEEDING PEOPLE DOG MEAT!" he screeched. "ALL THOSE PEOPLE YOU TOOK OUT THERE ATE DOG MEAT!"

"Carlos, I heard you, you don't have to yell."

"But Tío, all those FANCY PEOPLE ATE DOG MEAT!"

"Carlos, enough."

"No wonder our neighborhood is the only one in Santiago that doesn't have many stray dogs!" Carlos said.

"Oh, my God, where is my poor Jackie?" Sebastián joined in. He dragged Jackie, the German shepherd, into the middle of the patio, covering her ears with his hands.

"Jackie, don't listen to this horrible talk, we won't let them turn you into an empanada." Incredibly, Carlos and Sebastián never mentioned the dog meat saga to Judy or any of those other fancy people, and to this day I don't know if anyone I took there ever found out.

"So I've decided on my profession," Sonia told me.

"I thought you told me just last week that you wanted to be a lawyer," I said.

"I wanted to be a lawyer so long ago I can't even remember."

"So what do you want to do now?"

"I want to be an ambassador and have a great apartment like Tía Judy's. You can travel around the world and if you don't like the country, you just pick another one."

If Sonia had decided on her chosen profession (at least for the week), I was less sure than ever. For a long time I had been trying to convince myself that if I was to make a contribution in the world I had to become a doctor. This thought and the thought of going to medical school caused a great deal of anxiety. I would lie awake at night, thinking about taking organic chemistry and feeling guilty that I didn't get up and start studying from the chemistry book that I should have bought.

But somehow, over the past few months, the angst about going to medical school that had been such an all-consuming concern had lessened, until one day I realized I wasn't lying awake at night thinking about it at all. It had dissolved gradually, like snow on the peaks of the Andes Mountains, each day's difference scarcely detectable until I finally realized it had all melted away. Somehow I recognized that I didn't *have* to become a doctor, and the fact that I had so much anxiety about it suggested that it probably wasn't the right path after all. When I came to that realization, I felt an enormous relief.

Unfortunately, this revelation didn't give me a clue about what I wanted to do. I didn't know exactly why, but the fact that I didn't know what I was going to do with the rest of my life felt okay for the first time in a long time. A little frightening but manageable.

I did know that I wanted to study more, that I loved literature, that I wanted to write. One morning, the idea came: why not do something with that? Why not take literature classes right here in Chile?

TWENTY-TWO

THE UNIVERSITY

There was a marked contrast between summer and autumn in Santiago, so radically different that the city seemed to have a split personality. For a city of three and a half million people, the summer months of January and February were surprisingly tranquil. Schools, restaurants, and all kinds of shops simply closed their doors, especially in February—when trying to run an errand, you were likely to be met by a locked door and a sign saying, "See you on March 1st." Government-paid laborers had time to whitewash the walls and sides of buildings that had been spray-painted with graffiti and political slogans. In summer, a lazy life transpired on the beaches, and politics seemed forgotten. But come March, Santiago's residents returned to their capital to work, and students to their universities to protest.

Autumn transformed the face of the Andes Mountains day by day. Pablo Neruda wrote in "Autumn Returns" in *Residencia en la Tierra, II:*

> Todos los días baja del cielo un color ceniciento
> Que las palomas deben repartir por la tierra
>
> *Everyday a color like ash descends from the sky;*
> *which the doves must spread over the earth.*

Both the changing face of the Andes and the grayish-white doves seemed an integral part of autumn in Santiago. The birds invaded the capital city in the fall, flocking to the parks that dotted the city. On a March morning hundreds of the birds filled the quiet courtyards of

Campus Oriente of Santiago's Catholic University for the beginning of a new school year.

I had signed up for a linguistics class on Tuesday mornings. I arrived early on my bike for the 9 a.m. class, and before it started sat on a bench in the courtyard watching the doves. As the first students trickled into the university after their summer holiday, the doves waddled across the flagstone courtyard, reluctantly ceding their territory.

The truth was that when I had signed up for the class I had not totally recognized the difference between *Lingüística española* and *Literatura española*. Linguistics is the study of languages, how they are constructed and used, and it tends to be very theoretical. What I quickly learned was that what I had wanted was a literature class.

I was almost completely lost for most of the semester in my linguistics class, trying to decipher *gramática normativa* and *meta-lenguaje de la fonología,* and knowing that the latter translated as "meta-language of phonology" didn't help much.

One idea from the linguistics class stuck: that language—which is made up of individual words—was always a representation of something else. When we talked about *azul* we meant how the eye experienced a reflection of light in a particular way that we arbitrarily called *azul* in Spanish, while other languages arbitrarily used different words to describe it. In English we called it *blue*. It was easy to assume that the representations meant by the words *azul* and "blue" were the same across cultures and meant the same thing, that is, the translation "worked."

What I learned—some from linguistics class but even more from daily life in Chile—was that very often the translations didn't "work" for all kinds of reasons.

Something as straightforward as translating colors from one language to another is not as simple as it seems: "blue" is not always another way of saying *azul*. In English, we say, "I feel blue," meaning I feel sad or melancholy, which has no similar association in Spanish, as far as I could tell. For me, the colors "red, white, and blue" and especially in that order, meant something more than three colors: it referenced the U.S. flag, the star-spangled banner, and something about U.S. identity that a typical Chilean would not pick up on any more than they might associate "seeing red" with being angry or a yellow streak with cowardice. These are assumptions behind words in English that I had never thought about until I found myself in a place where people don't make the same assumptions.

Sometimes relations between these different representations were comic. In Chile, a *pez gordo*, a fat fish, was an important person; a healthy baby was a *gordito lindo*—beautiful little fat one—and even one's beloved spouse or girlfriend was called *gordita*, or "chubby one," language that probably wouldn't cut it in the United States. *Gorda* in Spanish is clearly not a pejorative term, as it is in English. *Seco*, the Spanish word for "dry," could also mean "awesome," almost the exact opposite in English. These different understandings of words and assumptions began to fill the pages of my notebook, and the recognition that even when you know the literal translation for a word in another language, you might miss the meaning.

Some patterns emerged. Chilean Spanish was much less direct than American English, and in Chile you almost never hear the word "no" used in direct response to a request. Instead I had a whole page of different ways of saying no in Spanish without ever using the word "no." The "no" list begins with *quizás* and *tal vez*, variations on "perhaps," and runs to phrases like *vamos a ver*, "we'll see," and *hablaremos*, "we'll talk"—which usually meant it was extremely unlikely you ever would. Most Chileans were very averse to conflict and indirect in their personal relationships, and the language reflected that.

The translation complexities were not just about translating individual words, but also about providing a context that gave meaning to the words. I came to realize how much of what I understood about the world was by analogy, so when I traveled to a town for the first time and learned that it had one hundred thousand people, that meant something because I knew that Fort Wayne, Indiana, where I grew up, had two hundred thousand people. I had a reference point.

Sometimes the translations didn't work because the reference points or analogies that underpinned the representations were different. Although my linguistics professor might have meant it in a slightly different way, I agreed when he said, "The key is getting the translation right." I began to be aware of the analogies I used and to ask myself if the analogy I had in my head was the same that they used here.

The first time I saw the bullet holes on the side of the Moneda Presidential Palace in downtown Santiago from the September 11, 1973, coup, the analogy I had in my head was clear: it was as if the U.S. secretary of defense had called the air force to attack the White House while the president sat inside.

If you had a different analogy in your head, as some clearly did here—say, that of the military supporting a citizen uprising overthrowing a tyrannical communist ruler—you gave the bullet holes a completely different meaning.

As far as I could tell, I was the only foreign student at the Campus Oriente that semester. Some features of the university experience were familiar; as in universities everywhere, students went from class to class, hung out in hallways and courtyards, drank coffee, smoked a lot of cigarettes, and carried backpacks filled with books, notebooks, and pens. Something less familiar was debating what form the protest would take and trying to guess what would be the reaction of the *carabineros*.

"When the police throw the teargas," Nancy, a third-year linguistics student, told me, "your best bet is to get away. But if you can't, the next best thing is to cover your mouth with a bandanna soaked in vinegar. Some people like lemon juice, but I think vinegar works better."

After one of my classes in April, a group of students had gathered in the middle of the courtyard. A banner was unfurled from a second-story balcony facing the street—"Necesitamos democracia ahora," demanding democracy now, each letter painted in a different color.

"Va a caer, va a caer, Pinocho va a caer," students began to chant rhythmically. "He's going to fall, he's going to fall, Pinocchio is going to fall," they'd cheer, using one of Pinochet's many nicknames, this one for the puppet whose nose grew when he lied.

By eleven o'clock in the morning, dozens of black-and-white police buses and vans lined the streets in front of the Catholic University. Some vans had been imported from South Africa, a country with real experience dealing with demonstrations, given its apartheid system. These vans had water cannons mounted on top that could turn 360 degrees. About one hundred *carabineros* stood at the entrance to the university. They wore riot gear: brown helmets with clear visors, padded olive-green jackets and pants, and high black boots. All carried guns or billy clubs, and many had large, clear Plexiglas shields. Some worked to hook up hoses to fire hydrants.

"Libertad! Libertad!" the students chanted. About twenty gathered inside the wide-arched entrance to the campus, taunting the police, yelling, "Asesinos!—Murderers!" The police opened up the water cannons, driving all the students back inside the university.

Although I knew I should flee, I was too interested in what was happening. I moved behind a stone pillar in the entranceway, and I felt like I was watching a movie. A *carabinero* loaded a canister into a wide-mouthed, short-barreled shotgun. I heard a thump and then the clatter of the metallic canister skittering across the flagstone courtyard. A noxious yellowish-white smoke began to fill the air. The last of the doves flew off. There was a second thump, a third, and a fourth. A dark-haired student wearing a red bandanna across his nose and mouth picked up one of the canisters and heaved it toward the police.

Less prepared than my fellow students and lacking a vinegar-covered bandanna, I covered my nose and mouth with my hand. The fumes burned the inside of my throat. Disoriented, I retreated with other students to a soccer field behind the courtyard.

"We're safe within the university walls," a student told me as we waited on the sports field behind the university for the air to clear. "In the past eleven years, the police have never entered the property of the Catholic University. They've gone into the public universities, but they're intimidated to come in here because of the Church."

By midafternoon the protests at the Catholic University had broken up. Some students took public buses downtown to continue the demonstrations, while others went home.

By late afternoon, the courtyard was silent. The air smelled like burned leaves, but the odor no longer stung my throat. A few banners lay abandoned on the wet flagstones. As the sun cast long shadows on the marble pillars and arches, doves came down off the rafters to wander the deserted courtyard, bobbing rivers of silver and gray.

A few weeks later, a group of philosophy students took over the Catholic University's philosophy building and demanded that the police release a philosophy student who had been arrested a day earlier. The police came into the university, broke down a barricade the students had erected, and dragged more than forty students off to jail. With that, any sense of security that some Catholic University students might have felt behind the walled campus evaporated.

WINTER IN A NEW NEIGHBORHOOD

It rained day after day, and everyone commented that it was one of the worst winters in memory. The Mapocho River that runs through downtown Santiago flooded its banks. Once clothes were damp, they seemed to take forever to dry. Almost no buildings had central heat, and once you were cold and chilled the feeling was hard to shake. Some of the poorest neighborhoods were along the river, and the simple wooden structures were knee-deep in water and mud. It was hard not to feel depressed.

One rainy evening on the bus coming back from school, I stood, wet and cold, staring hard at a lone policeman in a green *carabinero* uniform who had squeezed in next to me. He had a crew cut and pale, pimply skin and couldn't have been more than eighteen years old. He looked, even to me, like just a kid. He finally looked away, embarrassed, and I was the victor. I stood there wondering why I did it. Maybe because I was tired of living in a country where it seemed that everywhere I looked there was a policeman with a machine gun, tired of living under a military regime that decided what could be said, tired of watching people, especially young people with energy and visions of something better, being pushed down and harassed and beaten up by the police. I was tired of having Kafkaesque dreams at night in which the police came to the hogar and took me away because they found a crumbled piece of paper with a single written letter "C"—the only thing that survived when I burned all my notebooks. The "C" was for communist, the police told me over and over. I was guilty, and there was no need for a trial.

When we reached Vicuña McKenna Avenue, I looked up and noticed that a man in a brightly colored striped wool sweater had climbed onto the bus through the back door, guitar in hand, his hair wet from the rain. He began speaking in a ritualized way familiar to all the passengers.

"Pardon me for the inconvenience," he began, "but I am an unemployed father of three children . . . my intention is not to bother you, it is only to entertain you . . . this is how I make my living now." He sang, not especially well, yet with a force and an intensity that made me want to watch him. He had positioned himself, his feet spread wide, against a vertical rail at the back of the bus in such a way that he could play the guitar without being thrown around by the movement of the bus.

In the final song, each stanza ended with a deep and resonant "Alleluia!" which strangely gave me a heady, tingly sensation. The guitarist squeezed through the aisle and most everyone pulled out a few pesos. The man collected the money and thanked the driver as he got off. He moved to another bus stopped at the red light and, gesturing with his raised guitar, asked the driver if he could get on. The door opened; the man and his guitar were swallowed up by another bus.

I wiped the steam from the bus window and recognized that we were approaching my familiar corner. I pulled the cord for the bus to stop, then pushed and squeezed my way off the still-crowded bus.

With all the rain, the streets in our neighborhood had flooded as well. An old man in a gray jacket and black rubber boots had built a little bridge out of bricks and three wooden planks. He charged people five pesos to cross the street, placing his body between his bridge and any wayfarer unwilling to pay. A man in a business suit, indignant at the idea of having to pay money to cross his own street, rolled up his pant legs and tried to jump across the stream. He did not make it across, and his splash sent waves that rolled up where I was standing. I gave the old man five pesos to cross, even though I imagined that even if I stepped into the stream my shoes and pant legs could not get any wetter.

Walking to the hogar, I saw new graffiti on a red brick wall— "Manuel y Mónica" side by side with "Muera Pinochet—Death to Pinochet." The fluidity of the script and the white spray paint used for both slogans seemed to indicate they were written by the same hand. The dichotomy emerged repeatedly, inevitably—on city streets and in crowded buses, on brick walls and within myself—the tenuous relationship between perdition and redemption, the contradiction that it could be so bad and still be so good.

At the hogar, the rain ran off the roof in little rivulets where the gutter had broken. I opened the front door. At least everything was dry inside. Karen greeted me. I lifted her and made a "grrr" noise against her tummy. Héctor got off the couch and walked toward me, pulling up his sweater and exposing his bare belly, demanding, "Me! Me!"

That same wet evening, I met Marisol at the hogar. She was eleven years old and had short, wavy red hair—*colorina,* they called redheads in Chilean Spanish. With her broad swatches of freckles across her cheeks, Marisol could easily have been Irish. I met her and saw her plastic bag of clothes in the hallway at the same time.

Just the previous week, Olga and I had agreed that we were not going to take in any more kids. There was no more space or money, and if we kept taking in kids the place would lose its intimate, family-like feel. I gave Olga a hard look, guessing what was coming.

"Both her parents are dead," Olga told me, knowing that my rigid gringo mind would quickly move to try to enforce the agreement we had made the week before.

"She was living with her brother. He had some real problems. I'll tell you more later. Marisol doesn't have anyone else in the world, and she needs a place to stay, just for a while, but she's not moving in permanently," she said. "I promise," she added, not convincingly.

The first week that Marisol was living at the hogar, I mispronounced *colorina* as *golondrina,* which is the name for a bird from the swallow family. From that moment on, Carlos called Marisol nothing else.

"Golondrina, Tío Steve needs to talk with you," Carlos shouted at the top of his lungs. "Golondrina, you left a bag in the hallway."

Marisol quickly learned to defend herself.

"Cállate, cabro tonto," she snapped at him. "Shut up, you stupid goat."

"No te preocupes—don't worry," Marisol said to me warmly. "It's not your fault Carlos is an idiot."

That first night Marisol shared a bed with Sonia (until plywood was found to build another bunk) while Olga related the story of Marisol and that of her brother, Jose Luis.

Their parents had both died, and Jose Luis, who was only in his early twenties, was raising his eleven-year-old sister. He was a member of the opposition group called the Frente Patriótico Manuel Rodríguez, or FPMR. The little I knew about the FPMR came from their graffiti on walls throughout Santiago and from their claims of responsibility for bombing the power stations that had caused some blackouts. The group was committed to overthrowing the Pinochet government, but I knew little else except that association with it was extremely dangerous.

Olga explained that FPMR was named for one of the heroes of Chile's 1810 independence movement, Manuel Rodríguez. He was a national icon: Pablo Neruda wrote a poem about him, and there was a folklore dance in his honor. There were plazas and statues named for Manuel Rodríguez throughout Chile, and Manuel Rodríguez Street bordered our own Tupungato Street. I imagined that General Pinochet was not pleased that FPMR had usurped the name of a national hero such as Manuel Rodríguez.

A few weeks later I met Jose Luis, who went by the nickname Lucho. Like his sister, he had freckles and red hair. We stood together in the backyard under the grapevines, next to the cement block swimming pool. There was no small talk. He spoke of the "dificultades e incomprensiones que en ese momento enfrentaron los pioneros del rodriguismo."

I understood little of it. As he described the internal contradictions among the Communists and Trotskyites that made up the FPMR, I was confident I wouldn't be following it particularly well in English either.

He also told the story of the French priest André Jarlan, from the *población* La Victoria. A *población* was a poor urban area or shantytown, and La Victoria was famous because more than twenty-five years earlier it was the site of one of the first successful *tomas,* or "takeovers," of private land by the poor in Latin America. On the evening of October 30, 1957, some ten thousand *pobladores*—men, women, and children—had moved all their modest possessions onto the La Feria estate. They never left. La Victoria was one of the most politically active *poblaciones* in Chile.

During a recent protest in La Victoria, the police responded brutally. Jarlan was hit by a police bullet in the back of the head while reading at his desk inside his wooden house. He died almost immediately, and in the process had become a martyr for the FPMR.

"Los gringos are responsible for all of this," Lucho told me. "Tu gobierno—your government," he said, pointing his finger at me and, strangely, smiling at me at the same time.

"They brought Pinochet to power, and he's their puppet now. The CIA paid the military to do all this, even though we're a tiny country at the end of the world. The capitalist system you come from can't stand the idea that a country might elect a Marxist president. The CIA tells Pinochet what to do every morning."

I imagined that some of Lucho's version of the story about the U.S. role in bringing Pinochet to power was right and a lot of it was off. It was hard for me to believe that the CIA was directing the day-to-day operations of the Chilean military government.

"There are real divisions in the United States about what the U.S. is doing overseas," I began. "Lots of people in the U.S. do not agree with what our government did in Chile. Right now the Congress forbids the U.S. from selling weapons to Chile. I am sure the Reagan administration is doing everything it can to get around these restrictions, but I don't really think the CIA is running Chile's government," I said. I told him about the Church Committee findings, and the idea that parts of the U.S. government even investigated what other parts of the U.S. government were doing.

"You really think that your government tells you 10 percent of what it does?" he said, unable to control his laughter. "If you believe that, *hombre*," Lucho said, "you are so brainwashed by your government that you can't even think." I listened for a long time. We were about the same age, but talking with him made me feel very old.

Lucho smoked nervously, and the discussion turned more personal. He told me that he had been detained once by the CNI secret police and then was released a day later.

"If something happens to you, what will happen to Marisol?" I asked.

"The only way to help people realize the darkness they are in is to show them that the path to revolution is possible," he said. "The best thing I can do for my country and for Marisol is to fight for the revolution."

The word on the street was that the CNI were again looking for Lucho, and he spent his nights moving from house to house around Santiago. That one of the houses he occasionally stayed in was the hogar did not make me very comfortable.

TWENTY-FOUR

SEBASTIÁN

In September, after two straight days of rain, the skies around Santiago turned blue and clear at the end of the winter's gray wet season. I had been in Chile almost two years and had begun to think about leaving, but it was not easy.

There were so many things I loved about Chile: the incredible physical beauty of the Pacific coast; the low-hanging clouds hovering over the Andes peaks with the aura of a Japanese woodblock print; the smell of the eucalyptus forest near Santiago with its narrow rocky trails winding up through those giant trees; the constellations of the Southern Hemisphere—the winged Pegasus, the half-man, half-horse Centaur, and the brilliant Southern Cross that guided the earliest Spanish conquerors to this continent centuries ago. Now, in the first days of spring, all the scraggly fruit trees around Santiago bloomed at once, and whitish-pink blossoms filled the air with a syrupy scent.

In Chile, I had come to appreciate a simpler, less-hurried lifestyle. I took comfort in the warmth, generosity, and friendliness of Chileans, a people who relish family, music, and song. A single guitar could mean a party where everyone, including children, danced.

Other times I felt disoriented in Chile, living in a country where poverty, political repression, malnutrition, brutality, and alcoholism were overwhelming. At times, my strategy was to ignore the national woes and focus on the lives of the children at the orphanage. Like the pioneers of the American West, I wanted to circle the wagons and build a better future for those kids.

Many of those hopes and dreams were for my thirteen-year-old roommate, Sebastián. When Sebastián was eight there was simply no food in the house, and his mother sent him to live with an aunt, who in turn pawned him off on a cousin. Even though Sebastián is the most honest and earnest kid you could imagine, the cousin accused Sebastián of stealing and evicted him. Through the help of his second-grade teacher, he came to live at the hogar.

When Sebastián was seven years old, he took care of his two-year-old nephew, Daniel, and that sense of responsibility stuck with him. At the orphanage he would always look for ways to earn money to help us pay our monthly expenses. But this was also the same little boy who always wanted to play soccer until it got so dark he couldn't see the ball anymore or who would throw a plastic snake in the girls' bedroom to watch them scream. Many times he would get so excited when he wanted to tell a story or a joke that the words would come out in one big jumble. He'd say, "Espera . . . espera . . . espera—wait" and try again to get the words out but with the same unsuccessful result. Olga would have him run around the house twice, and when he returned he would be calm enough, albeit out of breath, to tell his story.

When Sebastián entered the fifth grade, it became increasingly obvious that he had a serious learning disability. It was frustrating for him because the harder he tried in school, the more problems he seemed to have. He would study for days for a social science test, memorizing all the definitions, and then on the day of the test either get nervous or not understand the directions. Inevitably he failed the test. He'd come home embarrassed, almost crying: "I knew everything," he'd say, "I just got confused."

That year, the three oldest children at the orphanage, Sebastián, Pato, and Sonia, were all in the fifth grade and went to school in the morning session while the younger children went in the afternoon. Every weekday morning the three oldest and I would rise at 6:30 a.m. and eat breakfast at the little wooden table in the kitchen before they headed off to school and I went to St. George's or to the Catholic University. We'd sit at the table whispering so as not to wake up the other children: Sonia complaining about the "gross" boys in her class, Pato laughing alone at his bad jokes, and Sebastián forever discussing soccer.

In Chilean style, breakfast was very light—usually a mug of hot chocolate and bread with margarine or jelly. One evening I forgot to buy bread, and the next morning there were only three stale pieces of bread in the bread bag from the day before. As the bakery didn't open until 7 a.m., I gave each of the kids a piece of bread, figuring I could buy something on the way to the bus.

Sebastián looked up from the table when I gave him the piece of bread, saying, "I already ate my bread."

"Huh?" I replied.

"You eat this," he said, passing me his piece of bread. "I already ate mine."

"You're crazy," I told him. "I counted the bread last night and there were only three pieces."

He looked down at the table, a little embarrassed, but smiling. "You counted wrong. I already ate mine. Anyway, you've got to have energy to teach your classes, so you've got to eat something," he said, repeating part of my "Eat a Good Breakfast" speech of a few days earlier.

We both laughed and split the stale piece of bread in half.

Even though it almost never got below freezing in Santiago, I remember being as cold in Chile as I had ever been anytime in my life. There was no central heating, and my clothes were almost always slightly damp so that once I got chilled, there was no shaking it. Sometimes on those cold, damp evenings I would enter my bedroom at the back of the house to find that Sebastián had made a coal fire in the tiny portable stove. It warmed my spirits as well as the room.

There was a two-week winter vacation during July, during which most of the hogar kids stayed with relatives or with families who had agreed to receive a child into their homes.

A year earlier, Sebastián had spent the winter break with a family with six children. Two of the boys were about Sebastián's age. For two weeks he had been the special guest who didn't have to make his bed, could play soccer until it got dark, and stayed up late watching TV.

But this winter, a few weeks before the winter vacation, poking at the burning coals in the stove with a metal rod, he told me, "I want to go and spend the two weeks at my mother's house. I can help out my mom. We never go hungry here at the hogar and I think it will do me good to go a few days without eating so much."

I saw him off at the bus stop, giving him bus fare and a pat on the back.

"Behave yourself, old man," I said. It later struck me how unnecessary that advice was. Two weeks later, he returned to the hogar. He looked thinner and when asked how everything went, he replied, "Fine."

"Can you help me save some money?" he asked me later that week.

"And why do you need money?"

"My mom's shoes have fallen apart, so I've got to buy her shoes, because if I give her the money, she'll spend it on food." I remembered when

I was Sebastián's age that all the money I saved from my paper route was used to buy cassettes and Siamese fighting fish for my aquarium.

"Maybe you could sell the macrame plant hangers you've been making," I suggested. In a few weeks' time, he had made a dozen hangers and sold them to visitors who came to the hogar.

This done, Sebastián and I set off for downtown on the bus to buy the shoes. We visited four or five shoe stores before he found a pair of size thirty-two shoes he thought his mother would like, brown suede boots with a fuzzy white lining. With the shoe box under his arm and a confident look on his face, Sebastián and I got back on the bus for the hour-long bus ride to the Pudahuel, near the airport.

As we rode out of Santiago, the roads worsened, and the brick houses were gradually replaced by wooden shacks, many with plastic sheets for windows. In front of many of the houses were little brick buildings that looked like toolsheds. A few years ago, Sebastián explained, the government built these little attachments designed to be a bathroom and a kitchen in front of each house. But government funds ran out and the project was abandoned. A few had running water. Most families, like Sebastián's, merely got a brick skeleton.

As we neared his house, he excitedly pointed out things in his old neighborhood.

"That's my godmother's house, and that's the soccer field where I used to play, and that's the kindergarten where my two nephews, Daniel and Cristopher, are in school."

We got off the bus and walked on a muddy road past a string of wooden hovels. Standing at the corner was a skinny, gray-haired man in baggy gray pants and a dirty brown jacket. He looked up at us through bloodshot eyes.

"Hola, hijo," he said. "How you doing?"

"Bien." Sebastián answered and kept walking, quickening his pace.

"Who's that?" I asked when we had passed the man.

"My father," he said, looking down at his feet as he walked.

I stopped him.

"You never told me your father lived here in Pudahuel." I always thought that Sebastián's father, like many Chilean men unable to find work and unable to deal with the misery of day-to-day life in a country where a bottle of wine costs the same as a soft drink, had taken up drinking, abandoned the family, and simply disappeared. That was certainly the impression Sebastián had always given me.

"I forgot to tell you . . ." Sebastián said. "My father likes to drink, and I never got to know him very well. I don't know where he lives now."

We continued walking down the road in silence until Sebastián stopped in front of a wooden shack that looked identical to all the rest. Sebastián opened the gate and stepped from rock to rock across the mud yard.

"Hello!" he yelled.

Three children ran out of the house, all three with runny noses and grimy blue jeans.

"Tío Sebastián! Tío Sebastián!" Sebastián hugged each of them and introduced me to his two nephews and his niece. Three-year-old Cristina's face was framed in curly light brown hair. Five-year-old Cristopher had a wild look in his eyes that reminded me of Andrés. Cristopher never stopped moving, twisting, turning, and pulling. Standing behind the other two was Daniel, who had dirty-blond hair.

"He just turned six," Sebastián told me, putting his hand on Daniel's shoulder. It was immediately apparent which of the three Sebastián had helped raise. Sebastián gave each of them a yogurt we had bought downtown.

"This is sooo good," Daniel kept repeating. It was the first thing he had eaten all morning.

Sebastián's mother, a short, heavyset woman, invited me into the house—a square, wooden room of ten feet by ten feet with a mud floor. A clear plastic sheet separated the room into a kitchen and a bedroom. Three narrow beds pushed together filled the bedroom.

"Please, Tío, sit down," Sebastián's mother said, pointing me toward the single chair. She pulled the plastic sheet aside and sat on the end of the bed.

"Has Sebastián been behaving himself?" she asked, rubbing her hands together. Her gray hair was pulled back with a rubber band; her ankles and wrists were swollen, her eyes puffy, her skin wan.

"We never have any problems with him. He really helps out a lot," I said, a little overwhelmed, as rambunctious Cristopher jumped on and off my lap. Daniel sat quietly next to Sebastián on the bed.

"Mommy, I have something for you," Sebastián said, handing her the shoe box. She opened the box and looked at Sebastián and then at me with a confused look.

"They're for you, Mommy," Sebastián said.

His mother took the shoes out of the box, running her hand across the white lining of the shoe.

"Sebastián saved up the money he made selling plant hangers and bought them for you," I said, trying to interject something. His mother continued to move her hand across the lining, as if petting a cat.

"Come on, Mommy, try them on," Sebastián said.

She tried but could not make her swollen feet and ankles fit in the narrow shoes.

"I'm just too fat for these nice shoes," she said.

There was an awkward silence.

"We can go back into Santiago this afternoon and exchange them," I suggested. Sebastián readily agreed. Sebastián and I stayed for lunch—a plate of runny rice and a lettuce salad, something I knew I shouldn't eat, given my recent bout with paratyphoid. I ate it anyway.

As the invited guest, I was seated on the only chair while the others sat on the bed balancing plates on their knees. After lunch, Sebastián, his mother, the three little ones, and I boarded a Pudahuel bus for downtown. Sebastián sat next to his mother, with Cristina and Cristopher squeezed in the same bus seat. Daniel sat next to me, holding my hand.

"Tío Sebastián gave me a new pair of shoes last time he was here," Daniel said. He held up his feet for me to see. He was wearing a worn-out pair of brown school shoes without laces. I imagined Sebastián must have scrounged them up from our junk shed at the hogar.

Downtown we exchanged the boots for loafers that his mother could slip on more easily.

"I can't remember the last time I had new shoes," she said. The three little kids' shoes were just as bad as their grandmother's, if not worse, so I bought three pairs of cheap off-white sneakers. They were all excited, so excited in fact that Cristopher, jumping up and down, wet his pants. Daniel, still holding my hand, told me three times, "I will take good care of my new shoes."

As we waited for their bus to take them back to Pudahuel, Daniel bent down with a Kleenex and saliva-wet fingers to wipe mud off of his white sneakers.

As Sebastián and I rode the bus back to La Granja, I pressed my forehead against the moist windowpane, looking out on a darkening Santiago, the sky bearing the final traces of the reddish-orange sunset behind the Andes. It was so false what I was doing, I thought: the gringo who visits bearing a bag of yogurt cups and new white sneakers like manna from heaven. These were inadequate gestures attempting to rectify a problem that wouldn't be solved by yogurt and sneakers. But at the same time, I thought, seeing my face reflected in the window, I had resources to make a difference. I could make sure these three little kids saw a doctor and a dentist and received supplies for school. I could probably get the wood to put a floor in Sebastián's house. Things could be done here, but the crucial issue was how. I could give the initial push, but the key was for Sebastián to take on the responsibility. If I bought lumber, he could build the floor. Or, better yet, he could save money from selling plant hangers and buy the lumber himself. When I got back to the orphanage, I told Olga about the trip to Pudahuel, the shoes, the mother, the house, the little ones, and about the ideas I had for helping.

"Steve, don't get too attached," she said, deflating my creative ideas. "You're only going to be in Chile a few more months . . . and what then? They've gotten dependent on you, and you take off. Take it slow." This had become something of a refrain of hers—"Don't rush so bullheaded into things. Take it slow." I found her maddening at times, in part because she was always telling me things that in the back of my mind I knew to be true but ignored because they always presented obstacles in my relentless desire to move from point A to point B.

About a week later we were in the bedroom, and Sebastián said, "We have to talk," motioning me to sit down.

"Do you think it's possible, that maybe, we could, maybe, let Daniel live here?" He continued but now talking faster. "They treat him real bad at the house, you know, they hit him. They say he's a *maricón*—a queer—because he never fights back. Daniel's six and Cristopher's only five and Cristopher always beats up Daniel. Don't you see?" Without giving me a chance to say anything, he continued, "My sister Ana doesn't take care of him, a lot of times she doesn't even send him to school. She had Daniel when she was seventeen, and then she moved away and my mommy took Daniel. . . . Ana doesn't even think of Daniel as her son. Don't you see? And my mommy can't take care of him. He wouldn't be any problem here, I promise."

"But Sebastián," I began, "you know that we don't have any more beds here in the house . . . and also, if in the future we do decide to accept another child, it will only be a child truly abandoned, who has no one else in the world to look after him. Now think about Daniel. He has a house and a mother and a grandmother to look after him. And what about the other two kids, would it be fair to them, to take Daniel and not them?"

"Just the other day," I continued, "we heard about a woman who has cancer and is going to die. She has two little girls, and when she dies those girls have no one else in the world."

The example came out almost unintentionally. It was true that we knew of such a case, but the woman had not come to talk to us directly. Nevertheless, I pursued the point. "Which do you think we should accept, the two girls or Daniel?"

Sebastián paused and conceded: "You're right, you should accept the two little girls. But if there's no room for Daniel, I could leave and Daniel could take my place. Don't you see?"

"Sebastián," I began again, "how are you going to be able to help out your family in the future if you don't get a good education here?" Tears ran down his cheeks. It had been a long time since I had seen him cry.

"Daniel can't live here, but maybe he can spend more time here," I said. "Next weekend you can go and get Daniel and he can spend the weekend here." Sebastián agreed, nodding his head.

That Friday, Sebastián spent the night at his house in Pudahuel and then came back to the orphanage Saturday morning with Daniel. When Daniel arrived he was a little overwhelmed with the number of people, but he soon made friends with Andrés and Juanito. When we all sat down to lunch, Daniel ate everything on his plate.

"Esta comida es taaan buena," he said. "This food is sooo good," he repeated so many times that some of the kids started to giggle. Daniel ate seconds and then thirds. I could not imagine where he was putting it all in that skinny body. In the afternoon, Daniel sat next to me at my desk, drawing with Sebastián's crayons while I wrote letters. Daniel drew a house with two giant flowers and a rabbit. They were all exactly the same size—the flower stems were as wide as the rabbit's body. Daniel would color them one at a time, touching me on the arm between each effort to ask, "¿Está bien? Is it all right?"

I nodded, and he continued working, taking deep breaths and never going outside the lines where he was coloring. He carefully put each crayon back in the box after using it.

Sunday afternoon a group of St. George's high school students put on a birthday party for Keli, complete with a dozen colored balloons and crepe paper decorations. The students brought enough sweets for forty, and our kids gulped down Coke by the liter and wolfed down chocolate cake, ice cream, marshmallows, and cookies, producing a sugar-induced state of hyperactivity. Carlos punched Alfredo, Héctor wet his pants, and the five-year-old birthday girl Keli threw up all over her new red birthday dress.

Daniel just sat in his chair with a paper cone-shaped birthday hat on his head and a smile on his face, taking it all in. After the party we put the extra cake in a box and gave it to Daniel for his family, along with two balloons for Cristopher and Cristina. Late Sunday night, Sebastián guided me in the car through the Pudahuel's dark, muddy streets, the car sliding from one side of the road to the other on its bald tires.

Somehow we made it, and I parked the car in front of Daniel's house. Sebastián's mother opened the door. The electricity had been shut off in the neighborhood, and the house was lit by a candle that cast shadows over all the people present.

Sebastián gave the cake to his mother, and Daniel gave a balloon to Cristina and Cristopher. They immediately asked when they could visit the orphanage with Tío Sebastián. After an awkward silence I finally said, "Well, it's getting late and Sebastián and I should be going." As we were leaving, there was a voice from the bed on the other side of the plastic sheet.

"You're leaving and you're not even going to give your old man a kiss." No one paid any attention to the voice, and Sebastián's mother, shaking her head, half-smiled at me and motioned to an empty bottle of wine. Sebastián slowly moved toward the bed, leaned down, and kissed the man, saying, "Adiós, papi."

Sebastián and I rode back to the orphanage in the darkened car without saying a word, Chilean folk music playing faintly on the radio. I felt the same pit in my stomach that I had felt the other day on the bus, the same uneasiness about what I was doing, the uncertainty, if not the hypocrisy, of it all. We showed up in a car with birthday cake and balloons in a neighborhood that didn't have running water and then got back in that car and left behind the muddy streets and rows of one-room wooden shacks until these sights were only a tiny reflection in the car's rear-view mirror.

For the next few months, almost every other weekend we repeated the routine. Sebastián would go and get Daniel on Friday afternoon, and then the two of us would take him home Sunday night. Daniel generally had few problems at the orphanage; he got along well with the other children and continued downing amazing quantities of food. But while Daniel was at the hogar, Sebastián would act strangely. He would get overprotective of Daniel and follow him around all afternoon fearful that someone would criticize him or do something to hurt him. One afternoon I had to break up a yelling match between Sebastián and four-year-old Andrés. Sebastián had accused Andrés of stealing Daniel's plastic truck.

At the dinner table Sebastián once again tried to protect Daniel, this time from three-year-old Héctor.

"You should send Sebastián to bed, he's always the cause of the fight," Eliana, who helped out in the kitchen, said to me.

Sebastián stood up, shoving his chair away from the table.

"Nobody has to send me to bed. I'm going," he yelled.

"Sebastián, sit down," I said.

He got up from the table, stomping as he went. "Concha su madre," he mumbled, before he slammed the door shut. I got up from the table and caught him by the arm on the back patio. I physically sat him down on a concrete ledge.

"Young man, if you have something to tell me, say it to my face."

"You never listen to me anyway." He turned his head away, refusing to talk to me.

"Sebastián, now's your chance, I'm listening." He was still too angry to talk and stomped off to bed.

The next Saturday, the rain came down so hard it broke the gutter off the hogar's roof. Sebastián and Daniel arrived at the hogar soaking wet. Daniel didn't have any other clothes with him.

"Sebastián, you should have had Daniel bring a dry change of clothes."

"I'm trying to take care of him the best I can," he told me on the verge of tears. The rest of the day he did not talk to me. During those weeks, Sebastián was increasingly difficult to deal with. He fought more with the other kids and was disrespectful at times, something he had never been before. I wavered between trying to be understanding and coming down hard on him when he really misbehaved. I wasn't the best or most consistent of disciplinarians.

One Saturday morning, I was awakened at seven o'clock by a yelling match between Sebastián and Carlos. Not having any idea what they were fighting about, I sent Carlos to his room and Sebastián back to ours. There, he turned on the radio full blast.

"Turn that off and get back in bed," I demanded. He wouldn't and just stood there, staring at me with his arms crossed, daring me to take action.

I walked over to where he was standing, grabbed him by the arm, physically pushed him back down on his bed, and then turned off the radio. He was fourteen years old. The worn-out adage "This is going to hurt me more than it hurts you" didn't apply. We both hurt.

That afternoon I sat down with Olga, who had been working with children in orphanages for about ten years.

"I'm worried about Sebastián," I began, "He's been having so many problems lately, with the other kids, with the people who help out here, and you heard about what happened this morning. I know that fourteen is a tough age, but he seems really down."

"I know, I've been thinking about him a lot lately too," she said. "When do you think the problems started?"

"I don't know, but you've seen him. These last couple of months he seems to have had a hard time getting along with anyone."

"About the same time he started going to his house regularly on weekends . . . ?"

"Yeah," I said, feeling more than a little defensive because I was the one who had started and encouraged the regular visits. But it made me realize that before, when he had visited his family only once every month or so, things had worked out better.

"Think of Sebastián," Olga began again. "He's probably the most responsible and one of the best kids we've got here. If you tell him he's done something wrong, he takes it to heart and thinks about it for days. So imagine him now, how he sees himself here, with plenty of food, a good school, and lots of opportunities, and then every weekend he goes to his house and sees the hopelessness of it all . . . the poverty, the alcoholism, the filth, the lack of ambition. He knows that it is not his fault, but all the same he feels responsible. Responsible, especially for Daniel. He's only fourteen, but he feels like he should take over the role of the father and he can't do it. He can hardly keep up in school, and it's all too much for him to handle right now."

I paused and then said, "I think you're right. It's too much for him. But that sense that he's helping, that he's doing something for his family, is so important for him."

"I agree," she told me. "I think we should try to figure out a way he can continue to help but limit the involvement with the family to some degree. Don't tell Sebastián that he can't go so often but encourage him to get involved in other things. For example, if he joins an organized soccer team, like he's always wanted to do, then maybe his family would not be such an all-consuming burden. He could continue to help the family, but the other activities might keep things more in perspective."

Even though I agreed with her, I was disappointed because getting him involved with his family was every bit as much my project as it was Sebastián's.

"Don't worry," she said, "it's just that Sebastián needs a little more room to grow up right now, a little more freedom, so that when he's a little older he'll have the resources to be the type of man and provider that he's trying to be now at fourteen."

I went back to our room, where I found Sebastián seated at the desk trying to figure out long division math problems. Through gritted teeth he said, "Math is so stupid."

I sat down next to him at the desk.

"Just hang in there," I said, "and one day all the pieces will fall in place and you won't believe that it could all have been so simple." I showed Sebastián a math shortcut to make the long division easier. He understood the idea and he said, "And that's all you have to do?"

"Yeah, sometimes things only look difficult," I told him, wishing I could believe my own words.

Life never was so simple, though, and Sebastián knew that as well as I did. Things seldom fell into place as they should, leaving us groping for answers that were fleeting and elusive.

But still, occasionally, when I saw Sebastián, laughing on the soccer field, with that impish look in his brown eyes, there was that sense, that hope and yearning, that things might work out after all.

ᔕ

EXPLAINING A FEW THINGS

ᔕ

Clear that linguistics was not my thing, every Wednesday during the second semester, beginning in August, I found my way to the Catholic University literature course I had been searching for, taught by none other than the head of St. George's, Don Hugo Montes.

Don Hugo's course on Latin American poetry was one of the most popular at the university. In his literature course, I read poets from across the Americas, including the Argentine Jorge Luis Borges, the Nicaraguan Rubén Darío, and the Peruvian César Vallejo, as well as the Chileans Vicente Huidobro, Gabriela Mistral, Nicanor Parra, and, of course, Pablo Neruda.

An extremely literate man who knew Greek and Latin and had a doctorate in literature from Germany, Don Hugo had never completely mastered English. In what I considered an incredibly ironic twist, every Thursday I was also in class with Don Hugo, but it was in his office at St. George's, where I was teaching him English. At his suggestion, the classes consisted of reading books aloud, such as Ernest Hemingway's *The Old Man and the Sea,* and discussing them in English.

Montes had written a book entitled *How to Read Neruda,* and in it he discussed Neruda's multiple roles in society—poet and cultural icon, senator and Chilean diplomat in Burma, Sri Lanka, Singapore, France, Mexico, and Spain. In class, we read Neruda's poems and connected them with history and places. Neruda wrote *Explico algunas cosas,* "I'm Explaining a Few Things," about living in Spain during the Spanish Civil War.

Yo vivía en un barrio
de Madrid, con campanas,
con relojes, con árboles . . .

Mi casa era llamada
la casa de las flores, porque por todas partes
estallaban geranios: era
un bella casa
con perros y chiquillos . . .

Y una mañana todo estaba ardiendo
y una mañana las hogueras
salían de la tierra
devorando seres,
y desde entonces fuego,
pólvora desde entonces,
y desde entonces sangre.
Bandidos con aviones y con moros
bandidos con sortijas y duquesas
bandidos con frailes negros bendiciendo
venían por el cielo a matar niños,
y por las calles la sangre de los niños
corría simplemente, como sangre de niños . . .

Generales
traidores:
mirad mi casa muerta,
mirad España rota:
pero de cada casa muerta sale metal ardiendo
en vez de flores,
pero de cada hueco de España
sale España,
pero de cada niño muerto sale un fusil con ojos,
pero de cada crimen nacen balas
que os hallarán un día el sitio
del corazón.

Preguntaréis por qué su poesía
no nos habla del sueño, de las hojas,
de los grandes volcanes de su país natal?

Venid a ver la sangre por las calles,

venid a ver
la sangre por las calles,
venid a ver la sangre
por las calles!

I lived in a suburb,
a suburb of Madrid, with bells,
and clocks, and trees . . .

My house was called
the house of flowers, because in every cranny
geraniums burst: it was
a good-looking house
with its dogs and children . . .

And one morning all that was burning,
one morning the bonfires
leapt out of the earth
devouring human beings—
and from then on fire,
gunpowder from then on,
and from then on blood.

Bandits with planes and Moors,
bandits with finger-rings and duchesses,
bandits with black friars splattering blessings
came through the sky to kill children
and the blood of children ran through the streets
without fuss, like children's blood . . .

Treacherous
generals:
see my dead house,
look at broken Spain:
from every house burning metal flows
instead of flowers,
from every socket of Spain
Spain emerges
and from every dead child a rifle with eyes,
and from every crime bullets are born
which will one day find the
bull's eye of your hearts.

And you will ask: why doesn't his poetry
speak of dreams and leaves
and the great volcanoes of his native land?

Come and see the blood in the streets.
Come and see
the blood in the streets.
Come and see the blood
in the streets!

Riding my bike home from the university, rounding the Grecia Rotary, there were police cars everywhere. Army officers with machine guns stopped buses, cars, even the few crazy individuals on bicycles. The scene was the same at a dozen intersections on the way to the hogar. Documents were shown and kept ready until the next checkpoint.

That evening, after homework and dinner, the kids had settled in to watch TV. Sebastián changed the dial among the three channels. To his dismay, the face of General Augusto Pinochet was on all of them.

"Where's Sanduki?" demanded Karen, referring to her favorite television cartoon character. Once the kids realized the talking head of General Pinochet was not going to give way to anything better, they all went to bed. Pinochet was not the kids' favorite TV entertainment, but many adults watched him for the dramatic circus quality of his orations.

Pinochet almost always wore tinted glasses, which gave him a sinister look. He began in a calm manner, his hands flat on the desk, his facial features relaxed, as he talked about the progress the country was making in the restoration of family values. But before long, he began to talk of threats to these values. He banged his fists on the desk, and his face tightened. "These terrorists who are trying to undermine our system, these politicians and union organizers are raping our country of her values and democratic principles. These, these, communists . . ." he almost spat the words. "Communists! We need to send the politicians back to the caves where they came from!"

Lucho showed up at strange times, often late at night or early in the morning, to see his sister Marisol. His eyes were bloodshot, and he was extremely edgy. He never stayed for long.

"He's a *pollito*," Olga said of the twenty-three-year-old Lucho. "It's as if eleven-year-old Marisol is the grown-up." *Pollito* was one of those words that didn't translate well. Literally, in English, it meant "little chicken," or someone who was afraid, but when Olga called Lucho a *pollito* she meant he was "innocent" or maybe like a baby chick in need of care.

Marisol, though, seemed to be thriving in her newfound stability at the hogar. She did well in school and along with Verónica and Sonia fell into the rhythm of the older sisters of the group, helping take care of the younger kids.

The next few days turned unseasonably hot for September. At night, Marisol pulled off her blanket and complained, "Tío, I can't sleep. It's too hot."

"I can't either," I told her.

"Can I ask you something?"

"Sure."

"My brother told me if I didn't behave here that you were going to throw me out," she said.

"I think he probably just said that because he wants you to be a good girl. . . . You are doing great here, and no one is going to throw you out."

"But I don't think it's fair," she said, very softly. "I don't know why I'm here, and why I don't have a family," and for the first time since she arrived she began to cry. "I just don't think any of it is fair."

"You're right, it's not fair, none of it. But you're here, and all these other kids are here just like you, and all of us have to do the best we can with that. You are a terrific girl, and everything will work out."

I sat on the edge of her bed for a while, and she quieted down and finally fell asleep.

Three radios blared somewhere in the neighborhood. Babies cried. Dogs barked. I couldn't sleep either, so I got up and sat on the side porch, hoping to catch a little breeze. I took out my dog-eared journal. My T-shirt stuck to my back and my forearms to the table as I wrote. Even a bottle of cold beer couldn't make the oppressive heat go away.

The next day was September 11, the eleventh anniversary of the military coup that brought General Pinochet to power. The union leaders had called for a national strike. Although never mentioned by the media, announcements for a one-day national strike had been spray-painted on walls all over Santiago. The government was also active. Helicopters were dispatched and hovered over neighborhoods like ours. The helicopters could fly closer to the houses than airplanes, raising the dust from the unpaved streets, making their presence even more intimidating and thus more effective.

Andrés was making noise in the boys' room. He had a bad cold and was grumpy. He'd been in bed most of the day. I sat by his bed, and we talked for a while.

"Tío, I'm feeling bad. Can you tell me a story?"

"Do you want me to tell the one about the Selfish Giant?" I asked.

"No, tell me one about helicopters."

I made up a story about helicopters that brought gifts to little children. "That's not a good story," he told me. He probably meant it was not credible.

"You're probably right. It's late Andrés, time to go to sleep."

I finally went to bed. In the middle of the night, I was awakened by a sense that the room was shaking. Was I dreaming or awake? Was it a bomb or an earthquake? The trembling continued, and pencils rolled off my desk: who needed earthquakes with all the other problems?

Chile, like California, lies on a fault line. It was only a tremor, but it took me a long time to fall asleep again. When I did, I dreamed of a black sky and blood rolling down the mountains. Again I woke, wondering if the dawn would ever come. Someone once wrote that in true despair it was always 3 a.m. I didn't bother checking my clock.

When I next awoke, it was 6:30 on the morning of the national strike. Everyone else was still in bed. I unlocked the front gate and walked to Américo Vespucio, the main highway that circles Santiago. Its four wide lanes were empty.

Miguelitos, bent four-inch nails that stuck up to puncture tires, were spread out across the concrete pavement. At various points, protesters had piled rocks, branches, and rubber tires into barricades to prevent cars and buses from using the road. It was useless to send the kids to school. The teachers would just send them back home. So we kept them home, tried to catch up on homework, do some small projects around the house, and pretend that everything was normal.

Later that morning, I took another walk out to Américo Vespucio Avenue. The army had been called out from the barracks and worked with the police, sirens wailing, to maneuver around barricades and to clear the debris from the streets. Children in school uniforms, probably only eight and nine years old, threw rocks at the police and yelled, "¡Pacos culiados!—Fucking cops!" and then fled down alleyways.

The national strike was a confusing mix of images. Some people refused to work as a sign of protest or because they were intimidated by the protesters. Others went to work even more frightened at the prospect of losing their jobs. A fire was set in one of the stores along Américo Vespucio that had been open in the morning. It was a warning to any businesses that didn't close their doors. More sirens and fire trucks. By noon, businesses had given up any hope of staying open, and the buses were no longer running, so stranded people were forced to walk miles to their homes.

I was drawn toward the noise and action on the other side of Américo Vespucio. In the evening, the only vehicles on Américo Vespucio were an occasional police van, weaving around the piles of rubber tires that had been set ablaze in the street. The acrid stench of burning tires and teargas filled the night air, making my eyes water and my throat sting. Sparks flew in the night as young men from the neighborhoods threw heavy metal chains over the electric wires on the telephone poles. The electric lines came down, crackling and writhing on the sidewalk. All the lights in the neighborhood went out. A darkened street favored those who lived in and knew the neighborhood.

The police arrived with enormous searchlights. People scattered. There were shots. Were they teargas canisters? Real bullets? I started running. My heart pounded as a police van turned the corner and started to approach. Searchlights. Voices. I pressed against a tree. The van passed. I fled and didn't look back until I was home.

"You shouldn't go out on a night like this," Olga warned. "But tell me everything that's happening," she added. I described the details: a near miss with a police bullet, rocks flying, more bullets, the police catching at least two people and dragging them away. All the kids were already asleep, all except Andrés.

"I can't sleep because of the noise," he told me. As I sat next to him on the bed, I could sense his heart racing. I imagined he could sense mine.

"What's that smell?" he asked.

"It's teargas."

"Do they make it with tears?" he asked.

By 8 a.m. the next morning, the government bulldozers had pushed most of the still-smoldering tires, broken glass, rocks, and branches to the side of Américo Vespucio. The buses ran and people went to work.

Both sides claimed victory. The morning headlines read, "Government Considers Strike a Complete Failure," while a statement from the leader of the National Workers Coalition called the strike, "An event of historic value, legitimizing new forms of pacific struggle in an attempt to reassert the rights of the workers and a return to a democratic system."

One morning paper listed the casualties: a nineteen-year-old police officer defending a fellow officer, a five-year-old boy playing in the street, a mother inside her wooden house. For a time, I was determined to write the name of each person who died in protests in my journal. The list simply got too long, and I gave up. Stories circulated that a young boy was shot and killed as he spray-painted "Stop the Violence" on a brick wall.

TWENTY-SIX

ഗ

YOU'RE GOING TO DO WHAT?

ഗ

Our scheming began innocently enough, with a run that meandered up the foothills of the Andes Mountains. The dirt trail took us through a forest of giant eucalyptus trees, the muffled crunch of blade-shaped green leaves under our running shoes. My Chilean friend Blas Zenteno led the way as the path grew steeper, rockier. The sun was hot, our shirts were soaked with sweat. We made sharp turns between jutting rocks and shortened our strides until we were nearly walking, but the movement of our upper bodies told me that we were still running. Blas came to a level spot and stopped.

"Listen," he said.

I heard the sound of water bubbling over rocks. Blas smiled and signaled me to follow. We climbed over a pile of boulders and saw a stream that ran crystal clear over whitish rocks into a small pond. Blas stripped off his shirt and shoes and dove in. I followed. The snow-fed water was so cold my fingers and toes stung. We emerged and lazed on a sun-heated rock, sitting in a comfortable silence for a long time.

"It's good to run so hard that the only thing you think about is putting one foot in front of the other," Blas said. "Kind of simplifies everything."

Blas's life was anything but simple. When I had first met him nearly two years earlier, he was in the Holy Cross seminary studying theology and philosophy at the Catholic University. Even then he had doubts about becoming a priest. When he met Liz, a strawberry blond from Texas and a recent graduate of the University of Notre Dame who was working as an English teacher at an inner-city Santiago high school, he clearly recognized that he would not have a vocation as a celibate priest. Blas left the seminary. Liz was coming to the end of a two-year stint in Chile as part of a volunteer program run by Holy Cross priests of Notre Dame. She was planning to return to the United States about the same time I was, in about six weeks. Both Liz and Blas were uncertain about what came next for them.

The sun began to cast long shadows over the rocks.

"It gets dark up here real quick," Blas said, as he put on his running shoes. "Whoosh, and you can't see a thing." I lingered at the water's edge. Santiago was spread out in a crisscross pattern in the valley below, bathed in the reddish glow of the late afternoon sun.

"This is the only good thing you can say about all the air pollution in Santiago," he said. "You get incredible sunsets."

Blas scampered down the rocky path easily. I fell a little behind. He noticed and slowed down. After the run, Blas and I retrieved our bicycles and rode to Genaro's Pub. The outdoor patio was nearly full on this cool October evening. Genaro's offered some of the best sandwiches in Santiago: *barros lucos* with steaming, thin-sliced ham and cheese, and *churrascos* with roast beef, melted cheese, and green beans. Local draft beer called *schop* was served in quarter-, half-, and full-liter glass mugs. If you drank two liters of *schop,* you won a certificate. Blas and I set our aspirations high: we planned to drink four liters each. Since we were both on bicycles, we decided to spend the night in one of the spare bedrooms at the seminary across the street from Genaro's where Blas had been living.

First liter. Blas related his most recent adventures with Liz: they had undertaken a ten-day round-trip bike trip from Santiago to Mendoza, Argentina. "The worst was crossing the Andes. For an entire day we climbed up. I got a flat, then Liz got a flat. But once we reached the top it only took thirty minutes to ride down the other side. It was amazing." I told Blas about a wonderful three-week, seven-hundred-mile bike trip I had taken through northern Wisconsin and Minnesota along the shores of Lake Superior.

Second liter. We talked about the future. I was planning to return to Indiana in December. Blas was considering joining Liz in Texas in December. Blas, though, didn't have enough money for the airfare. I had saved just enough for my flight to Indiana but not enough to travel more in Latin America. But I desperately wanted to see more of this continent.

Third liter. "It would be great to go overland to the States," Blas suggested. "We could bring the bikes along and bike through some of the interesting parts. It would sure be a lot cheaper than flying."

Fourth liter. "Why don't we ride our bikes back to the United States?" I proposed. "I read this story once in *National Geographic*, or some magazine like that, about a guy who biked across Africa. If somebody could ride across Africa, we could certainly ride from Chile to the United States."

"Maybe we could get a bike company to underwrite the trip," Blas contributed to the beer-induced fantasy. "We could ride Bianchi bikes . . . they're Italian and they're the best . . . and we could wear their shirts. Maybe they would even pay us to do it."

"Yeah and I could write stories for a magazine or newspaper. Maybe, send back weekly installments." We schemed on into the night. The words slurred together, but that night the ideas seemed crystal clear.

"Are you guys done?" a waiter asked abruptly, making it clear it was time to go home. The patio was nearly empty. Eight empty liter mugs were spread out on the table like trophies. I stood up, my head swimming and my legs rubbery. Genaro signed two certificates verifying that we had each consumed four liters of *schop*. I lost my certificate on the two-block walk to the seminary.

Blas fumbled with keys and showed me to a bedroom. I lay down on the bottom bunk, and the seminary bedroom spun like a giant whirlpool every time I closed my eyes.

"Gringo, are you coming down with something? You look so pale," Olga asked when I returned to the hogar the next afternoon. The previous evening's achievement had lost its luster.

"No, I just stayed up too late last night. I'm fine," I said, feeling as if I would throw up at any moment.

Instead, I tried to focus on the bike trip. I explained the plan to Olga. There was not overwhelming support for the idea.

"Explain this to me again," she said.

"Well, we get a bike company to donate bikes for the publicity and then we ride along the PanAmerican Highway through Chile, Peru, Ecuador, Colombia. We might skip Central America, I'm not sure. Maybe we'll get an ocean liner from Panama back to the United States."

"If you go up the Pacific side, you'll have to cross the Atacama Desert," Olga said. "It's one of the longest and driest deserts in the world, you know."

"Well, I biked a lot in the United States, and Liz and Blas crossed the Andes Mountains from Chile to Argentina . . . and everybody thought they were crazy."

"So where do you sleep in the desert?"

"We can get a tent," I said, annoyed at her lack of enthusiasm.

"Umm hmm, and aren't there parts in Colombia where there aren't even roads?"

"We'll figure that one out when we get there."

"Gringo," Olga concluded, "you're even crazier than I thought."

Crazy or not, I began to ride my bike more than just the thirty miles round-trip from the hogar to St. George's. I took detours, pushing myself up steep hills and roaring down the other side. One afternoon, I skipped out of the university and rode my bike downtown to see *Chariots of Fire*. I'd seen it twice before and knew it would inspire me to take on the new challenge. As the trainer Sam Mussolini told Harold Abrams after Abrams had won the Olympic gold medal, "We have the day, and no one can ever take that from us." I daydreamed of my day, of a five-thousand-mile bike trip through deserts and jungles and over mountains. I made a mental note to check the exact distance of the proposed route.

Blas took responsibility for trying to get the Bianchi Bike Company to sponsor us. I investigated the newspaper and magazine possibilities. To get my foot in the door, I tried my hand at writing and publishing an article about the hogar. I truly believed the story was worth telling: how Olga had begun the hogar four years earlier with almost nothing and what a success the hogar, modeled after a family, had become. I also wanted to discuss, in concrete terms, the dimensions of the crisis of abandoned and abused children in Santiago. I would include suggestions for getting involved, through adopting, supporting a child on a long-term basis, or volunteering at an orphanage. And as was always the case, there was the hope that this effort would bring in more financial support for the Hogar Domingo Savio. Finally, like anyone who considered himself a writer, I wanted to see my name in print.

I showed Olga a draft of the article. She liked my description of the orphanage but cautioned me about the press: "The press here in Chile always needs an angle, and I just don't think you can trust them."

"But, Olga, the article does not refer to the children directly in any way which would embarrass them or make them feel bad. Maybe I should read it to them before I do anything else and make sure they're comfortable with it."

So instead of the usual bedtime story, I read the kids the article. There were stories about the antics of Andrés, Marcelo, Keli, and Carlos, although I generally didn't mention the kids by name. They laughed at all the appropriate places, and I felt reassured that it was a good idea to try to publish it.

"It's a nice piece," one of the editors at the *Las Últimas Noticias* tabloid told me, after the more-respected *El Mercurio* newspaper had turned my article down.

"I won't change a word when we publish it in the Sunday magazine. That way people will know a gringo wrote it." He patted my back as we stood up. We talked for a few more minutes in the hall outside his office; about the orphanage, about my teaching, about Blas's and my plans for the bike trip.

"If we took a bike trip from Chile to the United States, would you have any interest in publishing the stories?" I asked. "For example, I could write one about crossing the Atacama Desert on bicycle."

The publisher laughed. "That should be quite a trip, but I can't promise you anything on that. I'd have to see the stories first."

"Fair enough. Next time I see you, I want to talk about the best way to send you the stories once we're on the road," I said as I left his office, my head swimming with ideas.

~

TWENTY-SEVEN

GROPING IN THE DARK

~

Olga boarded a train for the twenty-hour ride to southern Chile in a flurry of goodbye kisses, hugs, noise, and smoke. It was the first time she had been away from the kids for more than a few days in the past four years. A friend had invited Olga to travel to a part of her country she had never visited: the volcanoes and crystal-blue lakes of Puerto Varas and the remote islands and lush green forests of southern Chile. She definitely needed this ten-day vacation, and I was glad to have the opportunity to run things my own way for once.

Back at the house, Olga had left a note with a few final instructions. At the bottom she wrote, "Good luck, Steve, and try not to hurry so much." I thought to myself, with some guilt, how relaxed it would be not taking any orders from Olga or having her looking over my shoulder.

That Saturday evening, I relocated from my bedroom at the back of the house to Olga's more centrally located room. As I got ready for bed, I glimpsed the crescent moon through Olga's window. Later, I woke up in a fog, groping, disoriented in a bed that was not my own. When I finally figured out where I was, I heard coughing in the girls' room: a dry, raspy cough. I hit the light switch and was greeted by more of the timeless darkness. I looked out the window. The streetlights were also out. I fumbled in the desk drawer in the dark for candles and then searched through the box on top of the refrigerator, my hands struggling to find matches. I struck a match and sent strange shadows dancing across the kitchen ceiling.

The coughing continued. I stood with the candle in the doorway to the girls' room.

"Tío, my throat hurts," Karen said.

I had Karen open her mouth, but the candle flame cast nothing but shadows in her mouth.

"Here, this will help," I told her, offering her some cough syrup.

She sat up and took the medicine from the spoon. The red syrup dribbled down the front of her pink nightgown. Karen, still half-asleep, clumsily brushed her hand across the fabric trying to wipe it off. She went back to bed and immediately fell asleep. I assumed it was nothing serious, but irrational parental paranoia pervaded. Shouldn't I wrap her in a blanket and take her to the hospital this minute?

I had planned to get up early that morning and try to catch up on my homework for my literature class at the university. I set the alarm for 6:30. But by six o'clock Karen was coughing loudly enough to wake me. I gave her orange juice and more cough syrup.

The bathroom door creaked open, and I heard the sound of running water. Three-year-old Héctor came out. His pajamas were wet and reeking with diarrhea. I cleaned him off, changed his pajamas, and sent him back to bed.

About half an hour later, I heard bathroom noises again. I found Karen and Héctor in the bathroom, both of them barefoot on the cold cement floor. Héctor had another bout of diarrhea. Karen, it seemed, had instructed Héctor to remove his pajamas and had a wet washcloth in her hand. She was still coughing.

"Héctor doesn't know how to wash himself," she explained.

I sent her back to bed. She waved goodbye to him as she went. Héctor played "spot the diarrhea" by pointing to his ankle, his hands, his legs. He seemed as much amused as penitent. I made Héctor swear to tell me when he next had to poop. He smelled of soap and clean pajamas when I finally got him back to bed.

"Tío, will you get my bear in Tía Olga's room?" he asked. There was a loud noise, like a sledgehammer crashing against a wall, in the girls' room. As I rushed past, I stared longingly at my notebook, which lay open on the desk.

Carlos and Alfredo were wrestling—"professional style," they called it, with dramatic body slams and exaggerated cries of pain. Having awakened all the boys, they had moved the match to the girls' room. It was seven o'clock.

I grabbed both Alfredo and Carlos by the arms, lifting them both off the floor.

"If I hear a single word, one single peep, out of either of you before 8:00 a.m., you will both be working for me until dark."

I entered the bathroom, lit the water heater with a match, emptied my pants pocket on the counter, turned on the shower, and waited for the water to warm as I undressed. Yoana banged on the door: "Tío, I can't hold it anymore." I let her in and stood with a towel around my waist in the hall.

"Tell the girls to be quiet," I told her when she finally left. I returned to the bathroom and realized the two five-peso coins I had left on the counter were gone.

"Yoana," I yelled.

"Do you want me?" she asked nonchalantly.

"Give me the ten pesos," I said coldly.

"What?" she stammered, her short, uncombed dark hair sticking up all over her head.

"Give me my ten pesos," I repeated.

"I didn't take anything . . . I promise," and she started to cry.

"Yoana, you were the only person in the bathroom. I just took the money out of my pocket one minute ago!"

"But I swear I didn't . . ."

How many times had I repeated this situation with Yoana? How many times had Olga gone through the same routine? Yoana regularly stole trifles—an eraser, pencil sharpener, apple, or ten pesos—and then denied having swiped them. We always found the things hidden, days later, under her pillow or in her closet. When she was younger, Yoana had lived with her alcoholic father, who used to send her out to beg for money. She talked about those days in the same way other little girls talked about playing house. She would spot a person, usually a man, and follow him, begging, until he gave her a coin. Sometimes she would pick flowers from gardens and put them in men's lapels and then ask for money. If that didn't work, she would wait until a shop owner was not looking and steal bread or a piece of fruit.

"Give me the money, Yoana." I held out my hand.

She reached in her pocket and pulled out two coins.

"They were just lying there. I didn't think they were anybody's."

She set the coins in my hand, her eyes avoiding mine.

"I know you hate it when the other kids call you *ladrona*, but if you do things like this, they're only saying something that is true. Do you want that?" She shook her head, tears streaming down her cheeks.

Those early morning events set the pattern for the day. Héctor's diarrhea seemed to have given way to an incessant chorus of "I want" and "give me."

I spent the day yelling at kids.

"Quit fighting," was the most persistent plea, but I also resorted to others. The afternoon became an orchestra of maxims and orders set to a score of minor crises:

"Don't run around without shoes" (after Alfredo stepped on a nail with his bare feet).

"Don't jump on the bunk beds" (after Carlos broke the slats in one).

Later that afternoon, Keli's screams drew me to the girls' room, where I found Karen wearing Keli's new red dress.

"Karen, take off her dress," I demanded.

Verónica walked in and said, "Keli is so selfish, *la chanchita*, the little pig."

I grabbed Verónica by the arm and before I said anything, she said, "Tío, you're hurting me."

In the kitchen Marisol and Yoana were making a cake: there was flour on the countertop and refrigerator, a sink full of greasy pans, egg shells and milk on the floor.

"Wash the dishes," I told Marisol.

"But Yoana made the mess, and the little boys were in here. It's not fair that I have to do everything."

"All right, you and Yoana clean up this mess." I left the kitchen before I heard Yoana's reaction.

The boys returned from playing soccer covered with mud. I made them all take showers. I stood by the bathroom door and heard Sebastián tell Alfredo three times, "Tío Esteve said the last one out has to clean the bathroom."

I had said no such thing, but Alfredo started whining because it was obvious he was going to be last. I stuck my head in the bathroom door and said, "By the way, Sebastián's cleaning up the bathroom."

Alfredo laughed and Sebastián glared.

I called all the kids to the table. Only chubby four-year-old Juanito sat down at the table. He was always ready to eat.

"Fine," I yelled so everyone could hear me, "last one to sit down at the table has to wash the dishes."

There was a desperate scramble to get to the table. Sebastián flew out of the bathroom. Doors slammed and chairs scraped the floor. Verónica and Carlos ran in together, and Carlos pushed her out of his way to get to his seat first.

"Carlos, you pushed Verónica down and you're washing the dishes," I said.

At dinner, Carlos and Verónica were sitting cheek to jowl. Their bickering continued. I tried to regain my patience, but Carlos started yelling at Verónica. My patience evaporated like the last drops of water in a steaming kettle. Carlos stuck his elbow on the table in front of Verónica to annoy her.

"Carlos, leave me alone!" she cried.

I stood up and banged my fist on the table and yelled, "Knock off the fighting!"

As the words came out of my mouth, Carlos said, "But Tío, she started it."

I screamed at the top of my lungs, red in the face: "Don't you understand? Just quit fighting!"

There was no movement, complete silence. Then I started talking again, quietly this time, "Everyone complains, but nobody helps. Nobody thinks of the other people in this house, nobody tries to help. . . . Tell me one thing you did today, Carlos, other than fight? Verónica? Alfredo? Sebastián?"

Carlos had a response to everything, so I should have known better than to give him license to respond.

"I took all the little kids to the field to play this afternoon," he said. "But you, you said that the last one to sit down at the table had to wash the dinner dishes. I wasn't the last one, but you still say I have to wash them."

"You weren't the last one at the table only because you pushed Verónica out of the way. You weren't legally the last one, but you didn't play fair."

"But you weren't fair with me either," he yelped.

I whispered, "Thank you, Carlos, for how fair you've been with me. You only took the kids to the field to play because I forced you to stop fighting with Yoana. Yes, thank you, Carlos, for helping me, thank you for your support, your encouragement, your fairness."

There was no sound, no voice, no fork touching a plate. Tears ran down Carlos's cheeks. He said nothing.

"*Bueno*, Carlos, maybe we all have to improve," I said.

The rest of the dinner was eaten in near silence. My plate of soup was cold, and I dumped it in the sink. Carlos lingered over the dishes for an hour.

"No bedtime story tonight," I told Andrés.

All night I was restless. Carlos asserted his revenge by entering my dreams. He appeared as a grown man, close to my age, refusing to do anything I told him. "Carlos, wash the dishes," I told him over and over. He only rolled his eyes back, as he always did in real life, exactly the way I had to infuriate my father when I was Carlos's age. In the dream, I grabbed Carlos and tried to drag him to the kitchen, but he pulled out a huge butcher knife that glistened in the light. He chased me around the kitchen swinging the knife over his head and chanting, "I'm going to kill you. I'm going to kill you."

I woke up sweating. It was already 6:30 a.m., nearly time to prepare the kids for school. The morning was sunny but cool. I pulled on a sweatshirt. I walked into the boys' room. Andrés had kicked off all his sheets and was lying spread-eagled on his back. Alfredo had his pajama top wound around his neck and his pajama bottom around his knees. He was as messy asleep as awake. Carlos was on the top bunk. Sunlight came in through the Venetian blinds, etching lines across his green bedspread, the light not quite reaching his head. I leaned against his bed. He was already awake, watching me.

"Yo soñé contigo," I told him, which literally means, "I dreamed with you." I told him about the dream and the knife. He reached up and wrapped his arms around my neck. "No, Tío," and then, again, as he hugged me more tightly, "No, Tío."

I woke the other kids for school and mixed the powdered milk for breakfast in the kitchen. Five kids entered the kitchen and in five different ways inquired, "Tío, what can I do to help this morning?"

I was a little more than halfway through my ten days *solo,* though I couldn't honestly say I was running the place by myself. Eliana had been here the entire time, and she did a lot of the cooking, cleaning, and shopping. Some of her assistance, however, wasn't so helpful.

"Pato doesn't show any respect," she told me. "You have to discipline him or else he'll never learn," and then later, "You need to spank Sebastián for the way he talked to me."

"You can sure tell that Tía Olga is not around," she told me when I refused to spank Sebastián.

Having full responsibility for running the hogar for a mere ten days had made me more nervous, tired, and ill-tempered than I wanted to admit. It also made me realize how truly remarkable Olga was to manage this whole operation for so many years with so much grace.

"My knee hurts," Andrés sobbed, pointing to a knee that looked exceptional only in how dirty it was.

"It's fine," I told him. "All you need to do is wash it."

Half an hour later Andrés was back on the couch, holding his knee with both hands. "My knee still hurts," he insisted. Though there was no visible wound, the knee had swollen significantly.

Having no other options, I took him to the Sotero del Río Emergency Clinic. I'd grown to hate the place. After a long wait, the doctor set Andrés on the metal examining table and pressed firmly on the knee. Andrés began to cry. She pushed his swollen kneecap from side to side with her fingers.

"Make her stop," Andrés pleaded, big tears falling from his dark brown eyes. The doctor stuck a hypodermic needle into the knee, and the tube filled quickly with yellow liquid.

"Do you have a car?" I nodded yes.

"You have to take this boy immediately to the Hospital Luis Calvo McKenna. Do you know where that is?" I nodded again. "It looks like he has some type of infection, probably blood poisoning. They'll probably have to operate on the knee. We can't do it here. Take the liquid with you. They can test it when you get to the hospital," she said as she handed me the vial.

I ran out of the clinic into the damp night, trying to balance Andrés, his shoes, and the vial of yellow liquid. I unlocked the car door and juggled him into the seat, not wanting to overturn the vial. I sped out of the gravel parking lot through the dark streets of Santiago, the vial of liquid wedged between the two seats of the car. Andrés was silent, his blue stocking cap pulled low over his brow.

"Do you want to hear a story?"

He shook his head no.

"Andrés, when we get done at the hospital we'll stop and get some ice cream. Andrés, everything will be fine." No answer.

"Everything will be fine," I assured him again, trying to believe it myself. I thought back to happier times and a healthy Andrés. Just yesterday I had found him lying on his back in the grass looking up at the sky, his fingers clasped behind his head.

"And the clouds—who lives in them?" he had asked me.

At the hospital, it seemed to take forever to get him registered.

"Explain to me again your relationship to the boy," the nurse demanded.

"The doctor at the clinic said it was an emergency," I said, holding Andrés wrapped in a blanket in my arms.

"We must have this information before we can check him in," she told me coldly. "What is the orphanage's insurance number?"

Finally we saw Dr. Graciano Corbera, a man with slightly thinning hair and piercing, dark eyes.

"Andrés, tell me if I'm hurting you," he said. Doctor Corbera examined Andrés thoroughly, in a way that seemed less clinical, more human. He drained Andrés's knee again. Andrés whimpered.

"What a brave boy," Doctor Corbera said. Andrés sat a little straighter and smiled.

"If he has a systemic infection we'll have to operate immediately," he warned me. "It'll take an hour for the test results."

Andrés and I moved to the waiting room. Andrés filled the pages of my beat-up blue journal with doodles. Blue ink circles with protruding spokes covered three pages. Some were bicycles, he explained, and some were butterflies.

"These are children playing," he said, pointing to one series of spokes. The jagged lines were mountains. He pointed to another series of jagged lines: "These are the teeth of a vampire." We were called back into Doctor Corbera's office.

"Andrés may have had something in his knee, possibly a small piece of metal. That was why his knee is swollen. But there's nothing there now we can see, and the tests show there is no systemwide infection."

I wanted to hug him. Instead I shook his hand.

"We probably won't have to operate," Doctor Corbera told me. "We should keep him over the weekend for observation."

It was well past midnight on Friday night as an orderly wheeled Andrés through the basement corridors of the hospital.

"You can't come any further," the nurse at the entrance to the children's wing told me.

"I just want to make sure he gets settled before I leave," I suggested.

"We'll take care of that. You can come visit him on Sunday afternoon between two and three."

"Can I just stop in tomorrow?"

"Visiting hours are on Sunday between two and three," she barked.

"You mean I'm not supposed to come back until Sunday!" I complained. "If I brought a healthy four-year-old to the hospital and abandoned him for two days, he'd probably get sick."

"Those are the rules, and if you don't leave now I will call a guard," she said as her final words.

I turned to Andrés. "Bye, Andrés, don't worry, I'll see you soon." Andrés was quietly crying. At the front desk, as I signed more papers, a nurse told me, "Tomorrow you will need to drop off a towel and clean pajamas for the boy."

I finally got home about 2 a.m. The house was silent. I slept fitfully, dreaming that Olga came home, and her first words were, "You didn't paint the house? You mean we bought the paint and you had all that time, and you didn't even paint the house?"

At nine o'clock Saturday morning, I was back at the hospital with a towel, pajamas, a toothbrush, and an armload of storybooks. "No one is allowed in the patients' rooms outside of visiting hours," another nurse told me. With their white uniforms, white caps, and serious faces, they all looked identical.

Nevertheless, to drop off the things I had to walk right past Andrés's room, so I stopped in the doorway and talked to him for a few seconds.

"Andrés, there are some great books for you. All the kids are waiting for you back at the house," I said. Andrés smiled.

"You have to leave. We get in trouble if people are up here," a nurse instructed me.

"Bye, Andrés. I'll see you tomorrow."

"How is he doing?" I asked the nurse. "Does he have a fever?"

"I can't give you that information. You should not be back here."

"Who can give me any information?" I asked.

"His doctor," she informed me coolly.

"But Doctor Corbera will not be in until Monday morning," I said.

"Then you will get the information Monday morning," she replied. She was obviously agitated, but I was more so.

"So who is the doctor on duty right now?" I asked.

"I can't give you that information."

"Who is your supervisor?"

"You have no reason to ask me that," she said tersely, "and I will call the guard if you don't get off this floor this instant."

I went to find the director of the hospital. He was also gone for the weekend. I sat in the modern waiting room, with its wood and upholstered furniture, an incredible knot forming in my stomach. I knew Andrés was getting good technical medical care here, probably as good as anywhere in Santiago: it just seemed that the medical "healing" was so divorced from the human needs. The assumption was that technical, mechanical approaches would solve the problem, that the staff knew best, and that people like me should stay the hell out of the way.

After dinner, my stomach was still in a knot. I sat on the back patio with three-year-old Héctor. The sky, with all the pollution, was a brilliant red, and Héctor pointed, "Look, look, Tío, a rainbow!"

For Héctor, a colored sky was a rainbow. He had me lift him up on the swimming pool's three-foot-high brick wall. The sun was just setting behind the Andes and in the few minutes we stood there, the sky changed from the vibrant red to a dull, grayish pink. Héctor lamented, "Oh, no, the rainbow, it's going away! Don't let it go away. Tío, don't let it go away."

Early the next morning, I walked to the corner newsstand to buy *Las Últimas Noticias* Sunday paper, as my article about the orphanage was scheduled to appear. I turned to the Sunday magazine section and there on the cover was a full-page color picture of Andrés in his red- and blue-checkered shirt. He was sticking out his tongue and smiling. On the same front page, there was a smaller picture in a box, with five of the kids and me sitting on a bed. The caption next to the picture read, "In a poor Santiago barrio, there is a special hogar where disadvantaged orphans are treated like little princes and princesses. An adventurous and romantic teacher from the United States writes a valiant and human report about this great house that began with so little." When I opened the magazine and turned to the article, there in great big letters, was "LOS NIÑOS POBRES Y UN GRINGO LOCO—THE POOR CHILDREN AND A CRAZY GRINGO."

I thought I was going to throw up. I stopped and closed my eyes and took a deep breath. Inside the magazine were more pictures of me with the children. In one, Karen was swinging her doll, Juanito was hitting Héctor, and I looked on with a stupid grin. Under the picture, the caption read, "I will never leave this home as long as one child needs help." The quote was in the article, but Olga had said it, not I, as the caption implied. There was only one small photo of Olga, blurred in black and white, with the caption, "One of the many *mamás* at this very special hogar." Olga's cautions about the press came back to haunt me. The article led off with an introduction written by the publisher:

> An orphanage of poor children in a barrio near Santa Rosa Street was at the point of disappearing. Today it is a modest but efficient hogar. A gringo loco, an adventurer and professor, writes this amazing story as he prepares to travel to the United States . . . on bicycle.

I wanted to hibernate and wake up about two weeks later when it had all blown over—when there was no article and when Andrés was not in the hospital. I figured everyone would see the article anyway, so I showed it at breakfast to the kids and to Olga's sister Vicki, who had shown up that morning. She looked at the titles and the pictures and without even reading the article asked disapprovingly, "How could you have done something so ridiculous?"

Néstor had learned that Andrés was in the hospital, and in the afternoon we went together to visit him. Néstor and I arrived a few minutes before two. Already, a group of about ten people had gathered at the doorway to the hospital room to see their children. There were four beds in the room, and the nurse had put a desk across the doorway: each person had to take turns standing at the doorway and yelling across the desk.

Andrés waved when he saw us. His color was better.

"Did you see the baby?" he asked, pointing to a little girl in a body cast. "She's real nice," he continued, "her name is Amelia."

Néstor held up the cover from the Sunday supplement with Andrés's picture. Andrés beamed.

"Can I see it?" he asked. The nurse had left the desk. Néstor moved the desk, darted into the room, handed Andrés the magazine, and gave him a hug. Néstor was out again before the nurse returned.

The nurse with whom I had had the discussion the day before returned to the desk. She glared at Néstor and me.

"Do you want to see my picture?" Andrés asked her.

He held up the magazine. She walked over to his bed.

"This is Karen, and this is Héctor, and this is Juanito," he explained to her, pointing to some of the other pictures.

"That's Tío Esteve," he said, pointing to me. The nurse eyed me suspiciously, then looked back down at the pictures. Giving these explanations, Andrés seemed so grown up: a little man inside that four-year-old body. More nurses gathered around Andrés's bed. He got lots of attention, and our presence was obviously not needed.

"Andrés, I'll be back early tomorrow," I told him. He looked up, smiled, and resumed talking with the nurses.

Early Monday morning, I returned to the hospital and sat in the waiting room as mothers tried to calm screaming babies and orderlies pushed carts back and forth. Doctor Corbera arrived and took me into Andrés's room. The nurses were all very friendly.

"He behaved himself like a king," my least favorite nurse said. Her attitude seemed to have changed dramatically since she saw Andrés on the cover of the magazine. Doctor Corbera examined Andrés's knee, which was no longer swollen. He looked at a number of X rays.

"We'll have to put Andrés's leg in a cast for a week so he doesn't move it, but I don't foresee any further problems," he told me.

"I want to see him in a week. Do you think you can keep him in bed that long?"

"Sure," I said, knowing as soon as the words came out of my mouth that I was lying.

Andrés was wheeled down the hall to another room. As a nurse molded the cast around his right leg he asked, "Could you put one on my other leg, too?" and the nurse laughed, a wide-mouthed, toothy laugh.

Upon returning to the hogar, I quickly learned what a wide reading audience *Las Últimas Noticias* had in our barrio. Walking home, a group of kids that I didn't know yelled out, "Hey, Gringo Loco, want to go for a bike ride?"

That afternoon, Yoana came home from school crying, "This boy in my class just kept calling me *princesa*. I finally hit him, and then *I* got in trouble! Why did you have to write that stupid article?"

Olga returned that evening, and we sat in the living room as I recounted the events of the past ten days. Sheepishly, I handed Olga the Sunday magazine. Olga read the title and captions and said, "That's the press." She was not at all bothered. She started reading the article and smiled. "I see they called you the Gringo Loco . . . but we already knew that."

∽

TWENTY-EIGHT

GOD WILL SEE US THROUGH

∽

The doorbell rang. It always seemed to ring as soon as we would get all the kids to sit down to lunch. Carlos and Alfredo scrambled to see who could get to the door first. Carlos knocked over his chair, tripping Alfredo in the process. Alfredo came from behind and body-slammed Carlos into the back of the door. There was shoving and pushing to get the door open. They went outside, and the room became suddenly silent. The two of them reappeared.

"Tía Olga, some lady wants to talk with you," Carlos said.

Carlos turned to Alfredo, "Por Dios, are you fat."

"Idiota," Alfredo said as they both sat down at the table and returned to their chicken *cazuela* stew.

Olga got up from the table, and after a few minutes she called me. Olga introduced Ximena, the visiting social worker. Ximena had heard about the hogar through a friend.

Ximena sat on the sagging brown couch and told us about Rosa and Sonia. The two girls were from a family of five children in Pudahuel.

"One night last winter," Ximena began, "about eight o'clock, people in Pudahuel started banging pots and pans in protest against the military government. A number of *carabineros* trucks, the big green ones, came into the neighborhood. People ran into their houses when they saw the police trucks, but they continued banging the pots and pans inside." Ximena paused.

"Some of the police started shooting at a row of wooden shacks that was producing the commotion. In one of the shacks, Rosa, Sonia, and their mother hid on the floor under the beds. A bullet came through the wooden wall of the house. It hit their mother in the head, killing her, and splattering blood across the room." She paused again.

"The police entered the house, found the mother's dead body, and then cut their bullet out of the mother's head with a bayonet knife. The girls watched. I guess the *carabineros* were afraid that the bullet could have been identified as a police bullet."

No one said anything. The afternoon sunlight filtered through the thin white curtains.

"Sonia is nine years old and Rosa is seven," Ximena said. "Even before this happened, the girls weren't going to school. They spend their days in the streets. The only food in their house is white bread and tea. Their father is simply unable to handle the situation. He is unemployed and unable to take care of himself, much less his children. He's probably an alcoholic."

"The father has decided to put the girls in an orphanage," Ximena said, rubbing her thumbs together nervously. "I've checked around, and I can't find any orphanage that will accept them both together. Since Sonia is nine years old and has never been to school, they want to put her in a special home for retarded children. Sonia's not retarded; she's just never had any intellectual stimulation. And you can just imagine how her mother's death has affected her."

Three-year-old Héctor walked into the living room. Without a word, he sat next to Olga, resting his hand on her leg. He sat very straight.

"Isn't there any way you could take them both?" Ximena asked. "I just don't know what will happen to them if they are separated."

Olga looked at me. She brushed Héctor's hair off his forehead. Olga said, "We have to talk about this first, but I think we may be able to do something." I nodded my head.

That evening, with all fourteen in bed, Olga and I sat over glasses of beer and talked about the implications of taking in two more children. We had always been firm about not wanting to accept more children. Fourteen was a handful, and any more would take away from the special, family-like quality of the orphanage. We had turned away children before, children in desperate situations: children without enough food in the house, a three-year-old without a bed, another abused by her mother. Olga or I would have to explain that we were full and try to make suggestions, but sometimes we would send people away with no ideas, maybe just a box of powdered milk for a baby. This time, though, I had a gut reaction, and I wanted to say, if we've already got fourteen what are two more?

But my voice carried less weight. I would be leaving in a few months, and the responsibility of taking care of the children would fall even more squarely on the shoulders of Olga.

Olga took a drink of beer. "You know, when we started this five years ago, we didn't have a thing, didn't know where we would get the money for the rent and for food for the kids. I remember that first winter when we were out at the farm. All those kids, and the mud from all the rain. We had to bake our own bread in a red clay oven outside." She pushed her black hair away from her face.

"I remember standing in the pouring rain, trying to get the stove lit, praying that the bread would rise and that we would get money from somewhere so there would be food on the table for one more day. Somehow we made it . . ."

I traced the moisture on the side of my beer glass. Olga continued, "Now look at the group we have, and how well they are doing, here and at school." She tilted her head back and looked at the ceiling. "I just knew, as I sat there listening to the story of Sonia and Rosa, that they needed a home . . . and that we have a place, we actually own this place, and that God will see us through."

Later that evening, Ximena brought Sonia. Her sister, Rosa, was already admitted to another orphanage, and it would take about a week to complete all the paperwork before she could live at the hogar. Sonia was a blonde, with a pasty white complexion and brown eyes. She looked as if she had never been in the sun. Since there was already another Sonia at the hogar, the new Sonia's name immediately became Sonia Chica—Little Sonia.

"Do you want to take a ride in the car?" I asked Sonia Chica on her second day at the hogar. She stared vacantly.

"Sonia, would you like to go in the car with me?" She somewhat absently nodded her head and I took it to mean yes. We went to the hardware store and the post office. Several times, I tried to initiate a conversation. It ended up being a monologue about what a good place the hogar was, about what a special group of children lived there, and about how nice it would be when Rosa came to live there. In her two days, Sonia had barely communicated with anyone, and with me it seemed especially difficult, probably because of my accent. Every time I asked her something directly, she gave me a puzzled, slightly angry look, and said, "¿Qué?"

My last stop with Sonia was at the Trappist monastery, where I had to pick up the monthly check. I was to meet Father George, the soft-spoken, efficient accountant of the monastery, who would jot down numbers in his tiny handwriting on the back of an envelope, always making sure the orphanage got its monthly four hundred dollars on time.

We arrived at six, but Father George had gone into Santiago and still had not returned. Sonia Chica and I sat on the front steps of the monastery's kitchen. Although the monastery was close to Santiago, I'd never seen the smog that blanketed the city reach it. The sky was blue. A few birds sang, and branches swished and swirled in the wind. A young bearded Chilean monk came out and sat with us for nearly half an hour and tried to get Sonia to talk. He coaxed her with food and plied her with questions, and even did animal imitations of a horse and a duck. For all his efforts, Sonia told him she was nine years old, holding up nine fingers.

Sonia and I took a walk down to the monastic barn, and I showed her the horses and cows. I repeated *vaca* several times, patting the cow on the rump, as if I were talking to a three-year-old. She stepped up to the brown animal, touched it, and said, "*Vaca.*" At 7:30 the bells tolled for vespers. I sat alone with Sonia, exhausted from my attempts to make conversation.

Father George finally arrived at about eight, delivering an envelope with the monthly check. We didn't get home until well after dark. Sonia had fallen asleep in the car, her face pressed against the door. After a few more days, Sonia Chica tentatively said a few words to Verónica and Marisol. She remained, all the same, terrified of Olga, ignored Eliana, and didn't appear to understand a word I said.

I spent a good part of one afternoon with Sonia Chica using the same first grade reading book that I had used with Yoana, Alfredo, and Marcelo about two years earlier. In the reader there were pictures of animals, with the words spelled out underneath. I was lucky if I could get more than a "sí" or "no" from her as I turned the pages of the reader. We came to the word *vaca* with a picture of a black-and-white cow standing in a field.

"Well, I'm sure you know what this is now," I said. She smiled like the Mona Lisa but didn't say the word.

It took nearly two weeks to get Sonia's seven-year-old sister released from state custody. Like Sonia, Rosa had short blond hair and a pasty white complexion. She also had freckles. Rosa was quiet but seemed to observe everything going on around her with her big brown eyes. Sonia spent their first afternoon together with her arm around the shoulder of her younger sister, breaking her previous silence to give Rosa a tour of the house, explaining who was who.

After two weeks here, Sonia Chica was like an old pro and explained what could and could not be done.

"You have to make your bed, and you have to flush the toilet or you get in trouble."

Later, when all the children were in bed, Sonia's voice emanated from the girls' room: "Rosa, do you have a pillow?" "Are you too hot, Rosa?" "Rosa, do you need anything?"

ᔥ

THE END OF THE ROAD

ᔥ

Igot up early, hopped on my bicycle, and headed to the university for my Latin American literature class with Hugo Montes. He was a wonderful teacher, in part because it was obvious he so loved the literature and poetry he taught.

Professor Montes had invited a guest lecturer, Oscar Hermes, an Argentine poet, to his class. Hermes talked about Argentinean authors I knew such as Jorge Luis Borges and Julio Cortázar, and other names I didn't know: Enrique Molina, Eduardo Gonzalez, and Olga Orozco. Hermes quoted from the German poet Rainer Maria Rilke: "If in your darkest hour . . . you know you must write . . . then spend your life in devotion to that art." He then read some of his poems. He spoke softly, yet the usually restless class was attentive, and his words took on a power that filled the room. Before Hermes left the classroom he quipped in Spanish, "English is the language with which you talk to the world, French the language with which you talk of intellectual things and love, but Spanish, oh Spanish, is the language with which you talk to God."

In one of our English classes, Montes asked me what I thought of Dante. I had to admit, slightly embarrassed, that I had never read him. After our class, I went to the St. George's library and checked out the *Divine Comedy*. Reading about Dante's travels from hell to purgatory to paradise offered an escape from my other responsibilities. The story began with a perplexed thirty-five-year-old Dante, serving as both pilgrim and guide. From the very first lines, I felt this was something I could identify with:

> Midway in our life's journey I awoke
> To find myself alone in a dark wood.
> Who knows how I came that way?

For a couple of weeks, I took the *Divine Comedy* with me everywhere. Perhaps I needed this fictional voyage, in light of the hunger in my neighborhood, the helicopters that flew low over our house every night, and the disappearances that occurred on a daily basis.

Since I didn't have to teach or to attend classes on Wednesday, I spent the entire day at the orphanage. While the older kids were at school, I took the six youngest to the fields a few blocks from the house. Andrés, Juanito, and Héctor kicked a soccer ball, and the three little girls ran through the field, picking flowers and waving at me from afar.

I found a big rock in the middle of the field, amid wildflowers and weeds, where I finished reading *The Divine Comedy*. I had a hard time plowing through the last section on paradise, my concentration wandering with all the "rapt with joys," "numbed with amazement," and "bursting forth from the heavenly spheres." Strangely, hell and purgatory seemed far more engaging and real.

One day after my literature class, I met my American friend and Blas's girlfriend, Liz Hellinghauser, at a sandwich shop across from Catholic University. She had come down on the program of the Holy Cross Associates and was teaching high school.

We talked about her teaching and mine, about Rilke and Chilean politics, about her romantic relationship with Blas and my family's upcoming visit. I told her I had invited my parents to come and visit Santiago before I left, and much to my surprise they decided to come.

Liz and I also talked about the future. After two years in Chile, we were both planning to leave in about a month. Liz would fly to her hometown of Midland, Texas, while Blas and I would travel overland by bike to Texas by some still-unspecified route, arriving a month or two after Liz. The plan was that they would get married once Blas got to Texas.

"I'm a lot more apprehensive about going back to the United States than I ever was in coming here," Liz said.

"It's scary thinking of going back," I concurred. "We came here on a big adventure, and now it's coming to an end and we have no idea what comes next."

"If you could do anything when you go back, what would you do?" Liz asked.

"I'd study literature and writing," I said after a long pause. "I'd learn to write well and be content just studying for a while, without feeling guilty about doing nothing else."

Liz smiled and said, "But after *this,* you know that will be impossible." I nodded.

Later, I reflected on her comment and wanted to ask: What was the *this,* Liz?—Chile, Latin America, the way our worldviews had changed, the way we had changed, the incredible needs all around, how those needs were tied to our own, the realization of how privileged we were and the responsibility that entailed, or this incredible gap between reality and our dreams? I was not sure which *this* it was, but I knew she was right. A few days later, Liz sent me a photocopied page from *Notebooks of Malte Laurids Brigge* by Rilke:

Ah! but verses amount to so little when one writes them young. One ought to wait and gather sense and sweetness a whole life long, and a long life if possible, and then, quite at the end, one might perhaps be able to write ten lines that were good. For verses are not, as people imagine, simply feelings (those one has early enough),—they are experiences. For the sake of a single verse, one must see many cities, men and things, one must know the animals, one must feel how the birds fly and know the gesture with which the little flowers open in the morning. One must be able to think back to roads in unknown regions, to unexpected meetings and to partings one had long seen coming; to days of childhood that are still unexplained, to parents whom one had to hurt when they brought one some joy and one did not grasp it (it was a joy for someone else); to childhood illnesses that so strangely begin with such a number of profound and grave transformations, to days in rooms withdrawn and quiet and to morning by the sea, to the sea itself, to seas, to nights of travel that rushed along on high and flew with all the stars— and it is not yet enough if one may think of all this. One must have memories of many nights of love, none of which was like the others, of the screams of women in labor, and of light, white, sleeping women in childbed, closing again. But one must also have been beside the dying, must have sat beside the dead in the room with the open window and the fitful noises. And still it is not yet enough to have memories.

One must be able to forget them when they are many and one must have the great patience to wait until they come again. For it is not yet the memories themselves. Nor till they have turned to blood within us, to glance and gesture, nameless and no longer to be distinguished from ourselves—not till then can it happen that in a most rare hour the first word of a verse arises in their midst and goes forth from them.

I carried that folded piece of paper in my back pocket for so long that the ink smeared and became almost impossible to read. And still I carried it with me.

The next morning, I left early by bicycle for the Catholic University library. I rode along Américo Vespucio at a good pace. Increasingly, I could keep up with traffic on long straight stretches and could go faster than cars if there was some traffic. My new, tighter toe clips on the pedals increased my speed. I was pumping along really well when I came to the Grecia Rotary, which has rows of squat three-story, low-income housing on one side and the Cousiño Macul vineyards on the other. As I entered the merging traffic, I stood up on my pedals to gain extra speed. At that moment, the chain came off and jammed between two back sprockets. The rear tire came to a sudden, screeching halt, launching me headlong over the front handlebars. As my feet were strapped into the toe clips, the bicycle and I did a full flip before landing in the middle of the rotary. Cars swerved to miss me. Flat on the pavement, I had a hard time untangling my feet from the toe clips.

"Get out of the road, *idiota,* you want to get killed!" a woman yelled at me as she drove around me. I limped off the road, dragging the bicycle with me. Neither of the tires would rotate. I sat alongside the road and took an inventory: my shirt was ripped; my sunglasses were cracked; my Casio watch had stopped ticking; my elbows, knees, and face were all scraped and bleeding, but miraculously I was not seriously injured.

A teenage boy walked over to where I was sitting on the curb.

"Are you okay?" he asked. "That was quite a crash."

"Yeah, I'm fine, but I don't think my bike fared so well." We looked at the mangled wheel, the mutilated chain, and the spokes protruding at every angle.

"I'll give you three hundred pesos for your bike . . . I need some parts for mine." Three hundred pesos was about eight dollars.

"No, thanks," I told him, as I got up and hobbled along with the bicycle. I tried to flag down a bus, but none of them stopped. Finally, the driver of one of La Granja's blue-and-white buses stopped and agreed to give me and my bike a ride. I handed him the fare.

"I've never taken somebody with a bicycle before," he said, "but you looked like you were hurting."

I abandoned the bike in a repair shop near Plaza Egaña. They told me they could fix it in a few days, but it cost more money than I had with me. Instead of going to the university, I boarded a bus for Blas's house. I sat on the bus wondering: what if something like this happened in the middle of a particularly barren stretch of the Atacama Desert? Actually, was there anything other than particularly barren stretches in the Atacama Desert?

I rang the bell at Blas's house.

I'd forgotten how beat up I must have looked until Blas's mother exclaimed, "Por Dios! What happened to you?" She directed me to the bathroom to wash the grease and blood off my arms, legs, and face.

"You know, when I left the house, I was on my bicycle," I told Blas from the bathroom and recounted the story of my crash. Blas smiled through the whole account, especially the part about the boy wanting to buy the bicycle.

"That's Chilean entrepreneurship at its best," he said. "Unfortunately, I haven't been particularly successful with my entrepreneurial efforts. I don't think Bianchi is going to give us the bikes."

As I sat on a chair in Blas's kitchen, my body aching from the crash, the magic of the bicycle trip back to the United States began to fade.

"You know," I ventured, trying to test the waters after so much planning for this trip, "we don't have to travel by bicycle. We don't even have to travel along the Pacific coast."

Blas picked up the ball, "Yeah, Argentina is fantastic, and I've always wanted to see more of Brazil. We could spend more time in some of the interesting places if we went by bus and train, and even hitch-hiked, and we could probably even get a ride on a ship from Brazil back to the United States. We could work on the ship so it would be even cheaper." I had never been to either Argentina or Brazil. Suddenly, my wrecked bike trip dream was transformed into a new, maybe better, vision of traveling over the Andes and along the Atlantic coast of South America.

"The only thing, Blas," I confided, "is that it will be kind of embarrassing because I told everybody I was making this bike trip, and they even published it in that stupid article."

"Well, at least in your neighborhood they won't call you the Gringo Loco anymore," Blas said. "From now on they'll just call you the Gringo Mentiroso—the Lying Gringo."

〜

THIRTY

THE DAYS OF WAITING

〜

T ío, the milk has big lumps in it," Keli announced as she stared down into her mug of hot milk at the breakfast table.

"Just stir it with your spoon and it will be fine," I told the five-year-old. The soybean-based powdered milk that had been donated to the hogar in forty-kilo bags always produced a lumpy, yellow milk no matter how long it was stirred. The kids hated it. I swallowed a big gulp of the foul-tasting milk to set a good example.

"Tío, even the dog won't drink this milk," Pato said.

"These little balls of powder in my milk make me want to throw up," Keli added, her comment threatening to incite an insurrection.

"Tough. Drink it, Keli," I ordered.

She grimaced, held her nose, and swallowed about half her mug in one gulp.

"I've got to go to the monastery this morning and I'll be back later this afternoon," I informed the kids assembled for breakfast. "Eliana's in charge." Eliana was nowhere in sight. Olga was visiting her mother in the seaside town of Viña del Mar. I looked at my watch. It was nearly nine. I needed to go to the monastery to pick up the foundation check, and Father George had said he would be there only until 9:30. It took at least forty-five minutes by car to get to the monastery on a good day with little traffic.

As I stood up to leave, I saw Carlos still in his pajamas in the boys' bedroom.

"Carlos, get dressed. I already told you once. Everybody else is already finishing breakfast," I said as I went out the door.

The white Suzuki car was leaning to the left. One tire was completely flat. I changed it as quickly as possible, cutting my hand in the process. I hurried back inside to wash the grease and blood off my hands. Carlos, still in pajamas, was now playing with his cars in the living room.

"You're not even dressed yet!" I yelled at him. Carlos stared at me blankly. I yanked him to his feet and dragged him into the bathroom.

"So you can't even wash your face and get to the table by yourself!" I said as I splashed water on his face, dousing us both in the process.

"Now, go sit down and eat breakfast," I commanded.

Driving to the monastery, I consciously took deep breaths to calm down. I imagined Carlos red-eyed and brooding at the breakfast table. I was confident he was not drinking his yellow milk—he wouldn't even drink the white variety. I knew how Carlos would behave because it was how I behaved when I was his age.

"Don't roll your eyes like that when I talk to you," my father had commanded me when I was ten.

"I'm not rolling my eyes at you," I said, exasperated, as I rolled my eyes. Carlos recited in Spanish my exact lines to my father of a dozen years earlier.

By the time I arrived at the monastery, Father George had already left without leaving the check. One of the monks told me he would return around noon. I sat on a stone fence and brooded, probably not unlike Carlos.

The monastery was completely surrounded by mountains, and as I watched the breeze push the clouds across an aqua sky, my head began to clear. An American Trappist monk joined me on the stone fence.

"I put this on when I saw you sitting out here," he said, pointing to the Notre Dame sweatshirt he was wearing over his ankle-length brown robe. "Notre Dame beat Navy last Saturday, you know," he said excitedly. "I get all the games on a little shortwave radio. You must think it strange that a Trappist monk would still be such a football fanatic."

"No," I lied.

I began planning for the ten-day visit in December of my mother, father, brother Phil, and sister Karla. There was so much I wanted to show them. While I was planning, I received this letter from my father:

196

Dear Steve:

These last two days I've thought of you often. Thanks for your call last week—your mother and I both slept easier. There's just been so much on TV about the political situation and the violence in Chile. I'm calling the State Department regularly for updates, but we're still planning to come.

We have been blessed with some great vacations but we have never been as excited as we are now about our trip to Chile. Karla and Phil being there is really a bonus. We are attempting to learn some Spanish. Don't be too disappointed with me if I rely on a lot of smiling and hand signals to get by. We would like to bring each of the kids a small gift. Please send a list with names, ages and any suggestions you might have.

Questions: Do we need any special vaccinations? Should we advise the American Embassy in Chile of our arrival? Do Phil and I need coat and tie if we want to take Olga to a nice restaurant? Any advice you can give us will be appreciated.

Peace. Dad

The political situation in Chile continued to deteriorate: the government declared a state of siege, the most serious of the four possible states of emergency and the one permitting the government to detain people arbitrarily for weeks at a time. Local community organizers were rounded up and jailed. Stories circulated of mass arrests and detentions in the National Soccer Stadium, a haunting reminder of the brutal 1973 coup, because then the National Stadium had housed thousands of prisoners in the first days after the coup. At the time, torture centers were set up in the locker rooms, and many did not survive the ordeal.

In late November 1984, the few opposition newspapers and magazines that had emerged were shut down, their editors jailed. A friend gave me articles from the *New York Times* and *Time* magazine so I could learn what was happening in Santiago. It seemed absurd to have to read from pages printed on a different continent about what was happening in my backyard.

There was a saying in Chile: "Let the weeds grow long so you can pull them out by the roots." Many people believed the government had done just that—consciously allowed a small amount of political openness so that community and political leaders would emerge and be more visible before this latest government crackdown, when they were pulled out by the roots.

The government had sent soldiers from the north and south to Santiago because it feared the soldiers in Santiago might sympathize with "the enemy." The enemy, I guessed, were the people in my neighborhood and others like them.

The minister of the interior, Sergio Onofre Jarpa, explained the rationale for the restrictions under the new state of siege in the morning newspaper:

> The government, in the name of his Excellency, General Augusto Pinochet, with the strongest of intentions, removing obstacles in the path of restoring a true democracy and a refusal to fall under a totalitarian dictatorship through the present subversion and terrorism hereby decrees the following. The suspension of the following magazines: *Cauce, Análisis, Fortín Mapocho, La Bicicleta* . . .

> If there are restrictions of information, it is precisely to avoid the spreading of rumors and lies. Only in this sense are there restrictions.

> Prohibited: any act whatever its origin, direct or indirect, that can possibly cause alarm, alter the tranquility of the citizens or the normal development of national activities.

> Prohibited: any acts defined as terrorist, as defined in law #18.314, such as . . . [too numerous to list]. Also, all meetings must have previous authorization of the respective government body.

I once thought such language appeared only in novels by George Orwell. There was only one institution in the country that had the political clout to question the current government's policies: the Catholic Church. The great majority of Chileans were Catholic, and General Pinochet considered himself a practicing Catholic and was said to take communion daily.

On a Sunday in early November, at every mass in every Catholic church in Santiago, a letter by the new archbishop of Santiago, Juan Francisco Fresno, was read. Until that time, Fresno had been reticent to speak publicly on such issues as human rights.

"I beg you, with patience, to hear these words that, before God, I believe it is my duty to pronounce," the letter began. "My obligation as Pastor is to be sincere in my convictions, but at the same time, to be prudent. Some people, all the same, have considered this prudence a weakness. My dear children, do not fool yourselves—I want to be prudent, but I will not be a coward."

In the letter, Fresno detailed the growing tensions that had arisen between the Church and government in the past weeks. The minister of the interior had accused the Church of making pacts with political parties. The government had refused to allow the vicar of Santiago, who had been traveling in Spain, to return to Chile. Within the normal execution of the laws of Chile, Fresno argued in the letter, the government had sufficient means to fight terrorists. The current state of siege was unnecessary. It was a great step backward in a journey toward peace.

"Therefore, I call upon every Chilean first to pray to God to help us discover the truth and to act on that. I also call for a national day of prayer and fasting on November 23, not as a political gesture, but one done in the biblical tradition of a hidden fast as an offering to God. Finally, respectfully yet firmly, the Church asks that the government take steps to restore personal liberty and respect the rights of each individual to help restore the peace that we all so desire."

This damp, gray November afternoon in Santiago reminded me of many damp, gray November afternoons in northern Indiana. In Indiana, November was autumn, and here it was spring. But this spring day in Chile was unusually cold and left me with scant hope. I had no expectation the state of siege would be lifted before my family arrived.

"What do you think your parents will say about the tank parked on the corner?" Olga asked.

"Hey, no problem, they see tanks all the time in my neighborhood in Indiana. My mom gets a kick out of driving them," I joked nervously.

On the eve of my family's visit to this long, beautiful country on the Pacific that I had raved about, helicopters flew low overhead, distant bombs exploded in the night, and the electricity was dead. There was a 10 p.m. curfew, and anyone caught on the streets without authorization to be there was taken to jail.

I wondered what my family would see of the Chile I had so grown to love. Would they be able to see beyond the tank sitting on the corner of Tupungato Street?

THIRTY-ONE

THE VISIT OF THE GRINGOS

$\mathcal{O}$lga, six children, and I waited at the Santiago International Airport for the overnight flight from Miami. Since we could not fit all the kids in the borrowed van, we had held a lottery to determine which of the kids could come to the airport on the illustrious occasion of the arrival of my mother, father, twenty-three-year-old brother Phil, and twenty-two-year-old sister Karla.

We stood behind the glass partition in the airport lobby with the six lottery winners, watching people emerge from immigration. The plane was late. Nevertheless, Verónica and Sonia held up a banner made from an old white sheet that read "Bienvenidos! Welcome! Tío Jim, Tía Jean, Tío Phil, and Tía Karla" for anyone who wanted to read it. Keli impatiently held two bouquets of daisies wrapped in newspaper.

Andrés asked questions: "Can airplanes fly when there are no clouds?"

"Sure," I answered.

"Then what holds them up?"

"Tío," Keli said, "Héctor just wet his pants." I glared at Héctor. He smiled back. Just then, I spotted my family. "There they are," I yelled excitedly. They weaved their way through the crowd, all four carrying their winter coats on this sunny morning. There were hugs.

Keli stepped forward and gave my mother and Karla each a bouquet of wilted daisies.

"Tía Jean," she formally said to my mother in Spanish, "somos los niños del Hogar Domingo Savio—we are the children of the Hogar Domingo Savio," and, as if speaking to the queen of England, Keli gave a little curtsy.

My mom hugged Keli. "Aren't you wonderful, aren't you all just wonderful . . ." she said, her eyes misty. The kids didn't understand the words, but they did understand the emotion.

"Now, you must be Keli," she began. "And you must be Verónica, and you must be Andrés, and you must be Sonia, and you must be Carlos, and you must be Héctor." She correctly named each of the six, having learned their names from their pictures.

"Hello, I am Olga Díaz," Olga said clearly in English, eager to be included.

"Really, really good to be here," my father said before giving Olga a big hug. "Mucho gusto—I'm very pleased to meet you," he concluded.

"Not bad. Huh?" he whispered to me in English.

The twelve of us squeezed into the van and made the trip to the orphanage. The kids never stopped talking, explaining things, and asking questions, as if they'd known my family all their lives, all in Spanish. No one in my family could understand any of it. I wondered about the wisdom of having invited my family to spend an entire week at the hogar.

"Héctor always wets his pants because he's too lazy to go the bathroom and pull down his shorts," Keli told my sister. "Tía, your hair is so blonde," Keli continued. "It's so beautiful." I translated to Karla what Keli had said.

"It's not the real color, you know," Carlos added. I decided not to translate everything.

"They grow corn here on large fields," Sonia said, pointing to the newly plowed fields.

"Do you have a television?" Héctor asked my father.

"Do you have police in the United States like we do here?" Carlos asked. "They're called *pacos*."

"That is the church we go to. It's called Santa Rosa," Verónica said. I tried to keep up with a rapid-fire translation.

Four-year-old Andrés pulled on my mom's arm, pointing to something outside the window.

"That man is drunk," Andrés said.

"What is he saying?" my mom asked me.

"He says he's really happy to meet you," I said.

My mother, still misty-eyed, said, "He's sweet. Tell him I'm really happy to meet him too."

When we arrived at the house, Eliana had prepared a typical Chilean lunch: empanadas with real beef, tomato and avocado salad, fresh green beans, and Undurraga white wine. The kids were on their best behavior at lunch.

"Dis is a pencil," Yoana said, repeating to each member of my family at lunch the only thing she had learned after two years in English class.

"Más ensalada, Tía?" Verónica asked my mother, dishing more salad onto her plate.

"Más vino, Tío?" Sonia asked my father, pouring my father more wine.

"This is amazing. There are twenty some people around this table and it runs like clockwork. Are these kids always this well behaved?" my father asked me.

"We told the kids," I said in English, "that they would have to go back to the salt mines where they would get only bread and water if they didn't behave themselves."

"Tío, what did you say?" Verónica asked me.

"My father thinks you're wonderful and I do too," I responded. Verónica beamed. I was glad to some extent, I guess, that both my efforts to teach the kids English and my father's efforts to learn Spanish had not been spectacularly successful.

By midnight, I was so exhausted from translating that I could not keep my eyes open.

"I'm going to bed," I said first in English, then in Spanish. I imagined, given that the translator was retiring, the party would end. No one moved.

"Good night," my family said.

"Buenas noches," Olga said. They continued drinking wine and, with only a few words in common and lots of gesturing, communicated.

The next morning, fourteen-year-old Sebastián told me in Spanish, "Your brother is teaching me English."

"What did he teach you?" I asked.

With rough pronunciation, Sebastián stammered in English, "I am party animal."

"Good, Phil," I said to my brother. "Thanks."

For my family, everything was new: the country, the language, and the customs. Now I was seeing them again with new eyes.

"What I can't get over is how clean everybody is," my father said. "There's a woman across the street. She lives in that house with a dirt floor and no running water. But in the morning she goes to work in a spotless white dress, looking like she just stepped out of the beauty parlor."

Phil couldn't get over how much energy the kids had.

"These kids are crazy," said my two-hundred-pound former football player brother, just as Héctor and Juanito tried to tackle him from behind.

My mother recognized the subtle differences (or maybe not so subtle) in my relationships with the kids. "You really care a lot about Andrés, don't you?" and "It's really hard for you to deal with Carlos, isn't it?"

I was amazed at how well my family communicated with everyone in Santiago. In fact, it was disconcerting how much better they seemed to be managing than I did when I first arrived. The difference: I had been so insistent on learning the right word in Spanish that it often got in the way of communication. My family was just interested in communicating however they could.

One of the few opportunities my family had to speak in English with someone other than me occurred late one afternoon when we visited Liz and the four other American Holy Cross Associate volunteers who lived in Peñalolén. It took about forty minutes on bus to travel from La Granja, one of the poor municipalities south of Santiago, to Peñalolén, an equally poor municipality to the east. Although the socioeconomic levels were rather similar, La Granja was very flat, whereas the modest wooden homes in Peñalolén clung, at times precariously, to the sides of the foothills in the Andes. The Holy Cross Associates lived up a steep hill in an unpainted wooden house with a dirt yard.

My family enjoyed hearing their experiences, and the time passed quickly over a simple dinner of chicken, rice, and a salad. Many of the associates had had experiences similar to mine, working in schools, orphanages, and with community groups. The exception was that they had all lived together in a community.

For all my complaints about living at the hogar, especially about my lack of privacy and the demands on my time, I was grateful I wasn't living in "community" with five gringos and their running debates about what solidarity with the poor really meant. There was an ongoing division I had listened to many times over the past year about whether or not to use the hot water heater they had in their bathroom. One camp argued that it should not be used, in solidarity with the poor; the other argued that regular illnesses were caused by bathing in frigid water in the winter and that it was ridiculous not to use it given that it was already there. They could not reach a consensus, and so the debate continued. In the hogar the decision was easier. If there was money for gas, we had hot showers; if we didn't, no hot showers. Showers were always short.

Blas was also there, and my parents got to meet my future traveling partner to the United States. "I have to say," my mother said to Blas, "I am kind of glad your plans for the bike trip didn't work out."

Liz pulled me aside about 8:30 p.m. "Sometimes at night it is hard to get buses up here, and with the 10 p.m. curfew, you might want to start heading back," she suggested.

My family was enjoying the opportunity to talk in English so much that by the time they all said goodbyes to their new friends and we were walking to the bus it was after 9 p.m.

Except for a few private cars, there was not a vehicle in sight. We began to walk down Peñalolén's central street.

"This isn't going to be a problem getting a bus, is it?" my mother asked.

"No, I'm sure one will come along," I said with a slightly sick feeling in my stomach.

By 9:15 p.m. it was completely dark.

"Do you think we should call a taxi?" my father asked me.

I had never called a taxi in all my time in Chile, didn't have a number, didn't know where a phone was, and was pretty confident that no taxi driver would mosey on over to the shantytown of Peñalolén a little before the 10 p.m. curfew.

"I'm sure a bus will come along shortly," I said.

No one mentioned the 10 p.m. curfew, although I'm sure there was nothing else on anyone's mind. At about 9:25 p.m., a blue-and-white bus came tearing down the hill. I was terrified it was going to pass us by, so much so that I stepped out into the road to wave it down.

The driver stopped, cursing *garabatos* under his breath and telling us to hurry up and get on. There were only two other passengers. The bus roared down an abandoned Américo Vespucio Avenue, going around the Grecia Rotary so fast that for a few seconds it seemed it was only on two wheels.

Soldiers and military vehicles were now almost the only things we saw on the road. At about ten minutes to ten, three blocks from Tupungato Street, I pulled on the bell, and the driver let us off. He was already pulling away before Karla had stepped off the last step of the bus.

Back at the hogar, closing the door behind us, just a couple of minutes before ten, my mother, the eternal optimist, said, "That was such a nice evening getting to know your friends."

We got a chance to practice more nonverbal communication when my family and four of the kids took a day-trip to visit Sonia and Alfredo's mother in Santa Mónica, about an hour and a half south of Santiago by car. Santa Mónica was a farming community with beautiful rolling hills.

Sonia's and Alfredo's mother, Olivia, lived in a one-room shack with a dirt floor with her two youngest children. There was no electricity. Near Olivia's shack, we ate a picnic lunch under a eucalyptus tree and then hiked in the woods. Alfredo was our guide as we traced our way along the banks of a stream, over rock fences, and through a huge eucalyptus forest. The sun beat down through the long, narrow leaves of the eucalyptus trees.

"I'm not feeling very well," Karla said. "I'm probably just overheated. Do you think I could go back to the house and rest a little?"

"I'll walk back with you," I told her.

"That's fine. I can find my way back by myself."

"Carlos can go back with you just to be sure," I suggested.

Carlos agreed, and the two departed. About an hour later, we returned from the hike.

Karla was sitting in front of the shack soaking wet.

"What happened to you?"

"I guess I had a slight misunderstanding with Carlos," she said charitably. "Carlos and I came back here together, and everything was fine. I lay down on the bed inside and rested. When I got up, the door was locked from the outside. I could see Carlos through the window. I told him to open the door. He pretended he didn't understand me, but it was pretty clear I wanted out. Finally, I got fed up and opened the window. As I was climbing out, um, he threw a bucket of water on me."

"Carlos," I said tersely, "I would like to have a little talk with you when we get back to the hogar."

Later that afternoon, back at the hogar, Karla observed, "I haven't seen my friend Carlos since we got back."

"Carlos decided he wanted to clean out the storage bin behind the house," I told her. "He may decide he wants to do other chores. Let's go and see how he's doing."

Carlos was dragging a wooden box from one side of the shed to the other. His eyes were bloodshot from crying.

"I was just playing," Carlos told Karla. "It was a joke, but not a smart one."

I translated literally what he said and then added, "I think that's his way of saying I'm sorry. Isn't that right, Carlos?"

Carlos paused and glanced around the shed. I was confident he was mentally calculating the remaining work available if he wasn't sufficiently repentant.

"Sí, Tía Karla," he said. "Lo siento mucho, mucho—I'm really, really sorry."

My parents had brought dozens of photos, many ten or fifteen years old. There were pictures of the five Reifenberg kids, of school plays, and of family vacations. There was also a truly terrible picture of me in second grade, a close-up photo that showed off my bucktoothed smile. At least by the time they had taken the picture most of my hair had grown back.

"You're afraid to cut your hair," my older brother Mike, who was in third grade, had taunted me one day after school.

"That's dumb, I'm not going to cut my hair," I told him.

"Cause you're scared," he said. "Look," and he took a pair of scissors and cut a few hairs off his head.

"You're a scare-dee-cat," he called out.

"No, I'm not."

"You're a woosey," he chanted. That was the worst name you could call anyone.

"I am not a woosey," I told him defiantly and took the scissors and cut out big handfuls of hair, proving definitively that I was a tough guy. I continued cutting for so long that even Mike got nervous.

When my mother saw my barbering job, she looked as if she was going to cry.

"Steve, how could you have done that? What will your father say when he comes home?"

My father didn't get home until late that evening. I lay awake in bed thinking about a missionary who had come to St. Patrick's grade school and made a collection for poor, starving children in India. I thought I'd be happy to trade places with any one of those kids right now.

When my father got home, I was called out of bed, and I stood in front of him in my blue-and-white-striped flannel pajamas. He told me to turn around. He didn't say anything for a minute. Then he threw back his head and laughed.

"Don't worry about it, Steve-o-rino, just don't do it again. And don't do everything your brother tells you."

The next morning at St. Patrick's grade school did not go so smoothly. My second grade teacher, Mrs. Handley, had me stand up in front of my classmates. She then had to wait for the giggles to die down.

"Steve," she said, speaking very slowly, "please explain to the class why you did such a stupid thing."

It was strange how one picture instantly could bring that all back.

"Who is that?" Sonia asked laughingly, holding my second grade picture.

My mother pointed to me. Sonia fell off her chair, and before I could grab the picture away from her she was out the door. Almost immediately, I could hear the howls of laughter from the next room.

Dad passed around a series of pictures of our house, including one of him shoveling snow from the driveway.

"Wow, they live just like the Eskimos," Carlos said.

"Why don't you have a fence in front of your house?" Marisol asked. Almost all houses in Santiago had a fence around them. "Aren't you afraid someone will rob you?"

"Look at the beautiful carpeting!" Verónica exclaimed.

"Are you rich?" Keli asked my father bluntly. I translated her question.

"Tell her," my father said, "that I've never been richer in all my life than right now in Chile."

After a week in Santiago, we fled the craziness of the hogar, all five Reifenbergs cramming into the little white Suzuki car, and drove to the Pacific coast. We followed our progress on a map, first on paved highways and then on dusty roads through a string of coastal cities, until we came to the town of Cachagua. A teacher from St. George's had lent us her family's beach house. From the wooden porch that protruded over a hill, we could see fields of wildflowers, pine trees, and, in the distance, the wide, deserted beaches of the Pacific.

The first morning in Cachagua, I got up early, as the sun broke through the mist. The ocean roared continuously in the distance. I sat in one of the chairs on the porch, which was still damp with the morning dew. In all the hustle of organizing, translating, and worrying about everything running smoothly during my family's visit, I had avoided focusing on the reality that in only a few weeks I would be leaving Chile. On a Friday morning in Cachagua, the sun just warming up the deck and drying the dew, I asked myself with just a little hesitation and a lot of uncertainty: It it really true I'll be leaving Chile in only a few weeks?

Back at the orphanage, my father, having heard so many stories about the four-year-old terror Andrés, had taken a special interest in him. The day my family arrived, my father had pulled out of his suitcase small gifts for each of the kids. They ripped through the wrapping paper like a plague of locusts, leaving only shreds of paper in their wake.

Later, my father approached Andrés.

"Hey, Andrés, buddy," my father said. "Do you like the car?" holding a red Matchbox car in his open palm. Andrés eyed my father suspiciously, grabbed the car, and after that moment did not let my father get near him. All my father's attempts to win him over were to no avail.

On his final afternoon in Santiago, my father confided, "It's been a great trip, and I only have one disappointment—I never really got to know Andrés."

Later that afternoon, my father was sitting on a squat concrete post in the front yard, drinking a cup of coffee and watching the younger children play. Without saying a word, Andrés walked near to where my father was sitting. When he got no reaction, he moved nearer and even nudged my father a little. Still no reaction. Dad did not look down but just sat on the slab and drank his coffee. Andrés got closer, then leaned gently against the inside of my dad's leg. My dad did not say anything. Andrés stayed there five, maybe ten minutes, leaning against my father. My mother snapped a photograph of them. In the picture, Andrés is wearing his red cotton shorts and light blue T-shirt. He rests easily against the inside of my dad's left leg. Dad looks off in the distance.

"How are you doing, Andrés?" my Dad finally said, and with that, Andrés drew away and was gone.

Andrés stood apart from everyone else as the children gave my parents, Karla, and Phil goodbye hugs and kisses. After we secured the luggage on top of the Suzuki with bungee cords, my family again wedged into the car, and we drove across town to the airport. It seemed

I had just picked them up. At international customs we said goodbye, my mother with tears in her eyes.

"It was the best vacation I ever had in my life," my father said. Maybe a little like Andrés, I didn't say anything.

"I learned a lot about Chile and about my son," he said. "I'm very proud of you," he added, and he gave me a hug.

I didn't say anything but just hugged him back.

THIRTY-TWO

SEARCHING FOR SOMETHING

Seeing my family off at the airport felt like a dress rehearsal for my own departure in two weeks. Although I knew I was going back to the States, I had no job lined up and no certainty about anything in my future. I wondered how and when I would ever get back to this country at the end of the world.

I did remember thinking quite consciously when I arrived at the hogar two years earlier that I wanted to have fewer grand illusions about coming to Chile than I'd had when I began teaching high school in Colorado. I wasn't going to let myself experience another tremendous letdown like the one I'd had while teaching in Colorado. I would be tough and objective and hope for something good, but not too good, and certainly not be too unrealistic. I would plant my feet firmly on the ground, work hard to learn the new language, and grow tough by learning to deal with difficult situations. I imagined that life in Chile was not going to be suddenly wonderful, though it might be interesting, and I certainly hoped there would be adventure. There might even be some magic, but I would never again be the innocent child who hoped for too much, who was too idealistic, who was too naive. I told myself those things over and over on the way down to Chile until I believed them as inevitable truths, like two plus two is four.

But I came to Chile, to Santiago, to the orphanage, and my objectivity, so stern and rational, had disappeared. Time after time people invited me into their homes and their families and gave me the best of what they had, generously, openly, with few expectations of return. Children threw their arms around my neck and needed me to tie their shoestrings or lift them up until they could touch the roof with their fingertips. There was that sense of belonging, an immediacy and urgency, the joy of a child on the first day of summer vacation when life was full of endless possibilities. I was needed and welcomed and taken in, and, yes, it was recaptured, that sense of belonging, but in a different, more complex way, with all the hardships of living with and loving so many people so intensely under one small roof. Sometimes the hardships seemed trivial. Other times they seemed more serious, until I felt I was going to lose myself in the whirlwind of people, demands, noise, and lack of privacy. The tension was made much more difficult because the pervasiveness of the brutality and oppression in this country affected everyone and everything.

Lucho arrived late one night at the hogar, after everyone had gone to bed. He rang the bell. I went to unlock the front gate.

"Apúrate," he said, as I fumbled, half asleep, with the keys. "Hurry."

"I need to talk with your friend, that lady from Australia," he told me once we were inside. Lucho had met Judy Betts from the Australian embassy on one of her visits to the hogar, and he knew that his sister Marisol had stayed at Judy's apartment on an outing with the other girls. From Judy, he had learned about the Australian government's humanitarian aid and refugee program.

Lighting another cigarette, he told me that his closest friend from the FPMR had been killed and that the CNI had almost caught him.

"I know they are going to torture and kill me," he said flatly. "I know it. I'm sure. I need to leave Chile."

My trip was suddenly not the only international journey on the horizon. The next day Judy came to the hogar and talked with Lucho and Marisol. The day after that she came back with two suitcases. Judy had made all the arrangements for the two of them to go to Australia as political refugees. Between them, Marisol and Lucho didn't have many things, and they could have easily put all their things in one suitcase. It was strange to think of Lucho, in particular, going to the land of the gringos.

Neither Lucho nor Marisol had ever been on an airplane before.

"Tío, what's Australia like?" Marisol asked me the evening before they were to leave.

"I understand it is a fantastic country and people are really friendly."

"Tío, have you ever been to Australia?"

"No," I told her. I wished that I had been there and could reassure her that I knew the place firsthand.

"Do you think they'll laugh at me because I look funny?"

"No, mi amor, my love, they will think you are the prettiest *colorina* in Australia. There are a lot more girls with red hair there than here in Chile."

"Do some people in Australia speak Spanish?"

"I think a few people probably will, but most people speak English," I said.

"That's what I thought. That only a few people in Australia speak Spanish, and they will probably speak it funny like you and Tía Judy."

"There are some Chilean families there, too," I said.

"My brother always talks about the Chilean exiles, *los exilios*. He says the dictatorship forced them to leave Chile, and they can't come back. But they don't sound very happy living in other countries. The good thing, though, Lucho says, is that when the dictatorship is overthrown all *los exilios* will come back, and they will all have a good home."

The good-byes were hurried. Marisol's eyes were red, but she didn't cry. Lucho looked on anxiously. A car was waiting. In her suitcase Marisol carried a small plastic bag with dirt from the backyard of the hogar.

"Spread the dirt on the ground when you get to your new house in Australia," Olga had told her. "Something beautiful will grow there, and you will never feel far from Chile."

Marisol, Lucho, and Judy got in the black embassy car with a driver, and the three of them left. Judy didn't want any of us to go, as she didn't want to draw any attention at the airport.

Later that evening, on the back patio, Olga pointed to a jet flying across the darkening sky. "Do you think that's their plane?" she asked.

My last days were a whirlwind of shopping, helping direct the kids' Christmas play, housecleaning, driving to doctors' appointments, and end-of-year meetings at school. I did copy one entry into my journal, part of a poem by T. S. Eliot, "The Journey of the Magi":

All this was a long time ago, I remember,
And I would do it again, but set down
This set down
This: were we led all that way for
Birth or Death? There was a Birth, certainly,
We had evidence and no doubt. I had seen birth
and death,
But had thought they were different; this Birth was
Hard and bitter agony for us, like Death, our death.
We returned to our places, these Kingdoms,
But no longer at ease here, in the old dispensation,
With an alien people clutching their gods.
I should be glad of another death.

My family's departure—and now Marisol's—had left me strangely nostalgic for something, but I was not sure what.

I remembered arriving at the hogar for the first time that November afternoon. The spring day was sunny and magnificent. I was full of energy and curiosity and moved by the littlest things: that Chileans give a kiss on the right cheek as a greeting; that a man on a three-wheel bicycle with a brightly painted wooden cart rode through the neighborhood in the early morning and the late afternoon selling still-warm loaves of bread; that the wale on corduroy pants ran across instead of up and down. All details at the time that seemed so important.

However, there was now a longing and a connection to something that was not Chile, a connection back to a land that held my history. Over the past two years, for all my frustrations, it had been rare that I'd been homesick or felt ready to leave Santiago. But now, with my visa about to expire, there was something exciting about the idea of traveling around South America with Blas, not on bikes, but on buses and boats, up the Atlantic coast through Argentina, Uruguay, Paraguay, and Brazil, drawing me northward, to what I was not sure.

The last days also connected with a sense of melancholy, the sad realization that many of my dreams in Chile had sputtered or failed: the vision of a self-sustaining family farm (an idea that had left a dead goat, a dead horse, and lots of dead chickens in its wake), my illness, my continuing struggle with Spanish even after two years of full immersion, my grand plans for a bike trip back to the States (now just a mangled and rusting bike frame), my onetime vocation as a doctor (now history), and more generally an enormous uncertainty about how, in some way, I might one day, somehow, make a contribution somewhere.

In retrospect, although I'd tried on lots of fronts, all my contribution paled in the face of so much poverty, repression, violence, and need.

My concrete accomplishments were strikingly modest. I had helped Yoana, Alfredo, and Miguel learn to read from their first-grade reader. Sebastián, who was now a teenager, knew he had a tío who cared about him. Olga felt supported, at least at times, and I had helped raise some money for the hogar. And maybe, if I stretched it, I could imagine that a few people in the United States were paying a little more attention to what was going on in Chile because I had written them letters or talked with them about this long, skinny country at the end of the world.

But neither the world nor my neighborhood had dramatically changed by my coming to Chile. What had changed the most was me. I had learned some things: that the world was a lot more complicated than I ever thought; that U.S. political decisions had reverberations in dramatic ways all over the world; that children were often incredibly resilient; and that interventions, especially when carried out with compassion and love, could make a difference. Finally, I learned to believe in the idea that maybe it was not a bad thing to have big dreams, even if sometimes they fell short.

〜

THIRTY-THREE

TAKING LEAVE

〜

I wanted all my good-byes to be well said and memorable, the hugs tender, and the leavings gentle. I wanted to spend time with each of the kids individually before I left. And on that last day at the hogar, I planned to get up early, while all the children were still in bed, kiss each one on the cheek and be out the front door into the quiet dirt street, as I had done on so many mornings for the last two years when I headed off early to St. George's or the university. Maybe I would linger just a little longer in the bedroom doorway, watching the sunlight fall on Keli as she slept under her red bedspread, or Alfredo tied up in a knot in his sheets, or Andrés spread-eagled on top of his bare mattress, the sheets, blanket, and pillow all dumped on the floor. I'd smile in the doorway and then be gone.

But nothing in those last days went as planned. The days before Christmas were brutally hot, and on Christmas Eve I started to feel sick with a headache and a fever. I went to bed early, while everyone else, in Chilean tradition, danced to that tinny *cumbia* music until three in the morning.

The next morning I lay in bed with a 103-degree fever, convinced I had paratyphoid revisited or hepatitis or some other rare and crippling South American virus. My waking moments were spent rereading *Where There Is No Doctor*.

Olga produced a different diagnosis: "You're just exhausted—it's a case of the nerves."

I wanted to scream at her, "A case of nerves? I have a 103 fever and you think it's all in my head?"

I did not say anything, though, just put my pillow over my head to drown out the tinny Christmas music on the radio and the screams of the children fighting.

Dr. Jorge Vivanco arbitrated, and it turned out neither Olga nor I was right. I had a seventy-two-hour bug that was going around. Nothing serious but bad enough to ruin all my carefully orchestrated plans for those final days. Since my visa was about to expire, there was no way I could stay and make up for missed time. Blas and I planned to cross the Andes on the twenty-seventh into Argentina with someone who had offered us a ride and then head north.

I told Olga of my plan to leave early on the morning of the twenty-seventh, while the children were still in bed.

"That's not fair to them, and it's not fair to you," she said. "At least stay through breakfast and say good-bye to everyone decently, and then you'll get a ride into town so you can meet up with Blas." I agreed.

On December 27, I woke up with the first morning light creeping through the thin curtains. I was more nervous than I could remember being in years, simultaneously wanting the morning to be over as quickly as possible and hoping for it to never end.

Sebastián was still sleeping in the bed next to mine. My mind flooded with details of the kids: how Sebastián threw back his head and laughed with his mouth wide open, his whole body shaking; how Sonia got her head soaking wet before she pulled her curls back tight with little brown combs; how Alfredo got so nervous his hands shook when he wanted to explain something important; and how Andrés did a somersault—a running, leaping, flying roll, ducking his head, his knees spread wide—on the mattress in the backyard. I knew how each of these kids brushed their teeth and washed their faces and how they caught a ball. I didn't know why, but all those details took on a powerful significance as I packed to leave. Maybe those were the only things I'd be able to hold on to once I'd gone.

I walked into the main house. Keli was awake in her bottom bunk. Her eyes were wide open, and she was sucking her thumb. I walked over to her bed, and she took her thumb out of her mouth. I bent down to give her a kiss and just as my face neared hers she threw her sheet over her head and whispered emphatically, "Don't kiss me!"

I sat down on the bed and slowly her sheet came down. First, Keli's dark hair showed against the pillow, then a brown eye peered out from under her sheet. As soon as she saw me bending toward her again, she pulled the sheet tightly over her head, creating what she believed was an impenetrable shield against a kiss on her cheek. I moved to the other end of the bed, pulled her foot from under the covers and kissed the white padded sole of her fuzzy red pajamas. As I was leaving, the sheet came down from over her head.

"That doesn't count as a kiss," she admonished me.

I gave her a kiss on the cheek.

Olga was already up, and we smiled as we passed each other in the hall, but we didn't say anything. She woke up the children who were still sleeping while I put on the two pots of water to boil for the powdered milk. The house was quickly filled with noise: water running in the bathroom; voices; the radio; bare feet slapping on the concrete patio.

"Get your shoes on!" I yelled from the kitchen.

I gave Sebastián one hundred pesos to buy two kilos of fresh bread at the bakery down the street. Olga got all the kids to the breakfast table. I counted fifteen heads, hair still wet and freshly combed. Breakfast ran as usual, but somehow the familiar routine seemed poignant.

"Tío, Héctor keeps pulling on my pillow," Keli said.

"Keli, will you please say grace," I asked.

"Dear Lord, bless this food that we are about to eat," Keli said, making sure everyone was watching, "bless the poor and the hungry and those that don't have this cup of milk to drink. Amen."

Keli was sitting on a pillow, which made her taller than Héctor, who was sitting next to her. As soon as Héctor figured this out, he climbed down from his seat and came back with two pillows.

Breakfast conversation centered on the proposed trip to El Quisco beach in January.

"It's really great," Carlos told Sonia Chica and Rosa, who had never seen the ocean. "You can play soccer on the beach and find snakes on the side of the road."

"Do you remember," Carlos asked the table at large, "when Tío Esteve told us he didn't want anyone climbing up on the three-story bunk bed in the beach house?

"I'll sleep there," Carlos said in Spanish, imitating my gringo accent, "because I don't want any of you kids falling off."

"Then, on the first night there, when everyone was asleep and quiet, there was this giant crash!" Carlos exclaimed as he brought his fist down on the table for dramatic effect. Rosa jumped in her seat. "Then, there, lying on the floor is Tío Esteve in his sleeping bag!" Carlos was laughing so hard he was finding it difficult to finish.

"There, there on the floor, Tío Esteve says, 'Oh, I must have been dreaming. I thought someone called me on the telephone and I was getting up to go answer it.'"

The story had been told many times before, but everyone laughed at Carlos's rendition all the same. Breakfast ended and chores were assigned—who would wash the dishes, sweep in front of the house, do the bedrooms, clean the bathroom, and prepare the food for the dog.

I stuffed my brown duffle bag with clothes, my journal, and my tattered Neruda book still held together by a rubber band. The older children finished up their chores, and the younger ones played with dolls and marbles on the patio. I did not know what to do. Finally, I went from room to room. "Why don't you go into the living room," I said. All the kids assembled. The five youngest ones sat on the couch. Keli sat next to Héctor and tried to push him off the end. Héctor pulled her hair.

"Tío, Héctor won't stop bothering me," Keli cried. The other children sat on the floor and in the few remaining chairs. Sebastián stood apart, leaning against the doorway.

I started, twice in fact, to try to pronounce the words I wanted to say.

"Tío, Keli keeps pushing me," Héctor whined, just before Keli did manage to push him off the end of the couch. He landed on the wooden floor with a thud and started crying. Finally, I did get out a few words. "I'm going to leave now, but even though I won't always be here physically, you will always, always be here in . . ." I wanted to say "heart", but the word wouldn't come. I only pointed at my chest.

I stared at the floor as I talked, and when I looked up Carlos had tears streaming down his cheeks.

"Always," I repeated belatedly. Marcelo was crying hard with an angry look on his face. I hugged him, then Alfredo, who had also begun to cry. I went around the room bending down to hug each one. Keli pulled up her knees and pretended that she didn't want me to kiss her and looked annoyed when I didn't play the usual game. I just kissed her on the forehead. Andrés stood rigid. I hugged him but he didn't move.

All the kids were crying; Verónica, whose eyes were red and puffy, and Sonia, who thought she was too old to cry, cried with me. I hugged each one of them. I came to Sebastián last. He was now sitting on the floor, and like Keli had his knees pulled up and his head buried under his arms, only he was not kidding. All I could do was put my arms around his upper body, his arms and shoulders, and hug him.

The words did come between the tears. "You're the oldest here and they are really going to depend on you . . . I am going to miss you so much."

I left the room and went to the back of the house to get my things. I took a couple of deep breaths. The sun was already high over the mountains, and I stood there looking at the clear Andean sky for a few minutes before I picked up my duffle bag to leave.

EPILOGUE

Much has changed in Chile since I first arrived at the hogar more than twenty-five years ago. The most dramatic change was the peaceful transition from military rule to an elected civilian government. On December 14, 1989, Chileans went to the polls to elect a president for the first time in nearly two decades. The following day, I sat in my rusting Dodge Colt on a frigid December morning in a parking lot in Cambridge, Massachusetts, mesmerized as I listened on National Public Radio to a story about the election results. A Christian Democrat, Patricio Aylwin, had won and, incredibly, General Pinochet had accepted the results and agreed to step down. The reporter interviewed a woman from a *población* who said, "At this moment, all I feel is pride that we, Chileans together, have done something good."

More than a decade and a half after the return of democracy, Chile is often held up as a model of economic development and prosperity. Among its neighbors in South America, Chile has the highest sustained level of economic growth and some of the safest cities in the region. Chile was the first South American country to sign a free trade agreement with the United States, with the European Union, and with various Asian nations. Since the return of democracy, Chile's media have also opened up, with the widest variety imaginable of publications, both serious and irreverent, competing for readership.

With the wide publication of information about human rights abuses under the military government, including the 2004 Valech Report documenting approximately thirty thousand cases of torture against Chilean citizens, few today deny that these crimes took place. Revelations of General Pinochet's multimillion-dollar bank accounts have further undermined the belief, even among some of his most hard-line supporters, that the general had been honest.

A significant number of Chilean families have found additional information about loved ones who had "disappeared." In some cases, this led to the exhumation of mass graves and individual reburials. Unfortunately, for all her years of desperate searching, Inelia never found her son Héctor or uncovered any information about why he was taken. His name, like some thousands of others who died in those terrible years, is carved on a white marble wall at the General Cemetery in downtown Santiago. Inelia died in 2006.

Many people saw 2006 as a watershed year for Chile. Early in the year, on January 15, 2006, Chileans elected their first woman president, Michelle Bachelet, a socialist and the leader of the center-left coalition. Her story is a remarkable one.

She is the daughter of a high-profile air force general who supported the government of President Salvador Allende in the 1970s. After the military coup in 1973, her father was arrested and tortured, and he died while under detention. She and her mother were later arrested and tortured, before going into exile—first in Australia and then East Germany. Michelle Bachelet returned to Chile in 1987 to continue her medical studies and then work as a pediatrician, while also becoming active in resistance activities against the military government. With the return to democracy, she served not only as Chile's first woman minister of health, but also as its first woman minister of defense.

In the 2006 presidential campaign, she promised to continue policies that open Chile's markets to the world, while increasing social initiatives to reduce the country's gap between rich and poor. In her acceptance speech Bachelet said, "Violence entered my life, destroying that which I loved. Because I was a victim of hatred, I dedicated my life to undo this hatred and convert it into understanding, into tolerance and, why not say it, into love. One can love justice and, at the same time, be generous." In the last days of 2006, as if closing a chapter in the country's history, General Augusto Pinochet died at the age of ninety-one from heart failure. While thousands of admirers attended his funeral, some opponents celebrated his death with champagne. Many more lamented that he had escaped justice for the violence that marked his seventeen years in power. He died on Sunday, December 10, International Human Rights Day.

Américo Vespucio Avenue, where I used to ride my bike past open fields and vineyards, is now a modern toll highway dotted with enormous malls and giant warehouse stores such as Home Center, the

Chilean version of Home Depot, and land values throughout Santiago have risen dramatically.

The Trappist monks sold the monastery's land near Santiago as they felt Santiago's urban sprawl encroaching too much on their solitude. Today, La Dehesa is one of the city's most exclusive residential areas with walled condominium communities and large modern houses featured in upscale design magazines. The monks used much of the earnings from the sale of the land to create a foundation for low-cost housing and resettled an hour's drive south of Santiago in a pristine valley set in the foothills of the Andes.

On many scores, Chile is the region's success story. At the same time, while many Chileans have moved out of poverty, the gap between rich and poor grows ever greater. Latin America has the most unequal distribution of wealth in the world, and within Latin America, Chile is one of the most unequal countries in the region. In some ways, in La Granja and in many other poor Chilean communities things are much the same as they were twenty-five years ago. A few blocks behind all the shiny developments on the speedy thoroughfares of Américo Vespucio, behind the giant Home Center, the back roads are still lined with the same wooden shacks and cinderblock houses. Even though Tupungato Street, where the hogar is located, is now paved, little else has changed. For those in Chile with opportunities, there are incredible opportunities. For those with few, there are pitiful few.

Olga Díaz's generosity continues to amaze me, along with her commitment to working with underprivileged children in Santiago. Her life's work is about creating opportunities where there are few. Domingo Savio still exists in the same house on Tupungato Street, although in the past few years there have been significant changes. Domingo Savio is no longer primarily a residential hogar but now is a children's community center, serving a much larger number of children from the neighborhood and integrating these programs with their families as much as possible. Kids from the neighborhood participate in a series of daily workshops after school—on theater, martial arts, dance, computers, and a course on *mi cuerpo,* "my body," as well as a program for *asistencia escolar* that tries to nail down basic reading, writing, and math skills that they should be getting in school but often aren't. Underpinning the programs are values that stress the importance of self-initiative, tolerance, and respect for others.

When I left Santiago in 1984, I wondered if I would ever see Chile or the children at the hogar again. Probably my biggest surprise is how connected my life has remained to Chile. For one reason or another, almost every year since 1984, I have found an excuse to return to Santiago. Part of the reason is that I have stayed so closely connected with Olga and the kids, serving on Domingo Savio's advisory board and continuing to organize an annual fund-raising campaign for the hogar. However, there were other reasons. In 1987, for example, during the summer between my first and second year in a master's program in public policy, I came back and worked as an intern at La Vicaría de la Solidaridad, the Catholic Church's human rights organization. From that experience, I came away even more impressed with the organization and its courageous underdogs.

On the personal front, life took unexpected turns. While Chris Cervenak and I overlapped for three of our four undergraduate years at the University of Notre Dame, we didn't meet there. In 1989, eight years after I graduated, I met her at a wedding in Geneva, Switzerland—she knew the bride, and I the groom. We realized that she knew many of my closest friends, and I many of hers. She recounts that it was during that wedding weekend, listening to my stories about the kids at the hogar, she became convinced that one day she would marry me. I'm not sure if that's true, but I am lucky that she did.

Since I graduated from Harvard's Kennedy School of Government in 1988, I've had the good fortune to work in a series of interesting jobs at Harvard related to international education and international negotiations. In 2001, toward the end of my six-year tenure as executive director at Harvard's David Rockefeller Center for Latin American Studies, I helped the university develop the idea of establishing a satellite office that would facilitate Harvard faculty and student projects in South America. The first office was to be located in Chile, and so when they needed an office director, I raised my hand.

In August 2002, Chris and I moved to Santiago with our three children, Natasha, Alexandra, and Luke, all under the age of eight. It felt like coming home.

St. George's College continues to produce thoughtful and engaged citizens, and we have enrolled our children there. As far as we can tell, among the nearly twenty-five hundred students in nursery through high school, ours are among a very few *gringos Georgianos*. The first Spanish word five-year-old Alexandra learned in kindergarten at St. George's was a long one: *solidaridad,* as she had arrived during Solidarity Week at school.

Since we moved to Santiago, my parents and siblings have visited Chile a number of times, and each time they reconnect with Olga and all their friends from the hogar. I too stay in regular contact with almost all of the "kids" from the hogar, although I shouldn't call them kids as they are all in their twenties and thirties.

Sonia and Alfredo, just as they had planned, worked hard, saved their money, and bought their mother a house and a car, and they have helped with their younger sisters' education as well. Rosa has been trying to make a career in preschool education, and her sister Sonia Chica worked as a maid in the house of a well-known Chilean actress. Sebastián is happily married and works for a fruit exporting company; Patricio is a lawyer and has two children, while his brother Carlos has had a much more difficult time and is searching for his path. Keli married a Peruvian man and has two children. Verónica is a dedicated single mother with two children who works for a travel agency, Santiago Adventures, that helps international visitors enjoy Chile. Upon finishing high school, Marcelo got a scholarship to go on an educational cruise to the Caribbean, where he worked for many years as a designer, and now travels back and forth to Santiago, speaking fluent English with a Caribbean accent. Marisol has thrived in Australia, where she is a teacher, while her older brother Lucho had real trouble adapting and learning English in Australia and has struggled there.

Héctor is married and has two children. I had the privilege to serve as the best man at his wedding shortly after I moved back to Santiago. Karen is a single mother, working in telephone sales and raising a son. Her brother Andrés lived a number of years on the street after he left the hogar at age sixteen and subsequently held a variety of jobs that included cleaning the houses of gypsies as well as a one-year stint as a messenger and assistant in the Harvard office in Santiago. During the time he was working with us, my office colleagues all agreed that life with Andrés would provide stories enough for another book.

I still don't have a very good answer to Sonia's question about my profession. When asked, most often I talk about what I like to do: managing programs, helping turn ideas into reality, creating opportunities for students to learn something new, and building bridges.

In addition to managing Harvard College's study abroad programs in Chile and the neighboring countries, I help place many Harvard students as interns at places like Domingo Savio and other community organizations, while more than a few Chilean Harvard graduates who had never been to a neighborhood like La Granja have found themselves in active roles as mentors to kids who live there.

I am convinced people are often searching for a way to contribute and sometimes don't see a viable path to get there. I feel fortunate that part of my job is helping create those opportunities.

Many of the incredibly talented Harvard students with whom I work have made all the *right* decisions and done all the *right* things to get to where they are. However, studying or working in an unfamiliar environment and seeing the inequalities through different lenses often raises all kinds of new questions. Many of these students are idealistic but are also anxious about how these unsettling experiences might influence their future. They fear that doing something *different* might be the *wrong* decision.

It is reassuring, to some of them at least, to hear that I was *absolutely* clueless about what I would do next when I lived here twenty-five years ago—I seriously doubted I would ever be gainfully employed, much less feel I was making a contribution.

A good guideline, I sometimes tell students, is that it is hard to make a *wrong* decision if you engage in things you care about, try your best to make a contribution to others, and continue to learn in the process. Struggling is an important part of the journey, and my hope in publishing this book, at least in part, is to reaffirm the belief that it is worth the struggle.

CPSIA information can be obtained at www.ICGtesting.com
Printed in the USA
LVOW11s1413290716

498065LV00002B/78/P